Praise for *The C*

CW00927356

[A] richly investigated chronicle…
seamlessly here with the bloodstained tale of a blasted region.
This book, in its sobriety, puts a human and—despite the
random, ritualistic violence—oddly sympathetic face on a part
of the world that history, ancient and modern, has brought
home to all of us. — Tracy Lee Simmons, *Washington Post*

A standout for its lucid historical overviews and, more
importantly, the dramatic intimate depictions of daily life.
— *Publishers Weekly*

Kremmer writes compellingly…Undaunted by the
contradictions of this strange world, he makes his way
through Afghanistan, Pakistan, Iran and other places much as
the reader might, with a normal terror of gunfights, in the
street but eager to meet people, to start conversations and to
listen. The politics may be incomprehensible, but the
ordinary people emerge from his story as real individuals we
can certainly understand…people who wipe the grit of war
from their eyes and beat it off their carpets and then,
somehow, carry on with their lives. Just as we do.
— Alan Ryan, *Chicago Tribune*

So good is *The Carpet Wars* that I predict it will outlive its
timeliness and join the ranks of those other two classics,
Eric Newby's *A Short Walk in the Hindu Kush*,
and V.S. Naipaul's *Among the Believers*.
— Pat Baskett, *New Zealand Herald*

…an informative and charming book.
— Christopher de Bellaigue, *Times Literary Supplement*

...this is a big book at work on many levels...certain to become one of the publishing events of the year...these are stories to test our own sense of humanity and wider knowledge...in dry good humour, Kremmer takes us cross-legged on a panoramic ride, from the tragic present to a complex past. — Jefferson Penberthy, *The Bulletin*

If you read no other non-fiction book post-September 11, don't miss this one. At the very least it will make premature judgments impossible. It is also a source of vivid, unexpected pleasure—sharp as the air in the Afghan mountains.
— Morag Fraser, *The Age*

This was a moving and enlightening book, a journey through the Islamic heartlands with heart and mind fully engaged in the task. *The Carpet Wars* is an invaluable read whether you want insight into Central Asian Islam or advice on how to spot fraudulently aged killims in a Peshawar bazaar. And above all, it's a warm portrait of the nation with the most tragic recent history in Asia—Afghanistan. Buy it, read it, savour it. — Daniel Lak, *Biblio*

I plunged into Christopher Kremmer's big, fat, richly packed book of journeys through the very heart of madness and religion—at least as we tend to see it...a spellbinding sense of landscape and history pervades this book...I doubt that you'll find one more readable than this.
— John Clare, *Sunday Life*

...measured, informed and sympathetic...will likely stand head and shoulders above any that follow...This book is a heady mix of carpet appreciation, travel, adventure and geopolitics and will appeal to anyone who wants to know more than the simplistic good versus evil view of the 'War on Terrorism'.
— William Gourlay, *Australian Bookseller & Publisher*

As with the finest carpets, this book has many strands…there is magic in the carpet as Kremmer explores its pervasive role as a barometer of human triumph and tribulation—as a currency, a treasured artefact and the region's largest industry outside oil. — Peter Rodgers, *Weekend Australian*

The life and times of this crossroads between cultures and traditions is described in descriptive, often poetic, prose. The writing brings alive a world of crowded cities with cubbyhole shops, tea-houses and chaotic traffic, juxtaposed in the middle of some of the most desolate and awe-inspiring scenery in the world…Highly recommended for everyone, and required reading for those seriously interested in the art, culture, people or contemporary history of West Asia.
— Soumyajit Mandal, *Sunday Statesman*

I was gripped by this book, intrigued and happy as I read…
— Kate Llewellyn, *Eureka Street*

One of the best books I have read this year.
— David Verran, *Sunday Star-Times*

BAMBOO PALACE

Christopher Kremmer

BAMBOO
PALACE

DISCOVERING THE
LOST DYNASTY OF LAOS

flamingo

An imprint of HarperCollins*Publishers*

Bamboo Palace includes some material which appeared in Christopher Kremmer's earlier publication, *Stalking the Elephant Kings: In Search of Laos* (Allen & Unwin, 1997).

Flamingo
An imprint of HarperCollins*Publishers*, Australia

First published in Australia in 2003
by HarperCollins*Publishers* Pty Limited
This edition published in 2004
ABN 36 009 913 517
A member of the HarperCollins*Publishers* (Australia) Pty Limited Group
www.harpercollins.com.au

HarperCollins*Publishers*
25 Ryde Road, Pymble, Sydney, NSW 2073, Australia
31 View Road, Glenfield, Auckland 10, New Zealand
77–85 Fulham Palace Road, London W6 8JB, United Kingdom
2 Bloor Street, 20th floor, Toronto, Ontario M4W 1A8, Canada
10 East 53rd Street, New York NY 10022, USA

Kremmer, Christopher, 1958- .
  Bamboo palace : discovering the lost dynasty of Laos.
  Bibliography.
  Includes index.
  ISBN 0 7322 7756 6.
  1. Kremmer, Christopher - Journeys - Laos. 2. Laos -
  Politics and government. 3. Laos - History. 4. Laos -
  Description and travel. I. Title.
959.4

Cover design by Christa Edmonds
Cover photographs courtesy Christopher Kremmer
Textile photographs courtesy Carol Cassidy, Lao Textiles
Maps drawn by Margaret Hastie
Typeset in 11.5 on 16 Bembo by HarperCollins Design Studio

Printed and bound in Australia by Griffin Press on 80gsm Bulky Book Ivory

8 7 6 5   06 07

In loving memory of
Sebastian Phua (1956–2003)

Foreword

The Greek philosopher Heraclitus said that you cannot step in the same river twice, 'for fresh waters are ever flowing in upon you'. While some of the material presented here appeared in a previous work, *Stalking the Elephant Kings*, this is a new book. Not only are the waters fresh, but this time, thanks to fate and not a little luck, they flow all the way to the sea of truth.

This book is based on a series of visits to Laos made in the context of a two-year posting as a correspondent to neighbouring Vietnam, followed by an extended stay of several months at the conclusion of my term in Indochina. It was a forgotten country that delighted and fascinated me, two decades after it disappeared behind the bamboo curtain of Asian communism following the revolution of 1975. At that time, my quest to determine the fate of the royal family of Laos ended in failure. In this book, ten years after I began, the puzzle is finally solved.

After the publication of *Stalking the Elephant Kings*, I was contacted by representatives of the Lao royal family in exile who put me in touch with a former colonel in the Royal Lao Armed Forces, Khamphan Thammakhanty. At first, I did not realise the significance of Khamphan's story and an account of his experiences was left to collect dust in a garage for almost five years while I followed my muse to Afghanistan and Central Asia, journeys that produced another book, *The Carpet Wars*. When eventually I got around to looking at the Lao material again, I was astonished and anxious; astonished that I might at last crack the mystery that lay at the heart of my quest, and anxious that the sole living witness able to talk openly about the events described here might have passed away. To my immense relief, and now joy, Khamphan is not only alive, but physically, mentally and emotionally in good form. His tumultuous life story provides much of the new material for this book.

Those sections of the original manuscript that survive have been redrafted and reorganised into new chapters, with a new structure based on the location of the events related. Revisiting my notes and tape recordings of various incidents and meetings allowed me to rescue small gems previously overlooked. An index and timeline should make life easier for the reader. The overall result, I hope, will reward both my original readers, and those coming to this story for the first time.

My thanks for their unstinting patience and support go to my agent, Tara Wynne, at Curtis Brown, and to Shona Martyn, Helen Littleton and Amanda O'Connell at HarperCollins. Many thanks also to senior typesetter Graeme Jones, typesetter Helen Beard, designers Katie Mitchell and Christa Edmonds, proofreaders Rodney Stuart and Pam Dunne, and indexer Madeleine Davis. To the people of Laos I owe a deep debt of gratitude. Among those who contributed to this story were members and officials of both past and present regimes, exiles and stay-behinds, numerous members of the royal family, former re-education camp prisoners, and both Lao and foreign diplomats who have served in Vientiane and abroad. Help with translations from the French was provided by Jean-Gabriel Manguy and Christophe de Neuville, and from the Lao by Teng Teng Kinnavong. Julio Jeldres provided access to the Sihanouk archives. The staff of the Siam Society and the *Bangkok*

Post's clippings service also provided invaluable help and quiet corners in which to escape the clamour and pollution of Bangkok. The staff of the Australian Archives in Canberra also gave of their time and resources. The head of the Digital Conservation Facility Laos, Dr Alan Potkin and Catherine Raymond, Associate Professor of Art History at Northern Illinois University, provided additional information on the menhirs of Hua Muang. For her hospitality and friendship in Vientiane, my thanks go to Felicity Volk, and to Aradhana Seth and Peter Launsky-Tieffenthal in Los Angeles. For their help and advice, I'm indebted to Caro Llewellyn, Ramona Koval, Garth Nix, Vladimir Lozinski, Sarah Rose, Christopher de Bellaigue, Graeme Dobell, Pepita Conlin, Susan Aitkin, Jan Forrester, Monica McInerney, Barrie Dexter, Rohit Jaggi, Polly Watkins, Lachlan Colquhoun and the late Roberta Borg.

To my wife Janaki, parents Ted and Marlene and sister Melissa, your patience and support was, as always, much appreciated.

Several of my sources, including Lao and foreign nationals living inside the country and abroad, requested that I use pseudonyms, rather than expose them to potential unpleasantness at the hands of the Lao authorities. I have also elected to use the current style for transliteration of Lao names, so that Sam Neua becomes Xam Nua, and Viengsai is Viengxai. All dollars are American.

Truth, I realise now, chooses when and where it will manifest itself. My naive conviction that Laos was the best place to discover the country's history has been qualified by the insights provided by the exile community. In this regard, I am indebted to the late Prince Khamhing, Sithat Sithibourn, Khamphan Thanmakhanty and the Lao royal family in exile. I thank Khamphan for giving me permission to use and quote from his account in Lao of his own experiences, and for helping me to bring closure to a dark and troubling chapter of Asia's history.

CONTENTS

I called to the Lord from my narrow prison and
he answered me from the freedom of space.

—Viktor E. Frankl

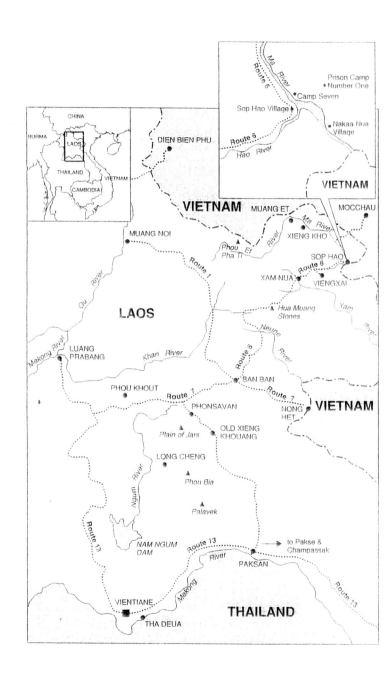

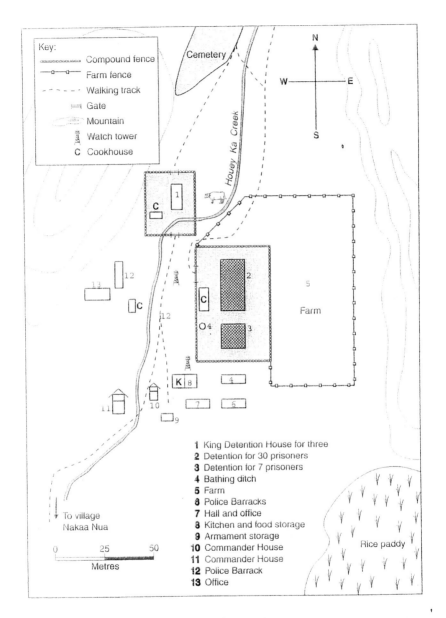

Key:
- ━━━ Compound fence
- ━○━ Farm fence
- - - - Walking track
- ⊨ Gate
- Mountain
- Watch tower
- C Cookhouse

Cemetery

N
W — E
S

Houey Ka Creek

Farm

To village
Nakaa Nua

0   25   50
Metres

Rice paddy

1 King Detention House for three
2 Detention for 30 prisoners
3 Detention for 7 prisoners
4 Bathing ditch
5 Farm
6 Police Barracks
7 Hall and office
8 Kitchen and food storage
9 Armament storage
10 Commander House
11 Commander House
12 Police Barrack
13 Office

Camp Number One, Sop Hao, Houaphan province.

Part One

LUANG PRABANG

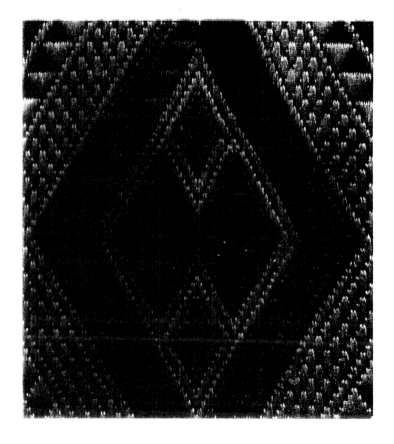

1

The White Parasol

On a promontory between two rivers in the jungles of
northern Laos nestles a small, gentle town of mouldering
villas and shuttered shopfronts. By day the dawdling streets of
Luang Prabang—'the place of the Buddha statue'—are dotted with
parasols. Life revolves around alms-giving and haggling. People
smile, and their smiles say, 'Leave us alone!' By night the black skies
are clotted with stars and thick with the scent of frangipani. You
might hear the song of a woman, unseen beyond a balcony; a
monk's chanted incantations; the steady gurgle of a stream. It is the
still eye in the typhoon of Indochina's history.

We had taken the plane because travellers plying the road to the
old royal capital had been attacked by rebels and bandits opposed to
the government in Vientiane, two hundred kilometres to the south.
The roads of the People's Democratic Republic were so bad and
airfares so cheap that even peasants flew, along with their livestock.
Caged sparrows twittered in the luggage racks and a dog slumbered
in the aisle. Barely clearing the heavily forested hills, the plane banked
hard and we saw our destination, buried in a palm grove at the
confluence of the Mekong and Khan Rivers. Then the pilot slammed
the plane down on the airstrip so hard that one of the mutts yelped.

In the terminal shack, uniformed guards slouched, armed with
rubber stamps.

'*Laissez passer*,' one of them grunted in French, demanding the document that even Lao citizens were required to carry when travelling outside Vientiane.

It was a sunny day, and a dry-season breeze flowed through the open galleries of the building, carrying off the slapdash formalities of tropical communism. Outside in the carpark, my rucksack landed with a thud in the tray of a motorised rickshaw, or *tuk-tuk*, whose driver hurled us across the bone-jarring ridges of a steel bridge over the Khan River towards Luang Prabang.

At the former royal palace, guides conducted tourists along zealously polished wooden corridors, through halls hung with portraits of kings and princes, heirs to the Kingdom of the Million Elephants and the White Parasol. The elephants represented power, the parasol protection, but the kingdom was gone and the heirs were missing. A different kind of aristocracy—the tough, opportunistic commissars and generals of a 'Peoples' republic—had replaced them. There were, however, a few vestiges of the old order to be found. Villa Santi was a small hotel that once had belonged to the royal family. Briefly nationalised, but now back in the family, its modest colonnades were flanked by pottery urns bearing the triple-elephant crest and the title 'Royaume du Laos'. Stepping onto the porch, I was surrounded by short, solicitous young men and women —the hotel staff—with hands raised as if in prayer, actually the *nop* of greeting. Seated with a drink in the airy lobby of the whitewashed villa, I awaited my host.

Santi Inthavong was a thirty-something scion of a family that straddled the royal–communist divide. Laos is more like a family than a nation. Surnames were considered unnecessary until fifty years ago, when the French administration made them compulsory. The Lao word for family—*vong*—is embedded in many names. The Inthas claimed descent from the king of the Vedic gods, who rode a white elephant and commanded thunder and rain. In the late eighteenth century, an Inthavong had ruled in Vientiane, but during

The White Parasol

3

the decades-long civil war the family split—spreading its risk, cynics said—with some members supporting the leftist Pathet Lao, and others fleeing abroad. The Inthavongs who stayed were in the hotel business, and Santi's father chaired the National Assembly's Economic Planning Committee. But as they had before the revolution, the big families still married among themselves, and Santi had wed a princess, the granddaughter of the last king.

I was observing a group of local women on the street outside, daintily covering their noses as they crossed an open sewer, when Santi swept into the lobby. Behind him trailed a silent, graceful young woman clad in the traditional *sin*, or wrapped skirt, who carried a brass tray with coffee. Compared to his serene servant, Santi had the harried look of a Gallic bourgeois, with tousled hair, a faded denim shirt and sunglasses.

'My uncle from France is here, and for the past three days it has been nothing but drinking,' he exclaimed in French-accented English, puffing up his cheeks with the stress of it all. 'So! What brings you to Luang Prabang?'

As the girl poured coffee, a minibus pulled up outside, and began unloading a party of European men fashionably dressed in jungle greens with their hair in ponytails, and carrying suit bags. Soon, my senses were assaulted by gusts of mosquito repellent, cologne and sunscreen, as the new arrivals invaded the lobby, their luggage forming a great pile on the floor.

'I've come for a rest…a holiday,' I told Santi, retrieving my gaze.

It was true enough. Life as a correspondent in neighbouring Vietnam was sufficiently stressful to warrant frequent bouts of rest and recreation. Usually, after a few days away from work, I would become bored and begin digging up stories. Santi seemed to sense that.

'A rest, *oui*,' he said, hiding a smile in his coffee cup. 'But I expect you will also find many stories in Laos. And for somebody like you, these are the best kind of stories—the ones that have never been told.'

LUANG PRABANG

4

The story Santi wanted told was about his efforts, and those of the Lao government, to get Luang Prabang listed on the United Nations' register of the world's heritage. He spoke of his work not only to restore the villa, but to revive the arts that had once enlivened the former royal capital. He had assembled a traditional dance troupe, clothing them in fine brocades and royal heirlooms. The authorities were supportive, but wary of glorifying the royal past. They had asked him to change the hotel's original name, the Villa de la Princesse, and insisted that he hand over the dancers' antique costumes, and replace them with copies.

'They're worried about the costumes being damaged. In the time of the king, the dancers might perform once or twice a year. Now it's once or twice a day,' he explained.

'And the name "Princesse"? What was wrong with that?' I asked, but he only shrugged, squinting through the smoke from his cigarette.

'You know, they asked me to join the party once. It was after the war with Thailand. I was wounded and given a medal, and then they said, "We need patriots like you." I was quite touched, but I said no. I couldn't possibly accept such an honour. From what I hear, being in the party is worse than being a monk!'

Returning from his studies in hotel management in France, Santi had married Sawee Nahlee. Her name in Lao meant 'Splendid Lady', but everyone called her 'Tin'. She may have been a princess, but her wardrobe matched her husband's casual elegance, as I saw for myself when she arrived unheralded to collect him. She was a young woman in her mid twenties wearing blue jeans with her hair in a bob. Jumping to my feet, I offered an ungainly *nop* which she reciprocated with a shy smile. I would see her around town in the coming days, expertly piloting a motor scooter. But her conveyance that morning was a battered blue Toyota, in which she and Santi drove off, leaving a trail of black smoke behind them.

Standing in the haze of their exhaust, I was left to ponder a past that, officially, no longer existed. It had been whitewashed like the old villas on Rue Sakarine, but as I would discover on subsequent visits to Laos, persistent, unsightly blotches kept reappearing.

For six hundred years, the territories of Laos were ruled by kings, but in 1975, the Vietnamese-backed Pathet Lao toppled the US-backed kingdom. Twenty years later, laconic Lao government officials were still parrying questions about the fate of Lao royalty with quizzical expressions, long silences and embarrassed giggles. The king had 'gone to the north', they said. Was he still alive? They didn't know. On a visit to Paris in 1989, the late revolutionary leader, Kaysone Phomvihan, had made the only detailed official statement that existed on the issue—all of three sentences.

'I can tell you now that the king died of natural causes. He was very old. It happens to all of us,' he said.

Three years later it happened to Kaysone, but his comments on a subject of intense interest to all Lao people were never reported in his homeland. Nor did his successors ever expand on them. The dead spoke louder than the living.

There was, however, one person who knew. And one day, he would speak.

2

The Salt Trader's Son

The Mekong is the ageless mother of the lowland Lao. Its annual inundation of chocolate-brown silt suckles their farmlands, and the river serves as the main commercial thoroughfare linking the Buddhist townships between China and Cambodia. In the 1930s, it was a highway for an itinerant salt trader from Don Kho in southern Laos who plied the river's broad girth in a cargo barge. The trader, Manoi, did good business hauling salt from the mines around Keun village, north of Vientiane, down the Ngum and Mekong Rivers all the way to Pakse, financing the return journey by buying porcelain plates made in Thailand for sale in Vientiane. A stable market, hard work and luck saw him grow prosperous. He married a young woman from village Pakhanoung, near the salt mines, and sent his three sons to school.

The eldest son, Khamphan, had a face both impish and wise. His eyes held the secret of some sly joke that also played in the corners of his mouth, and his ears flopped this way and that, twisted too often for stealing money from his father's wallet and chickens from the lady next door. His early life in the 1930s was a typical rural idyll, but at the village elementary school the impact of the twentieth century was beginning to be felt. Sitting for an exam one day, Khamphan was asked by a teacher to write his surname. Like most Lao people at the time, he didn't have one, nor did his father. Sent home to get a surname, he was told that his grandfather's name was Thamm, and his grandmother's was Khanty. Khamphan Thammakhanty, as the boy would henceforth be known, was a poor student, considered fortunate to complete elementary school. But in a country where, even today, two out of every three women cannot read or write, it was enough for him to qualify as a teacher. Aged eighteen, he took up his position at a small school on the road to Vang Vieng, transferring two years later to another school in his mother's village of Pakhanoung, where he would later meet and marry Singpheng, the daughter of the local county chief. In different times, Khamphan might well have lived the quiet life of a village headmaster. But history had other ideas.

With the advent of World War II, the French colonial administration that had ruled Laos for fifty years in concert with the monarchy collapsed, and the king fled to Thailand. After a brief Japanese military occupation, the French returned, restoring the king to his throne, but the twilight of colonialism and birth of Asian nationalism had arrived. In 1954, Laos gained full independence as a constitutional monarchy, but the new nation, like so many others, was soon split by the Cold War. Rightists supported the United States and the monarchy, while the Left wanted a Soviet-style people's republic. In between, the Neutralists struggled to keep the two sides apart and preserve the fledgling nation's fragile unity. Civil war loomed. In the midst of the struggle, Khamphan responded to the new government's call by joining the army reserve. While the royalists held the Mekong towns, the leftist Pathet Lao retreated east, launching a guerilla struggle backed by the like-minded government of neighbouring North Vietnam. Despite several attempts to patch up the rift by forming national unity governments, the fighting would continue for twenty years.

Within one year of joining the army, Khamphan was wounded in the leg fighting Pathet Lao units near the Xuang River north-east of Luang Prabang—but he was lucky. The wound was superficial soon healed, and was no obstacle to a steady rise through the ranks. Already fluent in French, the salt trader's son acquired a familiarity with English. There followed overseas postings to Malaysia to train with British intelligence, and Okinawa with the American occupation forces in Japan. In the early 1960s, with Singpheng, he built an airy, two-storey villa in Vientiane's Dong Mieng district that cost three million *kip* and took two years to complete. By 1968 he was a lieutenant colonel posted to Maryland, Virginia, where he studied counter-insurgency techniques along with officers from around the developing world.

The Lao communist movement was directed from its earliest days by the Vietnamese. The first Lao leftists like Kaysone Phomvihan, who studied law in Hanoi and whose father was Vietnamese, had joined the Indochinese Communist Party (ICP) formed by Ho Chi Minh in 1930. They later formed new parties with Lao names, and the guerilla army known as the Pathet Lao (Lao Nation). However, the symbiotic relationship with Hanoi was maintained. Although they denied it, their shared desire was to abolish the monarchies of Vietnam, Cambodia and Laos. The Pathet Lao stronghold in north-eastern Laos was a gift of the Vietnamese, who invaded and occupied Houaphan province in the spring of 1953. The ICP, controlled and dominated by the Vietnamese, continued to function secretly, and to boast senior Lao communists among its members. By working through front organisations they were able to advance a revolutionary agenda that, by one account, enjoyed 'almost no support' in Laos itself because it was 'antithetical to the notion of Buddhist harmony'.

By 1970, Khamphan had turned forty, and had two children. He had completed his officer training, and had been promoted to the rank of colonel working in counter-intelligence at Phonekheng military headquarters in the capital. That same year, he was reassigned to a politically sensitive new role in the royal capital. In

Luang Prabang he would be head of 'G2', the combat intelligence unit of the 1st military region that tracked Pathet Lao troop movements based on information gleaned from the interrogation of communist sympathisers, pro-government informants and refugees fleeing rebel-held areas. Occasionally, Khamphan would personally attend interrogation sessions. Sometimes suspects of particular significance were handed over to the American staff of the local station of the US Central Intelligence Agency. The United States was determined to stem the spread of communism, and Indochina was the frontline. The once somnolent royal capital buzzed with the activity of a large, but covert American military presence. 'Ravens', or US military pilots operating under civilian cover, flew thousands of sorties out of the town's small airport, acting as forward air guides for the B–52 strategic bombers spearheading the secret war in Laos. Khamphan's new job also would put him in close contact with the royal court, where he became friends with several princes, including Crown Prince Vongsavang, with whom he shared meals cooked by the Princess Mahneelai at their home. Soon, political upheaval would turn their world upside down.

In February 1973, the Vientiane Accords agreed a ceasefire between the Pathet Lao and the Royal Lao Army. The accords, in the language agreed by the royalists and communists, were 'in response to the supreme desires of His Majesty the King and the earnest aspirations of the people of all races throughout the country'. They committed both parties to defending the 'peace, independence, [and] neutrality of the Kingdom of Laos'. Recognising that the country was split into two separate zones of control, the agreement laid out a roadmap for reunification, and committed both sides to 'rigorously carry out the democratic liberties of the people which include: individual liberty, freedom of thought, freedom of expression, freedom of the press, freedom of assembly, freedom to form political parties and organisations, the freedom to appear as candidates in elections and the freedom of business and the right of private property'. The accords prohibited 'all acts of reprisal and of discrimination toward people who have collaborated with the opposing party during the war'. Although a ceasefire was in force, both sides continued to manoeuvre politically, with more and more territory falling under Pathet Lao control.

Having trained for two decades to defeat the enemy, it was difficult for a military officer like Khamphan to know how to react. His son, Pongsack, had been drafted into the new joint military units established under the accords, comprising royalist, neutralist and leftist elements. His own career trajectory, meanwhile, continued upwards. In early 1975, he was appointed assistant chief of staff for psychological warfare. Yet officially, the war was over.

For almost five years Khamphan and his wife had been living apart, Singpheng remaining in Vientiane with their daughter, while their son lived with Khamphan in Luang Prabang. The intricate web of Lao social obligations also saw him caring for two foster children belonging to a fellow military officer posted to the Plain of Jars, while Singpheng raised about a dozen children belonging to various members of their extended family. Like many Lao, Khamphan hoped the same strength and flexibility that held their families together would also keep the country unified. So many of the principal actors in the conflict were related by blood or marriage—above all, two princes related to the king. The 'Red Prince' Souphanouvong could use his influence within the Pathet Lao to ensure no harm came to the royalists, while his half-brother, the neutralist prime minister, Prince Souvanna Phouma, could ensure the Pathet Lao gained a key role in future governments. Yet as 'the two sides in the conflict circled each other, Khamphan began to question the old assumptions and wonder if he, like so many others, should consider fleeing into exile with his family.

Under the terms of the Vientiane agreement, the royal government agreed to 'neutralise' its two capitals—the national capital, Vientiane, and the royal capital, Luang Prabang. In practice this meant the redeployment of Pathet Lao armed forces to both cities. In Luang Prabang, hundreds of guerillas took up positions in the hills around the town, while their commander, General Saisompheng, took up residence in the town itself. Old enemies were now supposed to become partners. At bi-monthly meetings, Khamphan found himself seated across the table from General Saisompheng, discussing joint arrangements for the security of the town. Yet he never believed the leftists would keep their promise to share power.

At a reception at the palace he confided in Prince Thongsouk, the chief of protocol and brother of the king. The Pathet Lao were not honest, he told the prince. They would break all the agreements, and the law if necessary, to take over the country. Thongsouk, however, reassured him. The king, he said, believed that the superpowers would ensure that a balance of power prevailed in his strategically located country. In Vientiane, Khamphan asked his superior in the military, the intelligence chief General Lee, for his views. He too responded that there was nothing to fear. Life went on. Whispered anxieties and soirees took place at the palace in equal measure. Khamphan's closest contact in the royal family was the king's second son, Prince Sisavang. Aged in his early thirties, he managed the royal farm at Pak Xuang, and his regular visits to Luang Prabang were the occasion for much well-lubricated merriment between the two men. But as the royalists partied, their enemies circled.

One day in June 1975, the residents of Luang Prabang were bemused to notice a small demonstration snaking its way through the streets of the old town. The protest was unusual because those taking part were children from· local primary and secondary schools. Despite their tender years, the protesters' demand was pointed and political: three senior officials must be expelled from their positions in the royal capital. Among the officials who must leave was Khamphan Thammakhanty, and among the child protestors demanding his expulsion was his twelve-year-old foster son, Bounthiang.

'It was all organised by the Pathet Lao,' Khamphan recalled, a hint of hurt still in his voice years later. 'My foster son was an innocent recruit. They told him they were just going for a walk, to have fun.'

Anywhere else, the children's crusade might have caused barely a ripple. But in the increasingly surreal political atmosphere of the Kingdom of Laos, the protest caused heartburn at the highest levels. Along with demonstrations, labour union unrest organised by the leftists was putting further pressure on the regime. Desperate not to give his half-brother Souphanouvong any excuse to abrogate the Vientiane Accords, Prime Minister Souvanna Phouma intervened to satisfy the child protestors' demands. Khamphan and the two other officials were given air tickets, and told to be on the next plane out of Luang Prabang.

'The Pathet Lao targeted him because he was one of the few real fighting men in the Royal Lao armed forces,' said a Lao exile who has made a study of the period. 'He was hard working and incorruptible. He was known to be in the front line against the Pathet Lao. He was smart and he was a fighter.'

Yet far from placating the opposition, each small concession like the transfer of the three officials only exposed the weakness of the constitutional monarchy, and whetted the communists' appetite for total victory.

3

Across the Mekong

On Rue Sakarine, a street named after a king, the cool morning air was laced with incense, issuing from dozens of Buddhist shrines and temples, as I strolled towards the Mekong with my local guide and friend Boun Kham. He was another relic of the old days, a pilot in the Royal Lao Air Force who lost his job when the regime changed, and spent long years in one of the re-education camps set up by the leftists to punish their enemies. Denied medical treatment for an injury, he had lost the use of his left eye while in detention. Unemployed ever since, he had plenty of spare time, and had agreed to travel with me from Vientiane to help trace a few loose ends from the royal days.

At the point on Rue Sakarine where two cats carved in stone stood guard, Boun Kham pointed to a grand staircase that tumbled through the palm-fringed grounds of an ornate and beautiful temple. Wat Xieng Thong, the Temple of the Golden City, was built in the sixteenth century in the reign of King Setthathirath, who assumed the throne in 1550 after his father died in a fall from one of his two thousand elephants during a pachyderm rodeo before an audience of foreign ambassadors. Ten years later the grand temple rose on the banks of the Mekong River, and for over four centuries enjoyed royal patronage, its elaborate chapels and finials accumulating ever greater glory. Before a Lao prince could assume the throne he was required to cross the Mekong from Wat Xieng Thong to a temple on the other side. At Wat Long Khune he would spend days deep in meditation, cleansing his mind and spirit in preparation for the responsibilities ahead of him. It was a journey young Lao Buddhist men were still expected to make once in their lives, with the local *wat* becoming their springboard into adult life.

Standing on the bank, I hesitated to take Boun Kham's hand as he reached out to me from a *pirogue*, or canoe.

'C'mon, it's okay. No sweat,' he said, invoking the American slang of his air force days to coax me across the slippery riverbank towards a feeble, motorised craft carved from a single tree trunk. Beside him, the boatman smoked and yawned, a black felt Mao cap tilted rakishly as he waited for paying passengers to fill its seats. They soon came, scrambling up the greasy gangway in bare feet, T-shirts and sarongs, rocking the boat as they embarked. When every last seat was occupied we set off on a long, sliding arc across a swirling body of brown water that rose in Tibet and emptied into the South China Sea, over a thousand kilometres away. Close to the opposite shore the current weakened, and with an artist's judgment the boatman cut the engine and allowed the *pirogue* to drift slowly to the chosen spot onshore.

Following a track that rose steeply from the river, Boun Kham showed the way through the vegetable gardens that led to the village of Xiangmen. Less than a kilometre from the capital of northern Laos, the economy was based on growing vegetables and rice, and cutting wood from the forests. At a wooden bridge we passed a young girl whose eyes were blighted by cataracts but who gave us a ringing *Sabaidee*. There were stilt houses and marigolds, and we passed a *bonze*, or monk, carrying an umbrella the colour of turmeric that afforded little shade, but cloaked him in a radiant glow. Every time we passed someone Boun Kham would mumble a few words of greeting to them—cautious, staccato phrases delivered under the breath with a thrifty laugh, as if smoothing our way while checking for obstacles ahead. The old soldier was still operating behind enemy lines.

An arching bridge led into Wat Long Khune, a compound of whitewashed buildings with steeply raked, tiled roofs sweeping low to the ground. A novice asked us to remove our shoes and led us into the coronation room. When he pushed open the wooden shutters, light poured in on kings, lovers and the massed armies of the Ramayana, the Hindu battle epic still popular among Theravada Buddhists. The murals leapt out from the walls, recalling a passionate people who fought, thought, negotiated and celebrated, inspired by angels and terrified by demons. Statues of the Buddha were arranged at the end of the chapel, averting evil, making peace and asking for rain. They were very fine, more than a metre tall, and dressed in *pukhai*, the monks' orange robes. I had seen people washing and dressing similar statues during *Pimai*, the Lao New Year, in Vientiane. They handled them gently, as if washing a baby, with reverent affection and a touch of melancholy.

In 1905, King Sisavangvong, then a prince, had washed his spirit here. He donned the *pukhai*, lit incense and chanted the mantras given to him by the monks. He rested and took meals in the open gallery of the *sim*, or chapel. In the afternoons he listened to the breeze rustling the leaves of the banyan tree, and contemplated the roiling junction of the Khan and the Mekong rivers. In the late 1950s, the monks at Long Khune began to prepare for a new royal visitor, repairing the stairs and distempering the walls. Sisavangvong was dead, and his eldest son, Crown Prince Savang Vatthana, had been confirmed by the King's Council as the new king. He would rule for sixteen years, but he never made the ceremonial procession to Long Khune, nor was his coronation ever held.

Leaving the *wat*, we took the path back to Ban Xiangmen via the abandoned temple of Chompet and its 100-step staircase. A climb to the top afforded a panoramic view of the river and Luang Prabang. Chompet was in a terrible state, the stucco cracking and red clay bricks tumbling out. A carved floral motif above the locked entrance door had survived, but the wooden lintels were eaten away by termites. At the rear was an almost toppled *stupa* containing the ashes of one of King Sisavangvong's many wives. The old royal cemetery lay a few hundred metres downstream. Sala Tam Passar Luang had once been used for ceremonies and rites. Now some of the white plaster pillars had been vandalised, or defaced with charcoal drawings of skeletons with penises. Beyond the pavilion stood the charred brick pyres on which the bodies of royal family members had once been cremated. Behind the pyres, some smaller tombstones were almost overgrown by vines. Tourists never visited here. I sensed that Boun Kham was getting impatient, or was it uneasy? Soon we hurried away, as if there was a curse on the place.

4

The Aid Worker, the Explorer, the Hotelier
and the Dancer

Bad things had happened to nosey outsiders in Laos. Others had prospered there, attracting loyal followings like latter-day Lord Jims.

Word had reached Hanoi of an Englishman who had been living in Laos for several years and who knew the villages around Luang Prabang. Clive Rankin had been noticed exploring the upper reaches of the Nam Khan in a motorised canoe and penetrating secret valleys in a banged-up jeep. He spoke fluent Lao—not an easy thing—and had agreed to help me locate an equally intrepid, but less fortunate explorer.

In the nineteenth century, the Frenchman Henri Mouhot's travels revealed the glories of Cambodia's Angkor Wat. The son of a Protestant bourgeois, he set sail from London in April 1858, reaching Bangkok five months later. Travelling to Luang Prabang by ox-cart, he was welcomed by Lao royalty, and in turn, presented them with a rifle. Henri Mouhot had liked Luang Prabang in a detached, Eurocentric way. 'The situation is very pleasant…if the midday heat were tempered by a gentle breeze, the place would be a little paradise,' he wrote, before plunging into the jungles in search of his fate. He shot a tiger, witnessed a rhino hunt, and on 9 August 1860 left the royal capital, heading east. He was still out there somewhere in the jungles of northern Laos.

Clive arrived just after lunch, all sun-burnished sinew in an army shirt. He looked the part, and so did his overland vehicle, which resembled an amphibious landing craft. The staff at Villa Santi hailed him chattily in bubbling Lao, to which he responded with a variety of wicked teases. As we drove out through the town, he scanned the dozily deserted streets as if looking for someone to help, or something to improve. His projects had assisted rural communities to build the basic infrastructure that the Lao People's Revolutionary Party, for all its strident rhetoric, could not provide. Yet the slightest suggestion of laid-back Lao inadequacy made him bristle.

'Foreigners complain that this is the land of *baw pen nyang*, he said. 'You know: "We don't have it. We can't help you. Never mind." But I say this is the land of *baw mee ban haa*, which means, "We don't have what you want, but it's no problem. We'll do without, or we'll find another way." And when they say that, they'll smile. But it doesn't mean they're happy they've frustrated you. It means, "I'm terribly sorry, so why don't we sit down and think of a way to get around this problem."'

Henri Mouhot was another bearded European who had honoured his Lao associates for their abilities, but unlike Clive he could not befriend them. He was a hard taskmaster, and drove himself and others beyond sensible limits. His journal includes the advice of a Chinese mandarin that 'the only plan to get rid of all the difficulties which the Laotian officials will be sure to throw in your way is to have a good stick, the longer the better. Try it on the back of any mandarin who makes the least resistance and will not do what you wish. Put all delicacy aside. Laos is not a country for the whites.'

As I read out the quote, Clive looked horrified.

'Never lay your hands on a Lao!' he fumed. 'Try to behave as well as they do. Unfortunately, there are a lot of foreigners who don't always do that, and it causes shock in a place where they haven't had contact with Westerners for a long time. The Lao just can't believe that anyone can treat others rudely and aggressively.'

I'd had similar advice before. 'Never shout at a Lao,' the father of a Vietnamese friend once advised. 'For if you do, he will look at his shoes. And when you have finished shouting, he will go home. And early the next morning, he will swim to Thailand.'

Luang Prabang, with its 35 000 inhabitants, several hundred monks, dozens of *wats* and neat grid of streets had given way to ravines and scree. As the truck clambered through vast potholes we passed slick-backed buffalo, men harvesting teak and village weavers working at looms under stilt houses. A rudely fashioned bench seat signalled our halting place, marking the start of a track that took us down to the banks of the Nam Khan. Struggling to keep up with Clive's bounding gait, I followed him down the track, slapping on litres of insect repellent as we went. Mouhot had complained of fever, probably malarial. After he became ill, his Lao helpers advised him to write a letter to his family. He wondered at their strange suggestion.

'Are you afraid?' he asked them.

As we approached the river, its roar grew and roots twisted across the path like crude steps. Clive was waxing lyrical about the countryside, his big mountain boots making light work of the rugged track. He spoke of the ravines upcountry, and limestone hills similar to China's Three Gorges, heavily forested and cut through by fast-flowing rivers. Emerging onto a mud flat, we entered a bizarre riparian landscape in which flotsam hung from trees like Christmas decorations—plastic bottles, unravelled recording tape and pieces of wood snared in a recent flood suspended in mid-air. Blue butterflies fluttered through the rubbish, creating a scene of surreal beauty. The level of the Nam Khan had fallen since the flood, but it was still moving with apparent force, eddying across rapids, smooth in parts, but in others, white-capped and treacherous. The green hills rose steeply on all sides.

In October 1860, Henri Mouhot had passed this exact point, the ache in his brain magnified, roaring like a torrent. His diary entries became brief, dwindling like his hopes.

16th…
17th…
18th. Halted at H…
19th. Attacked by fever.
20th. Have pity on me, oh my God…!

As the fever consumed his famous energy and attention to detail, he wrote no more. He died on 10 November 1861, aged thirty-five. According to his brother Charles, the servants reported he had been insensible for three days. In their condolences to Charles Mouhot upon the death of his brother, members of the Société d'Emulation of Montbéliard wrote of Henri: 'His work remained unfinished, but it was gloriously commenced, and his name will not perish.'

Eventually, to our right, the dry bed of a dead tributary opened up, meeting the Nam Khan beneath an enormous banyan tree. Trudging into this ravine, over ants, creepers and worms, we came to a white concrete monument in the shape of a casket that marked Mouhot's resting place, rediscovered in 1990. The people of the explorer's home town had made the trek here to restore the grave. At one end was an inscription: '*La ville de Montbéliard est fière de son enfant, 1990*' [The town of Montbéliard honours its son, 1990].

Dark clouds had gathered and the sky was full of dragonflies. We stayed just long enough to wonder what morbid urge had drawn us there on a sightseeing tour, before deciding to return to Luang Prabang. But as it had with Henri Mouhot, fate took an unexpected turn.

Driving back through Ban Phanom, a village just outside Luang Prabang, Clive swerved to avoid a chicken crossing the road, but managed instead to decapitate the poor bird. He stopped, reversed, switched off the engine and waited. The body of the bird was still quivering, its black blood forming a pool on the road. A little boy ran out from the village to pick it up, head in one hand, body in the other. Hoisting the gory remains above his head he called to friends and family, 'Our bird! They've killed our bird!' A crone soon joined him, laughing at the display, or perhaps the unusual neatness of the job. She was followed at length by an elderly man with an impassive expression who took the body and head and examined them minutely, saying nothing. The crowd had built up to about fifty people. Many chickens had died crossing this road, but none had been beheaded so precisely. Was it a sign? The owner of the chicken paced back and forth, checking and rechecking the body of the bird and its severed head, weighing them in his hands. We braced for compensation, silently marshalling our arguments against his demands.

'This'll slow us down,' Clive groaned, explaining the frequency of such incidents on Lao roads, and the terrible intricacies of extracting oneself from them. It could cost as little as a dollar to settle on a dead rooster, but the haggling could consume hours. Time-starved drivers had taken to tucking generous wads of *kip* under the warm, quivering corpses of their road kill. Clive's kill was a full-grown hen, undoubtedly capable of extended egg production. The owner's minute inspection of its injuries had continued for several minutes, but his efforts at solemnity were faltering. At his feet, a wild tribe of children had struck up a dance in anticipation of that night's chicken feast. In the midst of this uproar, a strange voice—not unlike that of a policeman arriving just in time to foil a crime—announced a new player in the drama.

'You should be more careful, my friend,' cautioned the voice, 'driving on zis beezy 'igh-way.'

A stocky, silver-haired European gent sauntered into view, inspecting the evidence with summary disdain.

'Luckily for you zair is no 'igh-way patrol in zis area of La-oose,' he said, pausing to suck on his pipe.

'Allow me to introduce myself. I am Monsieur Perrot, and I am en route to see zer friend of my friend. Would you like to join me?'

The elaborate entrance was apparently for my benefit only. Clive knew the Frenchman, and a discernible tightening of his facial muscles suggested he did not care for him.

'Monsieur Perrot is an expert on Lao culture,' he said, with a hint of sarcasm, electing to stay put and complete his business. 'That's culture with a capital "C". You can learn a lot from him.'

'Today you are lucky,' Perrot declared. 'We will meet a famous dancer. Madame Peng Dee!'

It was an offer I could not refuse. A travel slut, I decamped with the flamboyant Frenchman, following him through neatly formed dirt streets lined by bamboo and thatch stilt houses, with stock animals corralled beneath. As we walked, Perrot told me that his father had come to Luang Prabang on horseback from Haiphong in 1924, staying in the country until just before the outbreak of World War II. He himself had spent forty years in the hotel business, in France, Africa, the Middle East and Polynesia, but this was his first time in Asia. Like Santi Inthavong, he had restored an old villa, once the home of Prince Souvanna Phouma, and had then been forced to change the name of his establishment by the Ministry of Information and Culture, which seemed to have problems with history. Originally, the hotel had been named after the prince. But much as a gecko will drop its tail to survive, it had dropped the final 'a', and was now called the Hotel Souvanna Phoum.

'You know who built zis village?' asked Perrot as we walked, while children danced around us and used long bamboo staves to pluck *markam*, green tamarind, from the trees.

'No. Who?'

'The king!'

'Really? Why?'

'For 'is concubine!'

In fact, Ban Phanom was populated by T'ai Lue people from China's Yunnan province, whose ancestors had been captured by a Lao army and held as prisoners of war. They'd been brought to Luang Prabang province from the northern town of Luang Namtha by King Sisavangvong, to satisfy his need for fine cloth and entertainment from their weavers and dancers. Before the revolution they'd been envied for their proximity to the court, after it, despised. Now, with tourists returning, their star was once more ascending.

One of the former dancers, Peng Dee, was sitting at a spinning wheel beneath her stilt house. She was a statuesque middle-aged woman with clever eyes and a determined jaw. She sat with her legs tucked beneath her to one side, watching her spinning wheel fashioned from a bicycle rim with a suspicious look, as if it might suddenly roll away. Perrot greeted her with a double handshake, introducing me as a journalist who had come to write a story about her. Immediately, the spinning wheel lost momentum and the air was filled with a melodious cackle. 'Everybody knows Peng Dee,' she said, adding darkly, 'but this is a jealous village.'

'Are all these children hers?' I asked, the kids having followed us in.

'Not all 'ers,' Perrot answered. 'They belong to 'er friend, who is een jail. Four months she is zair, all for love. Because she loved a *felang* [foreigner]. It is forbidden! More than one 'undred local women are in prison for similar offences.'

Who was this amorous *felang*, I wondered? Surely not Monsieur Perrot?

'Madame Peng Dee 'as eight children,' he continued, 'and is a widow. She was very close to zee old king.'

She was the sort of woman you passed in hundreds of villages, her hair tied in a modest bun, and wearing a colourful blouse over tanned shoulders and arms. But there was something different about Peng Dee. A theatrical animation could transform her features from moment to moment. She appeared at turns wise and sly, bawdy and matriarchal, warm and tough, all without shifting her gaze from her ever-spinning wheel. I suppose she had been beautiful, the village *belle* in her time. Born in 1942, she had begun learning the ancient movements of the *nan keo*, the Lao dance based on the Ramayana, when she was eight, and later performed for the king, who had created a full-time dancing troupe in the early 1950s. There were fifteen dancers, mostly girls in their teens, trained in the ancient rhythms of the court by a retired *danseus*. Peng Dee's family lived free of rent and taxes close to the palace for the six years her career lasted.

When the girls were not dancing they were weaving Laos' famous textiles, a skill that proved useful in later years when war and revolution swept away the monarchy and the favoured class of artists and artisans. It now earned Peng Dee the equivalent of $2 a day. She was also teaching her daughters to dance for the tourists. As we sat beneath the stilt house, two of the girls leapt spontaneously into the open air and began to perform, precocious arms weaving a spell their mother had taught them. Peng Dee beamed with pride and treasured memories.

'Those were the happiest days of my life,' she said, lifting her eyes momentarily from the wheel. 'In the evenings there would be great feasts, followed by the dancing. The palace was full of light, and the nights there were very colourful and exciting.'

Her children laughed self-consciously at Peng Dee, who was no shrinking violet and had strong opinions on most things, including the decline in the performing arts since the revolution.

'The dance they teach them nowadays is not the real dance,' she scoffed. 'They teach them in four months. It should take years.' To prove her point she twisted her arm, supple, graceful and alluring. She still had it. The king would have been pleased.

In the 1960s, Lao classical dancers were still performing *danse sourya*, the sun dance. It described the landscape at sunset along the Mekong, a river as important to the Lao Loum as the Nile is to the Egyptians. 'The sun at its setting falls slowly, spreading its rays,' the dancers would sing. 'The red clouds watch the forest, where the colours of the trees mix with those of the sun.' In the spirit world too, women danced for the *kinara*, a strange creature with the head of a man and the body of a bird which lived on mountains and in caves.

For six hundred years, the arts and religion and monarchy of Laos had formed a seamless whole, anachronistic perhaps, but indigenous. It was a world that collapsed with the abdication of the last king.

5

Dance of the Lost Puppets

On Rue Sakarine, the royal capital's modest ceremonial mall, the day began with an ancient act of submission. Since dawn, barefooted Buddhist monks swathed in burnt-orange robes had been filing out of the monasteries, each carrying a covered rice bowl. The daily ritual—as old as their faith—took them door-to-door around the narrow streets of the old quarter, where one member of each household, usually a woman, knelt on the doorstep holding another bowl. As each monk approached, the householder bowed her head, took a handful of rice and placed it in the monk's bowl. When their bowls were full, the monks would return to their *wats* for breakfast. In order to rid themselves of worldly concerns, monks are expected to give up all their possessions. They depend on the townsfolk for their physical sustenance, and in return, the people of Luang Prabang rely on the monks to sustain their souls and protect them from evil. This mutual dependence had deepened since the town awoke one morning to find that the holder of a sacred office, around which their lives had revolved for centuries, had disappeared without a word of explanation.

Somdet Pra-Chao Lan Xang Hom Khao Luang Prabang, the Lord of the Kingdom of the Million Elephants and the White Parasol of Luang Prabang, could trace his lineage back to Khoun Borom, the first Lao king, who according to legend descended from heaven to

27

rule an earthly kingdom near Meuang Thèn, somewhere in southern China. Khoun Borom's eldest son, Khun Lo, moved with his people towards the Mekong, settling at a place they called Muong Swa, south of the junction of the Nam Khan and Mekong, on the site of present-day Luang Prabang. Unlike the literate Chinese, he and his immediate successors had no scribes to chronicle their doings. Twenty-one kings followed Khun Lo, but it was not until the fourteenth century that history noticed one of them. A young prince, Fa Ngum, had been exiled and sought asylum at the Khmer court at Angkor, where he married a Khmer princess and became a Buddhist. Furnished with an army by his Khmer father-in-law, he fought his way back to Muong Swa, seized the throne and declared Buddhism the state religion of what was to become the Kingdom of Lan Xang. Pleased with the success of their protégé, the court at Angkor dispatched a delegation of monks carrying a 500-year-old solid gold statue of the Buddha from Sri Lanka, the *pra bang*, which they installed in the Muong Swa stockade as the kingdom's palladium.

In the late seventeenth century, the commercial agent Gerrit Van Wuysthoff of the Dutch East India Company found a grand kingdom on the Mekong where flourished literature written on palm-leaf paper, and music played on wooden xylophones, gongs and drums. Teak and gold decorated the kingdom's temples and palaces, and its people were clothed in fine fabrics woven on its many looms. In 1700, when a king died without leaving a mature heir, Sai Ong Hue took the throne with the help of the Vietnamese. His gambit split Lan Xang in three, with separate kingdoms proclaiming independence at Luang Prabang, Vientiane and Champassak in the south. Soon the new kingdoms were warring among themselves with foreign assistance. Burmese troops helped Vientiane conquer Luang Prabang, whereupon Luang Prabang conspired with Siam to topple Vientiane. In the end, Siam replaced Burma as suzerain. In 1828, King Chao Anou tried to reassert Lao independence, but in return a Siamese army burnt Vientiane to the ground, depopulating the city. By the end of the nineteenth century, Vientiane's population was still only a quarter of what it had been at the time of the war, and so weakened was the kingdom that when French explorers arrived, they found a land ripe for colonial exploitation. The French moved gradually, persuading the Siamese to allow a French vice-consul, Auguste Pavie, to be based at Luang Prabang. When Pavie personally rescued King Oun Kham during fighting between Siamese troops and Chinese bandits, the king asked for the protection of France. It was the start of a marriage of convenience between Paris and Luang Prabang. Oun Kham remained on the throne, but the role of his counterpart in the southern principality of Champassak was reduced to that of a local official in the French administration. French rule continued until after World War II.

In 1959, five years after Laos regained its independence, King Sisavangvong died in Luang Prabang. Tradition demanded that preparations begin immediately to bury the king and crown his successor, the young French-speaking Crown Prince Savang Vatthana. But the Lao are a deeply superstitious people, and when a sudden storm struck Luang Prabang, tearing the roofs from many houses and demolishing the funeral arches, the soothsayers made an extraordinary prophesy. The new king, they said, would never be crowned. Born in November 1907 in Luang Prabang, Savang Vatthana was educated at boarding school in France. Pictures show him on the eve of his departure for Montpellier, aged ten, dressed in Western clothes beside his proud father. After graduating from school, the young heir continued his studies in France. As king, Savang Vatthana was a thoughtful, sincere man whose personality combined a deep reverence for the past—his favourite book was Proust's *Remembrance of Things Past*—openness to foreign ideas, and a desire to modernise. His kingdom had an elected parliament, and a government formed in Vientiane—not in the palace in Luang

Prabang—which controlled the day-to-day running of the country. This suited the king, who was personally more inclined to cultural pursuits than political ones. Through the 1960s and 1970s, he would try to remain above the fray of the civil war, counselling both sides to bury their differences and preserve national unity. He repeatedly delayed his coronation—and the mystical journey to Wat Long Khune—in the hope that the war would end, and the ceremony itself could serve as a symbol of national rebirth and cultural continuity. A devout Buddhist, he became an authority on the *sangkha*, or clergy, and took his role as protector of the state religion seriously. However, he dispensed with customs he believed were anachronistic, such as polygamy. Savang Vatthana took only one wife. He had chosen her at a *fête* organised at the palace to coincide with a break in his studies in France. Of the fifteen of the kingdom's most beautiful princesses summoned to the celebration, his eye fell on one. Queen Khamphoui would bear him five children, including an heir, Crown Prince Vongsavang. Like most Asian royals, the family played tennis together, and liked to attend major tournaments on their travels abroad. Back home, however, their kingdom was descending into savagery.

Forced to choose between domination by the Vietnamese or by the Americans, the king chose the Americans, but this relationship would prove toxic to his life and kingdom. Strategic bombing of eastern Laos between 1964 and 1973 by B–52 'flying fortresses' proved ineffective in stemming the Pathet Lao's advance. The dropping of more than two million tons of explosives on the east of the country—more than was dropped on Nazi Germany—alienated the civilian population. It also sharpened the ethnic divide. The Buddhist Lao Loum, who account for two-thirds of the population, continued to live in relative peace in the lowlands along the Mekong. The brunt of the fighting was borne by the hardy, mountain-dwelling Hmong ethnic minority. Easily the toughest fighters in Laos, the mainly animist Hmong bravely held out against overwhelming odds, losing half their army of some 40 000 men. Another 125 000—or about half the total Hmong population of Laos—resettled after the war in the United States. The brunt of the bombing, however, fell on the Lao Theung, or people of the mountainsides, also animists but seen as allied to the leftist cause. American bombardment resulted in the deaths of more than 8000 people and razed more than 350 villages in Xieng Khouang province alone. As the bombing intensified, the rebel leaders, including the Red Prince, Souphanouvong, waited patiently for their day of reckoning. To them, the king was nothing but an American puppet, just as to many others the Pathet Lao were mere puppets of the Vietnamese.

After the fall of the monarchy, the streets of Luang Prabang had been given revolutionary new names. Cycling around town, I found that Rue Sakarine had become Xieng Thong, Rue Sisavangvong was Navang and Phothisarath was Phalanxay. Yet fly-spotted maps plastering government offices around town obstinately stuck with the old royal names: Sakarine, running from Wat Xieng Thong to the Ecole Primaire, Sisavangvong continuing to the Post Office. Twenty years since the revolution, the politically correct street names still seemed new and unfamiliar to most residents.

A more familiar sound—the tinkling of hammers on anvils— accompanied me down a narrow street to a two-storey building which was the home and workshop of Thitpeng Maniphone, whose family had been patronised for generations by Lao kings. A genteel man in his sixties, Thitpeng was sitting in his parlour with his wife, Chan, when I arrived unannounced. An open shed at the rear was occupied by several men earnestly hammering detail into silver scabbards and bowls. Sheet silver had been bent around moulds of a sticky brown resin called *kisee*, which gave it shape. After the item had been decorated, the resin would be heated and detached from the beaten silver. Thitpeng's methods had remained unchanged in his forty-three years as a smith. The silver ingots were still softened over charcoal before being hammered into shape. The craftsmen of the court had formed their own aristocracy, often intermarrying like the royal family did. Chan was a kind of precious metals princess, the granddaughter of Saene Makoune, a royal goldsmith whose work graced the ears of queens. The silverware produced by her husband and the works of the goldsmith Phia Thong had filled the palace and were often presented to visiting dignitaries. In 1972, at the age of forty-two, Thitpeng had been called to the palace during *Pimai*, to be presented with a royal award.

'When I went to the palace I joined a long line of people receiving medals,' he recalled. 'We were standing with our heads bowed. I didn't look at the king, and he didn't say anything to me. Later, in the evening, we went to a big feast inside the palace, with music and dancing. But the king sat in a separate room, and we didn't see him.'

The following year Thitpeng was called back to the palace, this time to receive a certificate of nobility. The monarchy produced awards and decorations the way a catherine wheel throws off sparks. One could be made a Commander of the Million Elephants and the White Parasol, a Knight of Civil Merit or an Officer of the Silver Reign of Laos. A medal featuring a portrait of Savang Vatthana had held pride of place in Thitpeng's home until 1975, when it was melted down for fear of punishment from the leftists, and hammered into a silver bowl.

'After the king abdicated it was dangerous to have such things around,' Thitpeng recalled. 'If you kept them, people might think you were against the new regime, and life could become difficult for you and your family.'

Life became difficult anyway. With the abdication of the king, and those closest to him fleeing into internal exile or sent to prison camps, Thitpeng lost his most valuable customers. His efforts to continue working were bedevilled by the new government's view of the petite bourgeoisie as exploiters of labour, and the economic downturn caused by their flawed policies. In 1977, like most other smiths and small businessmen, Thitpeng closed shop and dismissed his craftsmen. The clink of hammers was no longer heard on Kop Keah, 'the street of rose-apple trees'. Nine years later, when the government abandoned socialist central planning, Thitpeng decided the time might be right to reopen his business. His workers were recalled, and resumed hammering away.

Pedalling back along Rue Sakarine, I headed once more towards Wat Xieng Thong, where it was rumoured I might find the corpses of some tiny victims of the revolution. A Canadian aid worker, Roberta Borg, had told me the story of how, after the overthrow of the monarchy, another Lao institution had been smothered by the forces of progress. Roberta, a life-worn, chain-smoking veteran of bureaucratic aid battles, had been enchanted by traditional Lao puppetry, and thought it might be used to spread development messages in the backward countryside. Asking around Vientiane, she learned that the old art of *ipok* rod puppetry had died out in Laos. The only known troupe had been trained in fraternal Bulgaria, and used glove puppets. The traditional Lao puppet troupe based at Luang Prabang, and funded by the former king, had been disbanded in 1975.

In the old royal capital, people told Roberta there had indeed been a full-time troupe of fifteen puppeteers, who had performed with fine handmade rod puppets until the revolution. Most of the artists, now in their seventies or eighties, lived at Wat Xieng Thong. In their days as dependants of the royal family, they had lived in houses attached to the royal *wat*, where they were fed by the monks. During the civil war, in the late 1960s and early 1970s, their performances became less and less frequent. When the Pathet Lao came to power and cancelled the stipend which had supported the royal family, the troupe was done for. Of the original fifteen members, eight were still alive in 1991, including Souvanh, the keeper of the puppets, a stick figure of a man with shaved silver hair who still wore the trademark white jacket of the court. Souvanh told Roberta the king himself had helped make the puppets the troupe used. He dated the surviving ones to the 1950s, but said they were modelled on their predecessors 'like son on father', and that this passing-on process had been going on since antiquity. Every stage of the puppets' construction was accompanied by quasi-religious ceremonies, beginning with the blessing of the balsa-like tree from which they were made. Roberta asked if she could see the puppets, but Souvanh said the box had been closed for some fifteen years. The puppets were kept in the grand garage housing the funeral carriage of Sisavangvong, also within the Wat Xieng Thong complex. Aged in his seventies, Souvanh was the only one who could open the box because he alone knew the correct prayers for such an occasion. The prayers were in Pali, the language of the monks.

The Lao government agreed to Roberta's request through UNICEF to stage a performance by the royal puppet theatre. She had travelled back to Luang Prabang, accompanied by the Bulgarian-trained director of the national puppet theatre in Vientiane. After much cajoling, and promises to pay for the expensive ceremony involved, a reluctant Souvanh agreed to revive the sleeping marionettes. The director of the national puppet theatre had never seen the puppets, such was the self-induced cultural amnesia of the Lao revolution, and the opening of the box at Wat Xieng Thong seems to have been a profound experience for all involved. Roberta said it broke her heart.

'When they opened the box, there were various ceremonies they had to go through, these old guys and ladies. Even the act of touching the dolls required the permission of their keeper. It was a miracle the dolls hadn't been devoured by termites. And when they picked up these beautiful figurines that they had worked with so intimately for so many years, and were then parted from for decades, it provoked a complete physical transformation. Souvanh was like a sixteen-year-old. For him, they were not wooden dolls: they were alive, and the puppets themselves are of such a fine design and have such strong faces that you could easily believe they were real too. Once that box was opened, all this love started flowing.'

Hundreds of people were gathered in the grounds of the *wat* for the opening ceremony. The hushed crowd members were aware of magic in their midst. A pig had been slaughtered, and its grinning head was prominently displayed, surrounded by coconuts, bananas, buffalo liver, blood jelly and cans of 7 UP. All those items, not forgetting the *lau lao*, or rice wine, waited to be offered to the *rookatah*, or puppets, in a *baci* ceremony like those held to mark weddings, departures and other significant events in Lao life. In Lao tradition, the body houses thirty-two *khouan*, or souls, one for each bodily function and faculty. The *khouan* have a tendency to wander and when they do, sickness or disability results. In a *baci*, strings hanging from a flower arrangement are tied to the wrists to prevent the escape of the *khouan*. A feast of chicken, eggs, sweets and *lau lao* always follows.

Souvanh untied the knot that restrained the spirits, and cradling them in his hands, lifted one, then another, then another of the dolls from their sleep. There were about forty of them, their wooden faces polished to resemble porcelain, painted with flowing costumes in red, green and gold. The old man looked stiff and emotional. When the dolls had been taken from the box, he dragged deeply on a cigarette and began to blow smoke across their faces, then took a mouthful of rice wine and sprayed it over them. He lit another cigarette with a taper and placed it on the lip of one of the puppets. Buddhist novices with heads shaved listened intently as Souvanh spoke in long sentences, his voice rising and falling in waves of emotion, a voice in which to announce great things.

'Oh, after years, we see you!' he said.

Wooden xylophones chimed in with cascading scales, and cymbals clashed as the ensemble gained momentum, puffing and wheezing like a steam engine. Suddenly the old man began to weep, his conversation with the puppets breaking into wretched, constricted phrases. But they were tears of relief, for the puppets had partaken of the wine and their *phi*, or spirit, was now good. They would play well, and behave—important to know, for wayward puppets had a tendency to mischief and were feared as poltergeists. Souvanh kept putting a lit candle in his mouth, extinguishing it, and blowing the smoke over the puppets. Others passed the bottle of rice wine around.

'Remember the old movies where the ventriloquist's dummy takes over the ventriloquist?' said Roberta. 'Well, here it's for real. Puppets have a spirit, and you have to appease it before a performance, otherwise they can misbehave.'

No-one in the gathering was more awestruck than the young trainees from the national puppet theatre, who'd accompanied their director to Luang Prabang. The glove puppets they'd seen in Bulgaria, and which they had copied upon their return home, were crude figures. The royal puppets were smaller, dressed in wildly coloured frocks with tikka marks on their foreheads. Some were quizzical, others enigmatic. Their graceful hands were bent back 45 degrees at the wrist. The prince of the puppets was pearl-faced with fine features and a winged golden helmet. A demon puppet with a green face and white fangs protruding from blood-red lips wielded a sword. The smoking puppet ballooned his cheeks, a weedy fag on his lip; an internal tube allowed the puppeteer to smoke for him.

By evening, the crowd at Wat Xieng Thong had grown to almost a thousand, and after hours of unwrapping, wonderstruck fondling and renewing of vows, the old troupers were ready for their comeback. Their play told the story of a young and wayward prince sent out by his family to make his own way in the world. He marries, but his young bride is abducted. Three wives later he finds her again. Eventually Roberta realised she was watching one of the countless interpretations of the Hindu epic of Rama, Sita and Ravanna. The puppeteers, who also provided the narration and the voices, stood behind a thin bamboo screen on which scenery was painted. They supported the heads of their puppets with central rods made of bamboo and controlled the hands with two very narrow rods. Souvanh said his father had trained him in manipulating the rods by giving him a pair of chopsticks and telling him to play with them. Only after six months was he allowed to touch a puppet.

'But the puppet knows his own mind,' he said. 'The puppeteer is just a medium.'

There was no written script, and when one old woman couldn't remember all the words she'd learnt from her parents, the puppeteers began improvising jokes about individuals seated in the crowd, to the delight of their enraptured audience. When the time came to put the puppets to sleep, Souvanh was in tears, apologising to his wooden partner and wiping his eyes. He lapsed into Pali again.

'We brought all these things for you,' he told the puppets. 'We have head of pig, chicken. We will never see you again.'

'You silly old man,' called one of the others. 'Don't get so emotional.'

Souvanh picked up a plastic cup of rice wine, doused the tapers in his mouth and blew the smoke into the *lau lao*. He then took mouthfuls of the wine and sprayed it again into the puppets' faces.

'That's enough wine for you!' he said, thanking each one by name and stacking them back in their wooden chest.

Finally, coconuts were placed on top of the box, and a saffron cloth tied the puppets' spirits in.

When the new regime took power in 1975, local officials of the Ministry for Information and Culture had decreed that the puppets of Wat Xieng Thong should address each other as 'comrade'. The puppets had refused. Now, in their own modest way, the puppeteers of Wat Xieng Thong had cheated history. Lao puppetry had been born again. The one-off performance at Wat Xieng Thong inspired the Bulgarian-trained younger generation to set to work and reclaim their heritage. In the ensuing days they brainstormed with the elders, recording their stories and songs and unpacking the puppets again to photograph and measure them. Back in Vientiane they began making larger glove puppet replicas that could be seen at less intimate venues. The music, performed live in royal days, was taped. When they were done, they loaded the new puppets into a truck and drove them to Luang Prabang to perform before the surviving members of the royal puppet troupe, who pitched in enthusiastically with advice and storyline fragments recalled since their own performances. Suitably fine-tuned and lasting ninety minutes, the show then toured the province's villages. Roberta, meanwhile, set to work raising money to buy a glass case in which to exhibit the old puppets in the former palace. But, like the monsoon, the rain of enthusiasm had somehow passed, and the fragile figurines still languished in a box somewhere in Wat Xieng Thong.

Parking my bike, I crossed the temple courtyard, entering a vast wooden building decorated with the usual red and gold-leaf panels detailing episodes from the Ramayana. It was the garage of the funerary carriage of the last Lao king to be given a ceremonial cremation, Sisavangvong. I poked about among the boxes where Roberta had said the royal puppets resided, but saw none tied with saffron ribbon. Most of the space in any case was taken up by the grand carriage, built to resemble a *pirogue*. On its 'deck' stood three wooden urns said to have held the ashes of the penultimate king and queen, and one of their children. Another large metal urn had contained the king's embalmed body before his cremation. After that, Sisavangvong's ashes were entombed in the *stupa* at Wat That Luang, and the civil war resumed.

Returning to the cool comfort of Villa Santi, I spent the afternoon reading books and news reports about Laos.

'There are many tales about the fate of the members of the royal family, who disappeared after the communist revolution in 1975,' said a story clipped from the *International Herald Tribune* in June 1995. 'Some say they are still alive in a re-education camp...others say they perished in the limestone caves of Xam Nua, in north-eastern Laos, where they were being held by Pathet Lao officers... Others say they died of malaria in their garden in Luang Prabang, as there was no medicine available, certainly a plausible version since the Lao Revolutionary Museum in Vientiane proudly displays quinine tablets as part of the benefits of the 1975 revolution.'

Keesing's Contemporary Archives quoted a government spokesman as confirming that in 1977 there had been an unsuccessful attempt to rescue the ex-king by rebel elements, and that as a result he was well guarded 'far from the Mekong'. The most common interpretation of this was that the king and his family had been taken to the re-education camps in the remote north-eastern province of Houaphan, bordering Vietnam. Their departure date, at least, was known: 11 March 1977.

'It is as if, in British terms, Queen Elizabeth, Prince Philip and Prince Charles were taken from Buckingham Palace,' thundered the journalist James Pringle after a visit to Luang Prabang in 1989, 'and removed to the north—not to Balmoral, but to some workcamp in the Scottish highlands—never to be heard from again.'

6

The Empty Palace

A cool evening breeze wafted between the colonnades that formed the upstairs balcony of Villa Santi as I awaited the proprietor, whiling away time with a more recent copy of a foreign newspaper. A report from Moscow claimed positive identification of the bones of Nicholas II, the last tsar of Russia. Researchers had taken samples from a skeleton disinterred at Yekaterinburg, where Nicholas and his family were executed by the Bolsheviks in July 1918. Few were suggesting that the monarchy be reinstated, but finally knowing the truth about the country's history could only be good for Russia.

In Laos, there was no such certainty. According to various accounts, the king had died 'in 1981', 'in 1978', 'in or about 1979', 'in 1984 of malaria', or 'of a broken heart'. Yet others maintained, 'He lives normally in a villa in Viengxai, has a few servants and a garden he can tend.' Officials explained their reluctance to comment: 'Since 1975, the king has been an ordinary person, so if he died tomorrow, we would not print an obituary.'

How would the government react, I wondered, to a foreigner poking his nose into such a sensitive issue? The fate of the royal family was, it seemed, a state secret.

From the balcony I saw Santi arriving at the hotel. He had come alone.

'Is your wife joining us?' I asked hopefully.

'She sends her apologies,' Santi said. 'She has some family business to attend to.'

Mention of family—the royal family—was like salt to a wound. The mystery inside the conundrum submerged in the history of this backwater had begun to taunt the sleuth in me. Santi's elusive spouse, gatekeeper of a treasure-trove of secrets, was beginning to bewitch me. The disappointment must have shown on my face.

'Are you married?' asked Santi, ordering a whisky for himself and a vodka tonic for me.

'Oh yes, my wife is from India,' I replied, at which his face expanded like a balloon.

'But Indian women are very beautiful! She did not come with you?'

'She's in Delhi. I'll join her there. But I'm taking time to see Laos.'

That set him off again on his favourite subject—the delights of Luang Prabang.

'You've come to the right place. For me Luang Prabang is the real Laos. People are different here from elsewhere in the country. Religion is still respected, and once you're here you feel quite close to nature. It's something I can't find in Vientiane or other provinces. In all of South-East Asia, there are not so many places like Luang Prabang!'

It was such a pleasant afternoon that I soon forgot my intention of cross-examining him about the dead king. Together we wallowed in nostalgia.

'When I came here first,' he said, 'they had a very small dam. It looked like a paddy field! During the rainy season we had power. In the dry season, three days with, three days without. It was like that until, I would say, the middle of 1992. When we opened I told the guests, "We have power from 6 p.m. until 6 a.m. So wake up early if you have an electric razor!"'

The sun was dying, replaced by a wavering candle brought by one of Santi's softly shuffling staff. Its ghostly light flickered across the whitewashed arches that sequestered the balcony from the night.

'When I first saw this house,' Santi said, 'it was in quite bad condition. From outside it looks big. But once you open the door, you realise it's quite small. It was more difficult to renovate this house than to build a new one. In the French time, they built with sand, big bricks and plaster—no cement at all. So when I wanted to put in a new door, and I was obliged to break down the wall, I was really afraid the whole thing would collapse.'

It seemed a reasonable neurosis. So much else had. Santi's recollections coiled around their central theme—Luang Prabang— like copper wire wrapped around a guitar string, and as his memory plucked, they resonated.

'You know, this building used to belong to Queen Khammouane, the wife of Sisavangvong. When the king died, she gave it to the crown prince and Princess Mahneelai—that's my wife's mother. After 1975 Mahneelai lent it to the administration, and they used it as a warehouse. Then a couple of caretakers lived here. Today they still work for my mother-in-law.'

There it was again. The famous family. Princess Mahneelai was the senior royal still living in Laos, the wife of the last crown prince, and a granddaughter of King Sisavangvong. Like everything in the country, the details of her life were hazy. I asked if I could meet her.

'Unfortunately, she is not in Luang Prabang,' replied Santi. 'She is in Vientiane, awaiting a visa to Australia.'

Was this some arcane Lao torture, I wondered? You arrive in a strange nation, become intrigued by its history, then the person with the most direct knowledge of it departs for your own country while you're away.

'Her daughter lives there,' Santi added, rubbing it in.

Of Crown Prince Vongsavang's seven children, two had settled in Australia, two in the United States and two in France. Only one,

Santi's wife, Tin, remained in Laos. I had caught tantalising glimpses of her in town, around which she seemed to be in constant motion, from the hotel to her home, to the small souvenir shop she owned and, of course, to the temple. Apart from an enchanting smile and half a *nop* of polite greeting, she never gave me a word. Nor did I ask her anything, infected by the Lao custom of avoiding direct approaches. For all his trials and torments, the accursed Henri Mouhot had done better than me. He'd been granted an audience with the king himself. Writing in his journal, the naturalist crowed, 'After a few minutes more conversation, the king held out to me his hand, which I kissed, and then I retired, but had not proceeded far when several officials ran after me, exclaiming, "The king is enchanted with you; he wants to see you often."'

Finally, in desperation, I resorted to stalking the princess. Lying in wait at the hotel one morning, I cornered her, blurting out my obsessive need for a chat. Looking slightly unnerved, she agreed to see me over coffee the following day. At the appointed time, armed with a photocopy of the royal family tree from a book Perrot had loaned me, I positioned myself in the hotel lobby, only to be approached by a smiling receptionist.

'You are here for the meeting with Sawee Nahlee,' he stated with unusual directness. 'But I'm sorry, sir. She cannot come today. She wants to wait for her husband, Mr Santi, to come tomorrow. Then you can give an indication of what questions you will be asking.'

I unfolded my genealogical chart and showed it to him, pointing to the empty boxes I'd drawn where the princess and her children should be.

That night after dinner, I took my usual constitutional down to the confluence of the two rivers. A full moon cast diamonds on the water as it flowed free and wide, heavy with the silt of China. The sky was a lavish navy-blue lightened with clouds of luminescent white, and the hills were thickly thatched and dark. There were cars on the miniature colonial streets, but not many, and restoration was proceeding on a few of the old buildings, but not much. People stretched themselves on the pavements outside their shop stalls, yawning and playing with their children. I wandered in the moonlight into the deserted courtyard of Wat Xieng Thong. It was here in the 1960s that a tourist had asked an elderly Lao man to explain some aspect of the Buddhist religion. The softly spoken gent obliged, impressing the visitor with his encyclopaedic knowledge. Later, while handling some of the local money, the tourist recognised the man from his portrait on the *kip* notes—his guide had been the king of Laos.

There was one aspect of the lives of Lao royalty which the authorities were not at pains to conceal. There on Rue Sisavangvong it stood, a brazen monument to the good life they had lived. The palace was not only still standing, but open to the paying public, in other words, foreign tourists.

For centuries before the French colonial period, Lao kings had inhabited modest palaces built on timber frames with bamboo columbage walls daubed on both sides with clay and lime mortar, and roofs made from thatched grass. But in 1904, the French colonial administration began construction of a new palace in a blend of French and Lao architectural styles. The frontage was French, but its steeply sloping tiled roof resembled that of a Khmer Buddhist temple. Designed to symbolise the alliance of Paris and Luang Prabang, the new palace opened in 1909.

My guide from the local tourist office was a petite young woman called Somsanith, who as a schoolgirl had danced the *nan keo* for the king and his family at *Pimai*.

'We would come here every day after school for a year,' she said, pointing to the expansive lawns surrounding the palace, upon which chickens now roamed. 'We performed only once, on *Pimai*, in the open air. The king would often walk past while we were practising. He seemed a very kind man, always talking to the palace staff and enjoying walks in the grounds.'

As he strolled in the gardens in early 1975, dressed in a plain business shirt worn over *sampot*, the traditional baggy trousers, and watching the dancers practise, 67-year-old Savang Vatthana did not have too many pleasant strolls ahead of him. As a young man he had been politically active, leading resistance to the Japanese occupation and being exiled to Saigon for his trouble. But upon becoming king he confined himself to fulfilling largely ceremonial state and religious tasks. He had suffered from comparisons with his father, Sisavangvong, he of the mane of wild black hair, prosperous waistline and twelve—some say eighteen—wives, and at least twenty-four children. Undemonstrative and self-effacing, Savang Vatthana had one wife and five children, enough for a suburban solicitor perhaps, but not for a king. He was a tall man, with a tendency to talk in riddles, deeply religious and irretrievably superstitious, increasingly so as he got older. He had once lamented to his Cambodian counterpart, Norodom Sihanouk, 'Alas, I am doomed to be the last king of Laos.'

The well-groomed Somsanith guided daily tours around the palace, a job that paid better than her work as an accountant. Weaving a path through a newly arrived tourist group, we made our way to the gallery housing the symbol of Lao nationhood, the golden Buddha known as the *pra bang*. It stood in a room which opened onto the terrace, presenting the palms of its hands, which appeared dull and painted. Weighing more than 50 kilograms, it was kept behind bars which hardly looked robust enough to protect what the museum's printed guide called 'a chief source of spiritual protection for Laos since it was brought from Cambodia in the fourteenth century'. Members of the former royal family claimed that after the revolution the *pra bang* had been given to the Vietnamese by the Pathet Lao leader, Kaysone Phomvihan, to repay them for helping him gain absolute power, and had then somehow ended up in Moscow. Others claimed it was kept in the vault of the Central Bank in Vientiane. The genuine article was supposed to have gold leaf shielding its eyes and a hole drilled in one ankle. Somsanith blushed and smiled into her hand when I asked her whether the statue on display was the real thing.

'Maybe. I don't know,' she said, giggling like a schoolgirl.

In the reception hall we came upon the throne, a carved gilt monstrosity that turned out not to belong to the king, but to the country's chief priest. After the revolution the job of the *pra sangkharath*, or patriarch, was taken over by a government-appointed committee. The last patriarch, Boun Than, fled to Thailand, where he died.

In the 1930s, King Sisavangvong—whose statue still stands in the grounds—commissioned a French artist to help imbue the palace with the life of the country around it. Alix de Fautereau's frescoes depicted the village life of the Lao Loum, the chosen people of the lowlands, as well as the country's many festivals. Dressed elephants lumbered across one panel, while another showed a bamboo bridge across the Nam Khan, since replaced by iron girders. In a corner of the audience hall stood the bronze busts of three kings—Oun Kham, Sisavangvong and Kham Souk, or Sakarine as he was also known. The sculptor must have been a lover of continuity, for the dates he had chiselled in the bases ignored at least three interregnums. By early 1975, the Pathet Lao were rulers of Laos in all but name, and throughout that year the institutions of the 600-year-old monarchy and its elected government were gradually dismantled. The transfer of power resembled less a barnstorming revolution than a sleight of hand, the new leaders fearing a backlash if they moved too fast. Instead of giving reasons for removing the king, they said that because the coronation had not taken place, he had never formally become ruler.

'King Sisavangvong died in 1959,' said the museum brochure. 'He was succeeded by his son, Sri Savang Vatthana. For the coronation ceremony, the crown prince enlarged the throne room by adding two equal-sized rooms, one on each side. The establishment of the

Lao People's Democratic Republic on 2 December 1975 prevented the coronation from taking place. The king abdicated from the throne and was appointed Supreme Advisor to the President.'

Entering the throne room, Somsanith turned apologist for the regime.

'This is the throne,' she announced, pointing to the only chair with a back on it. 'The last king never sat there.'

Until the final week of November 1975, the Pathet Lao's intentions towards the monarchy were kept deliberately vague. The National Political Consultative Council, headed by the Red Prince, Souphanouvong, and based in the royal capital, had endorsed constitutional monarchy as the appropriate form of government for Laos. The new regime had even installed a previously ordered statue of the penultimate king in the palace at Luang Prabang the previous month. But it had also declared 12 October—the anniversary of the 1945 uprising, when Lao Issara nationalists temporarily deposed Sisavangvong—as the national day. Thirty years later, on the eve of the anniversary, Savang Vatthana summoned all able-bodied male members of the royal family to the palace and issued them with weapons from the armoury. Ordering them to stand guard throughout the celebrations of the new national day, he pointedly took no part in the official program of events. The king had been due to depart on a tour of Paris, Moscow, Beijing and Hanoi. In diplomatic circles there were rumours of exile, but in the event, the government—dominated by the Lao People's Revolutionary Party—informed the king that the timing of his proposed trip was inappropriate. The new national day was celebrated in Vientiane with a performance by Russian acrobats. But in the remote north-east town of Viengxai, near the border with Vietnam, a more exclusive and important gathering took place. Senior leaders of Indochina's three communist parties, representing Vietnam, Cambodia and Laos, met for the first time since coming to power. Representing Cambodia was Ieng Sary of the Khmer Rouge, who had arrived from a Phnom Penh already depopulated at the start of 'Year Zero', and who remained at Pol Pot's side until 1996. Twenty Vietnamese advisors were awarded medals for their contributions to the Lao revolution. Lao People's Revolutionary Party leader Kaysone Phomvihan said the revolution would 'speed up'.

At Kaysone's right hand was the king's cousin, Prince Souphanouvong, an aristocrat with a royal-sized chip on his shoulder. Born in 1909, the son of a commoner concubine, and thereby relegated to a lower rung of the royal family, he had picked up his socialism in France, and his wife, Viengkham, in Vietnam. A zealous participant in the failed revolution of 1945, he had fallen out with his nationalist colleagues after they agreed to restore his uncle to the throne. Expelled from the nationalist Lao Issara in 1949 for his extreme views, he helped form the Pathet Lao the following year. Souphanouvong saw himself as the Lao version of the great socialist leaders of the time, and moved around with a 23-member Vietnamese bodyguard. He was wounded in the anti-French struggle, escaped from prison (or was released after the intercession of his powerful relatives, depending on who you believe) and led a 'little Long March' overland to the safety of the Vietnamese border areas, where he spent a decade living in a cave during the American bombing. It was quite a legend, but it came at a cost. The Lao people admired Souphanouvong's willingness to forsake his royal birthright, but were uneasy about his Vietnamese friends. In return for Vietnam's backing, Ho Chi Minh demanded a decisive say in Lao affairs, subsuming the country within a Hanoi-dominated Indochinese 'federation'.

Events were moving too fast for the mild-mannered king, who began to show the strain. Staged protests against the monarchy were increasing and revolutionary committees controlled most cities and towns. Savang Vatthana told a Western diplomat that Souphanouvong had shown a lack of appreciation of Lao traditions, and suggested the country's future could be in the hands of a foreign power. By 4 November 1975, when another ambassador presented his credentials, even the king was no longer free to speak openly.

'The king was jovial,' recalled the ambassador, 'but he spoke of the need to adjust to the new situation, given the fact that there had been a complete change in Laos. He then remarked that he was by no means convinced that the monarchy was the best system for Laos, looking pointedly in the direction of the cabinet minister attending the ceremony, the Pathet Lao Minister for Religious Affairs.'

In Laos, for centuries, people had prostrated themselves before the king. The appropriate posture was no mere bow or curtsy. Demonstrating abject humility required that the subject grovel face down. Aware that the public reflex to honour the king would be difficult to eliminate, it became necessary to spirit away the object of that honour.

On 25 and 26 November, the National Political Consultative Council convened at Viengxai and decided to abolish the monarchy and declare the People's Democratic Republic. The next day, a rally in Vientiane denounced the monarchy and called for a popular regime. Prince Souphanouvong, who had been in Viengxai for the NPCC meeting, flew to Luang Prabang to propose to Savang Vatthana that he abdicate, and advise him on the appropriate form of words. Shaken by the demonstrations against him, the king had earlier told the British ambassador he intended retiring to his farm at Pak Xuang. Members of the Lao royal family living in exile in Paris claim the king rejected the prepared letter of abdication handed to him by Souphanouvong, and wrote his own.

On 30 November, Crown Prince Vongsavang carried the king's letter of abdication to Vientiane. The venue for the secret congress of people's representatives to which he travelled was Six Clicks City, an American compound besieged and occupied by the Pathet Lao in

May 1975. With its modern amenities and garden bungalows, it still had the feel of occupied territory. Party leaders had requisitioned parts of the compound for their own use, a potent symbol of their victory over the world's leading power. The crown prince had represented the king faithfully throughout his apprenticeship, travelling to remote and difficult parts of the country, including those few areas where the Royal Lao Army had enjoyed military successes. Vongsavang was impatient in matters of state, always questioning why the government was not doing more to defeat the Pathet Lao, but to him fell the bitter duty of announcing the end of the 600-year-old monarchy. Wearing a dark pinstriped suit with a small Buddhist medallion pinned to the lapel, a striped tie and spectacles, he read his father's letter of abdication with a dour face, unmoved by rousing applause. The only consolation was the careful wording of the letter which, as reported by the party newspaper, *Sieng Pasason*, handed power not to the Pathet Lao administration, but to the Lao people.

'Confronted with the new political situation in Laos,' it read, 'the co-existence of a monarchist regime, defined in the constitution, and the popular sovereign power is impractical and could be an obstacle towards the country's progress. In order to ease the path towards progress and to consolidate national unity, I solemnly renounce the throne from today, meaning I sincerely and completely renounce all goods willingly. I entrust the destiny of the country to the Lao people. Once more, this confirms the sovereignty of the population in all the territory of Laos. As a simple Laotian citizen, I sincerely address my best wishes for unity, independence, welfare and prosperity of the beloved Lao people.'

Vientiane Radio, by then under the control of the regime's propagandist, Sisana Sisane, broadcast an eight-minute report apparently based on the letter of abdication prepared by the government, but not signed by the king. It said: 'I agree to abdicate the throne, and from now on I dedicate my royal properties to the nation with a clear conscience. I agree to totally accept the new administration and put my faith in it. I ask the Laotian people to guide the future of the country, and to seek unity and a better life.'

Prince Souphanouvong's crowning victory was at hand. Since embarking on his long quest to shake Laos from its complacency, he had cultivated a ruddy, egalitarian manner, and was careful not to behave as a high-handed noble. To many he was a genuine patriot, but a Western diplomat who had contact with him saw 'a vain, ambitious snob. Emotional, with a savage streak, who commands respect because people are afraid of him.'

'He never really listened to you,' a member of the former National Assembly who'd spoken to the Red Prince in the dying days of the *ancien régime* told me. 'He had a pat answer for everything. It was impossible to have a normal conversation with him. It was always a cat-and-mouse game. And you felt like you were the mouse.'

In his usual robust and clear voice, President Souphanouvong addressed the congress.

'I am extremely happy in joining you here to celebrate the victory against imperialism and the destruction of the old and corrupt administration,' he told delegates. 'I am confident under the new regime, which will be adopted by this meeting, that our beloved country will have its independence, its unity and its prosperity, and that the Lao people will have a better life and greater liberties.'

He then proposed that the king become his 'supreme advisor' and that former prime minister Souvanna Phouma, another cousin, become advisor to the government. In early December, Pathet Lao radio reported that the former king was living on an orange plantation, probably a reference to his beloved orchard at Pak Xuang. On 6 December the *Economist* noted: 'The communist Pathet Lao put an end to the last pretences of coalition government in Laos on Wednesday when it forced the powerless but respected figure of King

Savang Vatthana to abdicate…the dream of a national reconciliation is clearly dead.' Some saw the hand of the Vietnamese behind the abdication. Arthur J. Dommen, in his book *Laos: Keystone of Indochina* said: 'The Vietnamese stage managers of this transfer of sovereignty were doing no more than following the pattern set in 1945, when the Emperor Bao Dai abdicated in favour of Ho Chi Minh's government in Hanoi. The Vietnamese communists basically are firm believers in tradition.'

At the palace, touches of grandeur survived in the king's private quarters behind the throne room, where four gigantic lamps stood at each corner of the royal bed, and a palanquin was parked outside the king's bedroom door. Glass cabinets lining the walls displayed royal orders from the emperors of France, China and Russia, none of them still in power—bad omens heaped one upon the other. The royal rubber stamps, now utterly useless, were also on show. On the king's king-size bed, ornately carved in teak with the initials 'SV' on the head, one of the ivory tusks was missing from the triple-elephant crest at the foot. The wooden frames for the mosquito nets were no more elaborate than the ones you could buy in Hanoi for a few dollars, and the dressing tables and chests of drawers resembled filing cabinets. Another feature of the bedroom was the enormous number of doors. No fewer than nine led to the king's suite, almost all of them windowed. The slightly seedy air of the bedroom was heightened by the placement of an old HMV gramophone outside the king's boudoir, primed to go at 78 r.p.m.

Turning a corner into what was once the ladies sitting room, we came face to face with Savang Vatthana, or at least his larger-than-life image in oils. In 1967, the Russian artist Ilya Gazurov had seen no trace of doubt about their future in the faces of the king, his queen and his heir. Their portraits exuded confidence and strength. Savang Vatthana wore an emerald silk tunic, an enormous belt with the triple-elephant crest, and baggy *sampot*. He carried a gold sabre, and over his shoulder loomed the Buddha. In a glass case beside the portrait was a red and gold silk tapestry sent to the king as a gift by Ho Chi Minh. Addressed to the *Roi du Laos*, and written in French and Vietnamese in 1962, the accompanying letter read:

> *Your Majesty,*
>
> *I would like to express my sincere gratitude to you for informing me of the appointment of Prince Vongsavang as heir to the throne.*
>
> *On behalf of the government of the Democratic Republic of Vietnam and myself, I would like to take this opportunity to extend our congratulations to you and Prince Vongsavang. I believe under your wise leadership the Lao people will embark on the path of peace, neutrality, independence and prosperity. May the friendship between the nations of Vietnam and Laos continue to grow.*
>
> *My sincerest regards to you and Prince Vongsavang.*
>
> *Ho Chi Minh*

Ho was perhaps being diplomatic. It was well known that the king had initially regarded Vongsavang as an unsuitable heir. The crown prince had not obtained degrees or diplomas from his studies in France, and he spoke French with a heavy accent, owing partly to his malformed front teeth. Ho's tapestry wasn't the only gift from across enemy lines. Prominently displayed in another glass case was the comb-and-mirror set given to Queen Khamphoui in April 1958 by Madame Viengkham Souphanouvong, the Vietnamese wife of the Red Prince.

What was the point of this bizarre exhibition? I wondered. Were the gifts and expressions of regard of the leftist leaders supposed to show what good fellows they were? Or was there something noble about rat cunning that I had missed? Were we supposed to wander awe-struck amid the evil wealth of the former king, which actually appeared to be rather modest? Or should we admire the Lao government for carefully preserving an important part of the nation's history, and encouraging foreign tourists, if not Lao citizens—who by and large could not afford the entry fee—to inspect it? Perhaps the Lao revolution craved continuity.

Somsanith drew close to me as I gazed up at the king's portrait.

'Now he is in the north of Laos,' she said, blushing.

'He stays there? Or...?'

'I don't know.'

Shaking her head, she led me into the next room, formerly the royal dining room, where more gifts to the king from foreign leaders were kept. These ranged from the banal—moon rocks brought back by the *Apollo* astronauts and presented by US President Richard Nixon—to some rather nice carpets from Iran, and fine Cambodian silver. The Lao flag carried to the moon and back by the astronauts bore the red and white triple-elephant symbol of the royal government. In hindsight, they might as well have left it there.

7

The Magic Buddha

The festival of *Kathin*, an annual presentation of robes and necessities to monks. was being performed all over the country at the conclusion of the Buddhist Lent. But the ceremony at That Luang in Luang Prabang had another purpose as well. It was 29 October, the anniversary of the death of Sisavangvong, whose ashes were interred in the gold-tiled *stupa* at the northern end of the *wat*. It was the only place in Laos where, once a year, the memory of a former king was honoured. The ceremony had been banned after 1975, but was revived in the early 1980s as revolutionary fervour faded.

It was my last day in Luang Prabang, and paper flags featuring the national colours were interspersed with Buddhist ones at Wat That Luang. The precinct of one of Laos' most important *wats* is one of the few places in the country that ever fell victim to bombastic Soviet ideals of town planning, the Pathet Lao authorities deciding to build a heroic stadium with the bleachers backing onto it. The project was linked to 1990's fifteenth anniversary of the founding of the People's Democratic Republic. Five years on, a triumphal arch stood isolated in a wasteland, a painted hammer and sickle—since removed from the national crest—rusting ignominiously. Clouds of grasshoppers rose before my feet as I picked my way across the abandoned open ground between buffalo pats and marshy patches.

The temple sat on a ridge, mist-encircled peaks rising behind it and a chorus of wooden xylophones and bells issuing from within. Beyond a steep staircase stood a large chapel and two *stupas*, one listing at a menacing angle. The collapse of old *stupas* provides a regular source of treasure for the nation's museums, as the shrines are repositories of votive statues of the Buddha and other valuables.

In the grounds of the *wat*, early arrivals—mainly elderly women—had begun burning incense and draping marigolds over the bases of the *stupas*. It was the strength of women like these that had bolstered the faith through the difficult years after 1975, when the government interfered heavily in Buddhist affairs. While the men of the Politburo banned alms-giving, their wives never ceased going to the temple. The new religious policy was quickly recognised as culturally unacceptable and abandoned. Lao women had stayed true to Buddhism all through their menfolk's fling with Marxism.

Churches have bells, but *wats* have drums, and the thunderous boom resounding from a drum tower outside heralded the arrival of the main body of worshippers. They came in a convoy of Japanese cars, *tuk-tuks*, a truck borrowed for the day from the local Sanitation Department and a tour bus that disgorged a squadron of monks. The lay worshippers all wore white sashes, and some of the women hived off to a communal kitchen where they not only prepared food but also worshipped. A US military parachute belonging to some long-lost pilot was slung between Sisavangvong's *stupa* and the chapel, billowing like a vast mushroom as it filled with the breeze, then sagged heavily under the sun it was supposed to protect us from.

Tin, the late king's great-granddaughter, had been up since early that morning preparing food. Arriving in a white pick-up truck, she began unloading large pots of victuals, robustly carrying the pots to the kitchen herself with a deportment that matched her flawless grooming. Her young son and daughter gambolled behind.

When her contributions had been arranged, she donned a ceremonial sash and rounded up the children.

Inside the temple the devotees were segregated, the men seated on the floor at the front. Their feet, which they were forbidden to point at the altar, were tucked beneath and beside them. Under a large statue of the Buddha painted in gold were collected dozens of cellophane bags containing washing powder, school exercise books, condensed milk, airmail envelopes and toilet-paper rolls for the *Kathin*. The uniformity of the offerings to the monks suggested they had been prepared en masse. Seated on the steps outside the crowded chapel, I could hear the tape-recorded chants issuing from a battered public-address system, but my view of proceedings was constantly hindered by crowds of inquisitive boys. When the tallest of them indicated that he would like my pen—my 'Bic', he called it—I gave it to him, causing much joy and envy. A few minutes later I had to buy it back for ten times its value, when I misplaced my other pen. Under the parachute marquee, Tin was standing alone with her children, facing the *that* of King Sisavangvong. Her hands were clasped in prayer before her face, and her children tried to replicate her devoted posture. She went down on her knees and lowered her head to the ground, and again they scrambled to follow. Then she began distributing garlands, incense and wax tapers to the children. A man went over to help her light the candles, and a waxy fragrance spread across the courtyard as the mother helped her children press the tapers onto an iron grille which bordered the *stupa*, pausing regularly to bow in obeisance before the monument, incense sticks clasped between prayerful hands. This simple act of remembrance by a young woman for her famous great-grandfather passed unnoticed by the bulk of devotees inside the chapel. Dusting off her knees, Tin dismissed the children and returned to the kitchen.

Dozens of helpers were soon carrying trays of food into the *sim*. Plates of sticky rice and bowls of meat floating in broth were passed inside from hand to hand. Tin shovelled ice into cups which were then filled with soya milk and again transported to the congregation. With the arrival of the food, the atmosphere around the *wat* lightened. The old women got excited and the children turned feral, sparing no effort to steal favourite bits of lunch. Buddha must have been smiling on me, for as I stood in the courtyard in the blazing sun he sent one of his devotees to feed me. She held up a tray of rice, pork and vegetables, and seemed genuinely happy to see me. It was Tin.

Then from a window of the *sim* I heard somebody calling my name in a shout disguised as a whisper.

'Hey, guy,' the disembodied voice said. 'Come sit next to me.'

It was Boun Kham. Removing my shoes, I squeezed inside and crawled in his direction.

'No sweat,' he said. 'No sweat. You came, uh? That's good. Lots of ex-ministers, even current vice-ministers are here. You eat with me. Last Supper, eh? Before we go back to Vientiane.'

As he beamed at me, his eyes darted self-consciously about the room. Sometimes he seemed to be flaunting his association with a foreigner to the assembled worshippers, but at other times I thought I caught the hunted glance of a fugitive or prisoner. As we ate our lunch, an elderly Buddhist nun seated in the midst of the assembly held up the new saffron robes and other donations in ceremonial recognition of the community's generosity. Then a *bonze* appeared, sporting his new kit with the creases in the robes still showing, and began to gather up the cellophane bags containing the groceries and carry them to the altar. Then the charity plate was passed and 1000-*kip* notes soon piled up on it. I threw in two, stirring a murmur of approval. It was the perfect moment to doze off in post-prandial slumber, but instead, Boun Kham launched into a diatribe the tenor of which reminded me of my father's after-dinner homilies.

'They told us Marxism was good and communism was strong, and the US was the enemy. But now, see what's happened in the

Soviet Union. So they were wrong. And Lao people know they were wrong,' he hissed.

Somehow, the speech lacked conviction. It smacked of bitterness rather than vindication. Stalinism may have collapsed in Russia, but it was alive and kicking in Laos. Instead of finishing off the satellites, the West was propping them up with recognition and aid. When Boun asked why, I murmured something about geopolitical strategy. We agreed to disagree, and to meet later at the airport.

Leaving Luang Prabang is always a melancholy experience. To cross the iron bridge over the Nam Khan is to wake from a dream, to break an ancient and mysterious spell.

'Such a pretty little mountain kingdom capital,' a well-travelled friend once told me, remembering those days before the revolution. 'Much like those in northern Burma or Thailand must have been. The small court, the craftsmen and dancers, and their majesties at the centre of all the ritual festivities and daily worship. All that semi-feudal apparatus that the Pathet Lao loathed. Such a pity they sent them away. In the normal course of events, a term of more than two years in a Lao prison was almost a death sentence.'

The brooding mountains reflected that mood as the hotel minibus bumped and jerked its way towards the airport. The other passengers were chatting around me, but I felt insulated, isolated by memories not my own. The previous afternoon, in preparation for my departure, I had purchased a small souvenir. Amid the antique royal costumes on sale at the Phukdee Friendship store on Rue Fa Ngum, I had found a statuette of Buddha which according to the shopkeeper was from Pak Ou, a settlement up-river. Opposite this town at the junction of the Mekong and Ou rivers perch the Tham Ting and Tham Phum caves, a tranquil sanctuary where pilgrims have installed thousands of Buddha figurines since the seventeenth century. The statues, ranging in size from tiny to tall, are arranged in massed ranks and smaller clutches, standing with arms at their sides in the Luang Prabang posture that calls for rain. In former times, the king and his family would travel to the caves once a year during *Pimai* by gilded *pirogue*, installing new statues commissioned from local artisans especially for the occasion. During the civil war, the royal boat's progress was observed by communist and royalist troops dug in at different points along the river, their commanders having been in the habit of declaring ceasefires out of deference to the king.

The wooden statuette proffered by the shopkeeper was tiny, about the size of my index finger, its exquisite features mottled in gold dust and soot. The asking price was $6 and I bought it without bargaining. Then, riding back to the hotel, something strange had happened. We were bumping along—me on the bicycle and the deity in the parcel rack—when an irresistible force seized the handlebars, turning the bike off the road and crashing it into a fence.

'What happened?' cried a startled householder, emerging from his cottage to inspect the damage.

'I don't know,' I said, dazed. 'The bike seemed to have a mind of its own. I couldn't stop it.'

A quick examination revealed that the bike's steering lock had engaged, probably due to the vibrations caused by the rough road. With the front forks straightened, and the bamboo fence repaired, I was back under way, my injured confidence the only casualty. But that afternoon, as I rested in my room, there was a knock at the door. It was Villa Santi's receptionist, who handed me a small package wrapped in brown paper. Opening the package, I was surprised to find the Buddha figurine I had purchased earlier that day. In the shock and confusion of the crash it had apparently been lost, forgotten as I pedalled off. A local sleuth had tracked me down and delivered it to the hotel. Inspecting the statue closely, I saw a hitherto unnoticed expression of mischief on its face. Emerging half-asleep from my room, I found Santi slumped on the lounge in the lobby.

'Have you had a nice time?' he asked, beaming as if there could be only one answer. 'Did you go to the Pak Ou caves?'

'No,' I said, still groggy. 'Why do you ask?'

'I first went to the caves in 1989,' he said, sipping his coffee. 'I was very impressed by the number of Buddhas there. They told me there were approximately eight thousand statues in the caves. Do you know how many there are today?'

I didn't.

'Two thousand, maybe three thousand maximum. Of course, all those Buddhas are not stolen by Lao people. For them, it's a sin. They're afraid to touch a Buddha like that. But for tourists, it's something else. It's a souvenir, or a decoration for their desk. If we select the good type of tourists, we can avoid this. But if we get mass tourism or backpackers in Luang Prabang, that will damage the town.'

Excusing myself, I returned to my room, and retrieved the figurine, which smiled enigmatically at me. Back in the lobby, I handed it to Santi.

'It is surely very old,' he said, poring over it. 'Certainly an antique, and from a temple...but probably from the caves.'

I felt about as small as my tiny Buddha. The craving for old things is one of life's more conflicted compulsions. I had seen for myself the pillage of Angkor Wat, and knew diplomats whose personal effects included whole periods of their host country's archaeology.

'Please, Santi, do me a favour,' I said.

'Sure. Anything.'

'How often do you go to Tham Ting?'

'Maybe once a month.'

'Next time you go, take this.'

I handed him the statue.

'Take it? Why?'

I told him about the strange force that had possessed the bicycle. Santi chuckled.

'Small but powerful, eh?' he said. 'Okay, if you wish, I'll take it back to the caves.'

'*Kop chai lai lai*,' I said. 'Thanks very much.'

It was my last night in Luang Prabang, and still I hadn't been able to talk to Santi's wife, Tin. Even better would be a chat with her mother, Princess Mahneelai, back in Vientiane. But to have any chance of meeting the crown princess, I would need to transgress the cultural taboos; I would need to force the issue.

'Santi,' I said, 'I need to meet your mother-in-law before she goes to Australia.' I muttered something about writing a newspaper article about her in time for her visit there.

'Well, I'd have to ask her first,' he replied. 'Many have asked for an interview, but the Ministry of Information and Culture has refused permission. You know, officially, you are supposed to give them a list of the questions. And then they probably won't allow it anyway.'

'Which is why I'm not asking for an interview. I can just meet her,' I said, a sinking ship.

'You know it can create difficulties for us,' Santi continued. 'We don't want to make trouble.'

'But what about your business? You need publicity so tourists will know about the hotel and come here, don't you?'

'Sure, sure.'

The silence rang with hopelessness.

'Look,' he said. 'Why don't you try to meet her when she's in Australia?'

'Santi…'

'Well…well, all right. I'll talk to her. But remember there is one French journalist from *Le Figaro* who will never be allowed to come back to Laos. He was supposed to write about the Mekong, but he wrote about the anti-communists.'

'I know.'

'Maybe I can ask her if she would like to meet you. But you must not ask her political questions, or questions about her personal feelings.'

'Of course not!'

'She is a hidden person. She has many painful memories. You shouldn't disturb them.'

Part Two

VIENTIANE

8

Meeting with a Princess

Vientiane was a low-slung, balmy town cradled in a bend of the Mekong River, where the only tension was an intermittent struggle between the rising dust and the lowering dampness of the air. And the dust was winning, settling in small dunes along the roadsides. The dunes encroached gradually on the narrowing roads, defying the efforts of grass to stabilise them, and of schoolchildren press-ganged on days of public service to sweep them away. On the city's main arteries, battalions of *tuk-tuks* and cars mimicked the Bangkok 'charge', careering between the handful of traffic signals.

My host was a diplomat friend who lived in the Sokpaluang temple district. In the immediate post-revolutionary period—when diplomats were prohibited from travelling more than 5 kilometres outside the capital, and their homes were besieged by police and spies—such an arrangement would have been unthinkable. Now things were considerably more relaxed, and my friend's home was an air-conditioned, bougainvillea-draped haven. The gatekeeper met me with a gargantuan smile and the housekeeper advised me to leave my shoes at the door.

Early next morning I set out by *tuk-tuk* for a meeting with a princess. Princess Mahneelai and her husband, Crown Prince Vongsavang, had been apart now for longer than they had been married. The two scions of the Lao elite, educated at Cambridge and Montpellier, had wed at the palace in Luang Prabang in August 1962. The bride, aged 20, was described in diplomatic cables as 'lively and intelligent…speaks fluent French and English and seems to have considerable influence over the husband'. When, in March 1977, the crown prince and his parents disappeared from Luang Prabang, his wife was left behind. Mahneelai had raised seven children alone in a whitewashed villa that was still her home. When I met her at a compound owned by the Inthavong family in Vientiane, she was fifty-four and her children were spread across four continents.

Knocking on the door of the bungalow, I was surprised to be greeted by a barefoot princess. There were no servants around, no-one else at all in the residence that showed few signs of permanent habitation. Although lacking shoes, the princess wore lipstick and polished nails. At 54, her hair was grey, with wild wisps refusing to stay in a bun, and her figure was draped in a simple brown *sin* which she constantly smoothed over her knees. Her title might be gone, but her beauty and dignity were intact. She had prepared for our meeting by dusting off an old photo album with pictures of her wedding. There they were, two young Lao transformed into avatars of an ancient culture. The bride's skin was creamy, as if washed in milk, her shoulders clad in heavily brocaded textiles and her hair bejewelled. Beside her stood the crown prince, ornate and grave.

I had with me my chart of the royal family tree, which I showed to the princess in the sitting room. Gold-rimmed spectacles perched on her nose as she pored over the genealogy of her family, a maze of cousins and half-brothers, descendants of the lusty King Sisavangvong. His first wife, Khammouane, had borne Savang Vatthana, the last king, but there were many other wives including Mahneelai's grandmother, Khamla, who had also done their bit to renew the pool of princes, nobles, diplomats, secretaries and eligible marriage partners for the king and his heirs. As a student of English at Cambridge, Mahneelai had met the crown prince in London during one of his trips to Britain, where he preferred to spend his vacations. He was at that time studying political science long and nonchalantly in France, where he was seen as a loner. Vongsavang had left Luang Prabang at the age of twelve to attend school in Hanoi when it was still under French rule. Mahneelai was the daughter of Khamphan Panya, the Lao ambassador to Washington. So although they had grown up in the same small town, the couple met on the other side of the world.

'When we first met in London, it was as cousins meet,' said Mahneelai. 'He was intelligent and he never smiled. I didn't dare love him. He was my cousin, but intermarriage was still the way at that time. In fact, you were discouraged from marrying outside the royal family. When Vongsavang fell in love with me, he told his parents and they agreed to arrange our marriage. The new generation marry Europeans and people abroad, and they choose their own partners…My daughter's husband, Santi, was not a member of the royal family, but they love each other. It's not like before.'

Before the wedding, the princess was carried in procession from her home—a villa near the Mekong—to the palace, where she and her betrothed were dressed in golden tunics and shawls. The groom held a gold sceptre; the bride was laden with jewels. The palace chief of protocol, Prince Khamhing, fussed over the arrangements while attendants in white dress uniforms squatted and cradled *baci* bowls in their hands, their faces grave lest the slightest hitch mar the occasion. The incantations of the shaman swelled and ebbed.

Vongsavang and Mahneelai did not have a honeymoon for the same reasons that Savang Vatthana was never crowned king. As the seers had foretold, the king's reign coincided with difficult years of war and political division, even within the royal family itself.

'For years we prepared for the coronation, but it never happened. We just prepared,' recalled Mahneelai. 'At that time there were two political parties within the royal family, and they were fighting. So they couldn't make the decision.'

The new king occupied himself with his projects, restoring Wat Xieng Thong, renovating the palace and developing his farm at Pak Xuang, 15 kilometres upstream from Luang Prabang, where he introduced new varieties of oranges and avocados to Laos. Foreign leaders playing host to the king were sometimes surprised when he digressed from matters of state to inquire about foreign varieties of eggplant or grapefruit, and whether they could arrange the import of seeds. Vientiane-based ambassadors lucky enough to be invited to the palace would find themselves issued with wellington boots to go trudging through the manure at Pak Xuang with the crown prince.

'The oranges were magnificent,' recalled Mahneelai. 'Once a year there was a ceremony for the threshing of the rice. Anyone who wanted to could attend, and many villagers would come.'

The garden at Pak Xuang should have impressed the Pathet Lao at least, but after his abdication in 1975 the king was no longer permitted to visit, and the farm was allowed to go to seed. During the fifteen months between his abdication and internal exile, the king continued to live in Luang Prabang, but was forced to leave the palace, which became a museum. He moved into a villa on the Mekong and was not allowed visitors. In 1977, when the king, queen and crown prince were taken away in a Russian helicopter, Mahneelai was pregnant with her seventh child. She became very depressed but was consoled by Anoulath, the head of the monks' school in Luang Prabang.

'He came to me and said, "It's not good for you to do like this." So the monk came and taught me every afternoon, about how the Buddha took five-hundred lifetimes to get over his troubles. And eventually I changed my mind, and accepted. I realised that if I allowed myself to succumb to my sadness, no-one would look after the children.'

Extraordinary as it may seem, the princess had never been informed officially about her husband's fate. When party leader

Kaysone announced the death of the king he did not mention her husband.

The royal family was no longer powerful, but in Luang Prabang Mahneelai enjoyed the respect of ordinary Lao who still bowed to her in the street. She was something of a Lao Princess Diana, her life glamorous and tragic. The mother of a Lao friend told me that, despite the fall of the monarchy, she would certainly prostrate herself if ever she met the princess. But as far as Mahneelai was concerned, being 'common' had its advantages.

'Now I can go to the market, or anywhere I like. When I was a princess even shopping like an ordinary person was not possible, unless I was followed by security people, and that was unpleasant. I'm free now.'

For most of her children, however, such small freedoms were not enough. In August 1981, two of her sons—Prince Soulivong Savang, then eighteen years old, and his seventeen-year-old brother, Thayavong—made a daring night crossing of the Mekong near Vientiane on a raft made of banana-palm trunks. The boys took their ageing governess with them, and a couple of young maids and guards. They ended up in Paris.

Ten years later, Mahneelai petitioned the local authorities to return the small, run-down villa on Rue Sakarine that had been 'loaned' to them after 1975. Under the new economic policy adopted by the party, her request was granted. Work began to restore the building and open the Villa de la Princesse (now the Villa Santi), which quickly built an international reputation, contributing greatly to the development of tourism.

'It's how I keep busy,' Mahneelai told me. 'It's how I forget the past.'

I began to see the resemblance to her daughter—the impression of strength combined with reserve. There was a rock-like immovability about the family. Fate had made them flexible, but also stubborn.

'I've adapted to the situation by going to the temple, and listening to the teachings of the Buddha. I don't think, like some others might, "Oh I'm very depressed." I learnt from Buddhism that life goes in cycles, and Buddhist teachings are not a lie. You must accept the good and the bad, the high and the low, and learn from them.'

She may be a princess, but at that moment her voice seemed universal, one of the thousands of voices lost in the abyss of war and revolution: a voice of resilience and survival and faith.

'You can escape the sun. You can escape the rain. But you cannot escape the cycle of your own life,' she said.

At one point in our meeting, the telephone rang and she went out to answer it. When she returned, I asked about the disputed authenticity of the *pra bang*, the gold talisman of the nation displayed at the palace in Luang Prabang. Was the genuine one really in Moscow?

'Nobody dares say that,' she warned, 'because if you say it, and you're wrong, Buddhists believe you will die.'

She laughed at my alarmed expression.

'Whether it's real or not depends on your heart,' she said. 'Even if not, we will still respect it, and that will make it real. At *Pimai* last year, the people came to throw water at the Buddha image. And one person came from the village, and he said, "Oh, this is not the real Buddha. It doesn't shine!" But I told him, "You shouldn't say that. It's been kept inside the palace for a long time, so it hasn't been cleaned. It's just a bit dusty." And the people all around us said, "Yes, Mahneelai is reasonable! Mahneelai is wise!"'

I felt I had imposed on her time and hospitality enough, even though there were many questions I had still not asked. My mere presence could potentially cause problems for a woman who'd already had her fair share. Santi had told me the princess preferred not to think about the past, but I had to know why, in her view, the monarchy had collapsed. If kingship was bestowed by the Buddha, was its destruction also a reflection of his will? Had the Elephant Kings lost the mandate of heaven?

'We've enjoyed good things in our past lives. Maybe our time has come to live differently,' she said, sidestepping the question. 'No-one knows into what incarnation they will be born. If they could choose their birth, everyone would be king. Even the women.'

She laughed joyously.

But could the monarchy ever return to Laos, as it had in Cambodia?

'We are still the royal family,' she replied. 'The royal spirit is in our blood. But now we live as ordinary people. It's difficult for commoners to enter the royal family and learn that style. But royalty can live as the common people. And we have. Yet we are still the royal family.'

It was an enigmatic answer to a political question, which I shouldn't have asked anyway, but repeated.

'It depends on the circumstances,' said Mahneelai. 'I don't think about it.'

9

The Purge

Returning to Vientiane in June 1975 after his humiliating expulsion from the royal capital, the salt trader's son turned intelligence officer, Khamphan Thammakhanty, found a city that was physically unchanged five years after he left it. Yet its political foundations had shifted irrevocably. Reporting for duty at the Phonekheng military headquarters, the career army officer was told there was no job for him. He was still a soldier, but the Royal Lao armed forces no longer knew what to do with soldiers. Instead of reassigning one of their most capable and committed officers, the generals at Phonekheng told Khamphan to attend the political re-education seminars being held every day in the headquarters' assembly hall.

Arriving for class early the next morning, Khamphan found about 150 other officers studying the Vientiane Accords. In the coming weeks, he would notice that high-ranking Pathet Lao leaders were frequent visitors to the general headquarters, where they would occasionally make speeches about the new political realities. One day at the end of June, the soldiers were told that a senior minister in the new coalition government would be addressing them. But instead of a speech to rally the flagging morale of the armed forces, Khamphan was astonished when the deputy Defence Minister, Khammouane Boupha, advised the men to consider their futures. The public mood was ugly, he told them, and for their own safety he strongly advised them to take refuge at the Chinaimo army cadet training school until things settled down. Next day, Khamphan's wife, Singpheng, drove her husband to Chinaimo. He had packed a trunk full of clothes and personal belongings, and carried a shoulder bag containing $270 and some important papers. For the next three weeks he would remain confined to the army base—now what was called a 'seminar' camp— visited only by his wife.

The seminar system was probably the largest and most organised social program ever implemented in Laos. Its immediate aim was to consolidate leftist control by isolating individuals whose loyalty and submission to the new order could not be guaranteed. A vast enterprise, it required at first voluntary attendance at classes by thousands of people associated with the former government. The Lao term *samana* refers to a gathering of friends, and this proved to be a useful ambiguity for the Pathet Lao. By 'inviting' such attendance, the authorities encouraged the widespread hope that the new regime was committed to national reconciliation. Instead, it flushed out the party's perceived enemies, allowing them to be systematically processed and eventually expelled from the capital well before the official declaration of the Lao People's Democratic Republic on 2 December 1975. For some, it merely involved a break from normal work to spend a few weeks attending classes at Vientiane's Dong Dok (formerly Sisavangvong) University. But for political prisoners it would mean years separated from family and friends, and sometimes death in remote corners of the country. The facade of a process that had anything to do with education soon fell away. No books or papers were issued at Chinaimo. The campus was merely a holding facility needed because there were not enough planes to transport the regime's prisoners to the new prison and labour camps springing up across the country. Perhaps the most egregious aspect of the internment program was that it was probably unnecessary. In the supple political culture of South-East

Asia, the tendency to adapt to changed circumstances was still strong. Having seized control of the government, army, intelligence apparatus, courts, police and media, and with the United States having withdrawn unequivocally from Indochina, it was unlikely that the Pathet Lao would have faced serious challenges from individuals associated with the old regime.

'We would have happily worked with the new government,' Khamphan said years later. 'It was unlikely we could topple them, so what was the point in opposing them? Everyone just wanted to get on with their lives.'

On 21 July 1975, just before lunch, selected prisoners at Chinaimo were surprised by an order to pack their bags immediately. There would not be time for their meal. They were leaving for the airport, and a flight to Viengxai in north-eastern Houaphan province. Returning to his bunk, Khamphan quickly packed his clothes and mosquito net, and made sure he had his shoulder bag with the money hidden inside. Still wearing his full Royal Lao Army dress uniform, he boarded the bus with the other prisoners. They went quietly, with no suggestion they might try to rebel.

As the bus rattled through Vientiane, the prisoners looked out at the country's largest city, some of them for the last time. They knew the reputation of Viengxai, the 'City of Victory', whose caves were the crucible of the Pathet Lao guerillas. They were prisoners of history, and knew how easily they could also become its casualties. As the bus headed along Samsenthai Road, with their luggage piled on the roof, Khamphan's heart leapt. He realised they would be passing the National Printing Office, where his daughter, Chan, worked as an accountant. Quickly, acting on impulse, he ripped one of his service medals from the breast of his uniform, and as the bus passed his daughter's office, flung it out the window. The decoration, once a source of family pride, landed on the dirt path outside the government building.

A janitor who happened to be passing picked it up on his way into the office.

'Look what I found outside,' he said to his colleagues when he entered the building. Told that Chan's father was a military officer, the janitor took the medal to the upstairs office where Khamphan's daughter immediately recognised the rare decoration as one she had seen on her father's uniform, and telephoned her mother. Alarmed, and acting on a hunch, Singpheng raced to Wattay airport in the family Volkswagen. There she found her husband, standing among a group of other detainees waiting to board a plane. Seeing his wife, Khamphan asked the guards' permission to talk to her, which they granted.

Khamphan told Singpheng where they were taking him, and asked her not to worry and to look after the children. Despite the obvious anxiety and confusion on her face, she did not weep nor become hysterical, but maintained a typically nervous Lao smile. As the guards called out that his group was leaving, Khamphan said goodbye to his wife, the mother of his children. But he did not kiss her, nor did they embrace or even hold hands. They did not touch because public displays of physical affection between men and women are not encouraged in Lao culture. They would not see each other again for fifteen years.

In June 1998, the US Central Intelligence Agency declassified and made public a secret 1992 report describing the Lao prison and re-education system. Although it contains a number of factual errors (one prisoner declared to have died in detention is alive and well and living in Portland, Oregon), the document is the most authoritative and detailed account of the Lao gulag yet published. The system, spanning eleven of the country's sixteen provinces, incarcerated at least 30 000 people, one-third of whom died from malnutrition, lack of basic medical care, starvation, or were executed. The report confirms that Vietnamese and East German advisors served in senior positions in the seminar camp system. It identifies the facilities near the village of Sop Hao as the 'worst camp system in Laos'. The Lao gulag would leave its mark on every part of the country, from Vientiane and Luang .Prabang, to Phongsaly in the far north bordering China, and Champassak on the Cambodian border.

The Lao government had arranged for me to meet Khammouane Boupha, the 62-year-old former deputy Defence Minister who had advised his senior officers to surrender to Pathet Lao custody. Mr Khammouane, now Minister of Justice, was one of the few figures from the old regime to make a smooth transition to life under the Pathet Lao. An officer in the Royal Lao Army, he had been serving in Phongsaly in the early 1960s, when the Pathet Lao occupied the province. Defecting to the leftist camp, he remained with them until 1974, when he returned to Vientiane as a Pathet Lao representative in the coalition government.

The waiting room of the minister's office, housed in a building opposite Vientiane's grand arch, modelled on the Arc de Triomphe in Paris, was the size of a broom closet. After a short delay, I was ushered into his room, in which the curtains were drawn and the air-conditioners operated on full throttle in an attempt to push back the torpid tropical heat. The furniture was chipped, a bathmat doubled as a doormat, and the plastic covering had been left on the sofas. Mr Khammouane was an imposing figure, solidly built, but strangely defensive, with a nervy, impatient way of speaking. His smile was more of a wince, and he wrung his hands as he began our meeting by reading from prepared answers to questions which had been submitted in advance.

'We're trying to take the state under law,' he said. 'Our system of law is based on the democracy of the people. Since 1991, we've passed fourteen laws. A criminal code, a civil code and an economic law.'

He spoke in the steel-trap jargon of a political apparatchik, machine-gun sentences shot off with a permanent glare that at first looked threatening, and later timid. The revolution, said Mr Khammouane, had made Laos free and given the people ownership of the country. The government had brought peace and was developing the nation, especially for the highland people, increasing their rights so that everyone could make their own choices and decisions. It was a better system that would make everyone equal.

'I had a part in getting rid of the old system,' he said modestly, when I asked why he had ordered his troops to lay down their arms. '...to create the new system successfully without bloodshed, just by campaigning and meeting with officials from the other side. Some people were sent to Xam Nua to understand the ways of the party and also the new government. Afterwards, they were put into the workforce, depending on their knowledge and ability.'

When his recitation of the written answers had finished, I inquired whether I could ask some unscripted questions. Mr Khammouane looked at his pencil-thin assistant-cum-translator, who smiled non-committally.

'What happened to the king?' I said. 'You're the Minister of Justice. Was it lawful?'

Mr Khammouane looked again to his assistant, apparently disbelieving the translation. Deep furrows marked the assistant's face. I repeated the question, my persistence verging on impertinence.

'They've made a film about twenty years of the Lao revolution,' the minister said. 'You should look at that.'

'Did the king do something illegal?'

Mr Khammouane took a deep breath.

'In 1977 it was the idea of the government to invite the king to Xam Nua. Some countries were trying to use him.'

To a question about political detainees, Mr Khammouane responded with a trump card in the unexpected form of his leathery little translator perched on the plastic-covered sofa. He turned out to be Houy Pholsena, the brother of Quinim Pholsena, the left-leaning Foreign Minister in a coalition government whose assassination in the early 1960s convinced the Pathet Lao that it was dangerous for them to remain in Vientiane. The brothers had been on opposite sides of the political divide.

'After the war, Dr Houy spent thirteen years in a re-education camp. Now I have made him the director of my office. When I'm away, and the vice-minister is not here, the director takes on the role of head, with all responsibilities.'

The little fellow perked up, smiling bashfully at being mentioned by his minister. He seemed resigned to his role of providing living proof of the government's generosity.

'To mend the damage of war, people needed to change their way of thinking,' said Mr Khammouane. 'Feelings of hatred must be forgotten. When that person fully understands the situation, he can come back. This is the Lao way, the Lao system. Some countries use weapons, but Laos doesn't use that sort of system. If the attitude of the person changes, then the sentence is quickly reduced. Those who understand the new situation are given jobs—for example, Dr Houy.'

Perhaps the minister had done this sparrow-like man a kindness by letting him work in his office. But I found their relationship somewhat repulsive. As he bowed and scraped, the prisoner in Dr Houy was never far from the surface.

10

Collective Amnesia

Twenty years after imposing their stern new order, the Lao leftists decided to throw a party. The anniversary celebrations of December 1995 were the opening I'd been looking for to gain access to people and places associated with the founding of the People's Democratic Republic. But the chasm between what I wanted to know, and what they wanted to project, would make for numerous difficult encounters. My determination to unearth the secret past was matched by their desire to keep burying it.

For weeks there had been no reply to my letter to the foreign ministry requesting interviews with all important officials from the president and party leader down. Camped in Vientiane as I awaited a response, I whiled away time visiting *thats* and *wats*. There was That Luang, the massive *stupa* painted gold on a hill north-east of the capital; the stately Wat Sisaket, whose scriptures had been carted off to Bangkok by marauding Thai armies; and the soothing Sokpaluang temple with its sauna run by nuns. But there are only so many temples you can take before retreating to the bamboo bars that perch along the Mekong levee, where the slow stupefaction of beery sunsets awaits you.

Then, out of the blue, came a telephone call from the Ministry of Foreign Affairs. I was to present myself before officials the following morning. The caller failed to identify himself, and gave no indication of the meeting's purpose, nor whom I was to meet. Told of the call, an expatriate friend forewarned me.

'The Lao have a reputation for being submissive,' he said. 'But among themselves they're quite ruthless. All that gentle stuff is eyewash for the foreigners. If you cross the line, if you're seen as interfering in their internal affairs, the gentility turns to obstinacy, and even hostility.'

The morning dew was evaporating, steam rising from the roads, as I entered the iron palisades of the Ministry of Foreign Affairs. Inside the large, undistinguished building, men in suits disappeared round corners in clouds of cigarette, smoke as I approached. In the outbuilding housing the press department, I was met by a stocky young man called Khen who sat me in a reading room lined with obscure works by the late North Korean leader Kim Il-Sung and his son Kim Jong-Il. After stewing in my thoughts—and those of the two Kims—I was led upstairs to meet Linthong Phetsavan, a polished diplomat who'd served as chargé d'affaires in Washington. He welcomed me warmly and asked how my visit was proceeding. As always, I had prepared a list of complaints—interviews not organised, a new and arbitrary service charge which had been imposed on journalists—ammunition with which to hit back, in case they had some complaint against me. But Linthong knew the first rule of diplomacy. He never stopped smiling.

'We highly appreciate your efforts to write about our country,' he said. 'We regard you as a friend of the Lao PDR.'

This worried me. Many times as a correspondent in Vietnam, I had been complemented before being denounced. Only a friend could become a turncoat and an enemy. It had never happened to me in Laos, and I looked at the floor, waiting for the verbal blow to fall. But Linthong simply wished to discuss my request to interview the prime minister.

'The government is considering your request,' he said. 'The questions you have submitted are very good, very constructive. We want to do this. But we need your assurance that you will stay with these questions, not other, unconstructive questions.'

Linthong reminded me that if he organised the interview and things went awry, he would get into trouble. Even if the prime minister smiled and was gracious in my presence, the trouble would come later. Concluding that any interview was better than none, I agreed to all conditions, confident that once bonhomie developed between me and the prime minister I could ask whatever I wanted and we'd all part beaming and embracing, as always happened at the end of a non-interview with a communist official. In the event, the proposed meeting never eventuated.

Returned to the custody of Khen, I was informed that Sisana Sisane, a founder of the People's Revolutionary Party, had agreed to meet me. Born in Savannakhet in 1922, Sisana had fought the French and fled to Thailand with the Lao Issara nationalists. He'd been imprisoned by the royal government in 1959, but escaped and joined Souphanouvong on the 'little Long March' overland to Xam Nua. Throughout the 1960s and early 1970s he'd run the Pathet Lao radio station, broadcasting propaganda designed to undermine the morale of the royalists, and after 1975 was made the first Minister for Information and Culture. Being in government, however, did not 'agree with him—or perhaps it agreed too well. In 1983, he was demoted for expressing 'anti-Soviet sentiments' and banished to Houaphan. Reliable sources had told me this period of re-education had more to do with personal problems than with political ones. Sisana's *faux pas* had occurred at a gala song contest he'd presided over as minister. The audience was large and enthusiastic, and Sisana, who enjoyed a drink, decided to perform one of his own compositions. Ignoring shouted requests for a popular Russian tune, he interspersed his tune with jibes at the crowd, the Russian song and the Soviet Union in general. Apparently it was quite a performance, but the Houaphan hangover proved sobering. In

1985, Sisana was rehabilitated as director of the Institute of Social Sciences and entrusted with producing an official history of the country and the party which, as far as I could establish, he had never completed.

For press-office minder Khen, the prospect of meeting such a high-ranking official was as daunting as it was unusual.

'There's not much time,' he said, bustling and flustering like a minion. 'We'll take your car.'

'You mean, my *tuk-tuk*.'

Khen looked at me in disbelief. What was the point of being a government official if you had to travel in *tuk-tuks*?

'*Baw*,' he insisted, getting quite agitated. 'We can't. We must have a car to get to Sisana's office.'

'Oh, really?' I said, taking perverse pleasure in his irritation. 'Does he live in a garage?'

'No, of course not. He's meeting us at Kilometre Six.'

I was dumbstruck. Kilometre Six, or Six Clicks City as it was widely known, had been off limits to foreigners since the revolution. It was the former compound of the United States Agency for International Development (USAID) which the Pathet Lao had besieged in 1975. American aid to Laos had been higher per person than that to any other country, and was the main means of support for the 25 000 troops of the Royal Lao Army. But when the US walked away from its allies, as well as its foes in Indochina, the fate of Laos, Vietnam and Cambodia was sealed. In April 1975, as Phnom Penh and Saigon fell, Pathet Lao troops attacked the strategic crossroads at Sala Phou Khoun that linked Vientiane with Luang Prabang and the Plain of Jars, and began to move into the Mekong River towns, the last bastions of the royalists. Pro-American ministers and generals fled across the Mekong to Thailand, and deputy Defence Minister Khammouane Boupha gave his infamous order to government troops to lay down their arms and turn themselves in.

At the celebrations of Constitution Day in Vientiane on 11 May 1975, Prime Minister Souvanna Phouma addressed an audience depleted by the heat and political uncertainty, but which included the king, who arrived in a black Russian limousine. Souvanna had come in a Ford, but his car was the only pro-Western statement made that day. The constitution they were celebrating was already a dead letter, one more worthless piece of paper, like the Vientiane Accords and the Paris peace agreement signed only two years earlier.

'The upheavals which have agitated our country for twenty years have clearly resulted in a new situation,' Souvanna said. 'It is necessary to look at the facts and prepare to arrive at an accord with history. Our population understands the situation well by instinct. We must stop the fighting. The war has reached an end.'

A few days later, leftist guerillas surrounded USAID's Vientiane compound at Kilometre Six on the road to Nam Ngum dam. As well as aid workers, the compound housed CIA staff overseeing the secret war in Laos. The siege was lifted only after the US agreed to withdraw the USAID mission and all its personnel by the end of June. A cameraman I knew who'd visited Six Clicks City during the 1960s and early 1970s had often spoken of the place as a sort of Shangri-la in the midst of the civil war, with sealed roads, bars, restaurants, swimming pools, tennis courts and saunas, a well-stocked commissary full of duty-free booze and, according to him, blue movies on video.

'It was magnificent, mate,' he'd told me, eyes watering over a soda, one sweaty evening at the Lan Xang Hotel.

A fond, foggy memory perhaps, but Kilometre Six had provided what every war needs; a bastion of splendour reassuring people that somewhere, somebody at least was living it up, a dream protected by barbed-wire barricades.

Khen had been a press guide since the early 1990s and had never been to Six Clicks City. Since 1975 no Western journalist had been there either. We ran to the *tuk-tuk* and headed for the Morning Market, where we hired a battered Corolla and driver and headed out past the Defence Ministry.

At 6 a.m. on 20 May 1975, the American residents of Kilometre Six received telephone calls ordering them not to attempt to leave the compound. The Pathet Lao had surrounded it and were in command of all exits. Anyone seen leaving or entering would be shot. The following day the Americans paid off their servants, who walked out and were immediately sent to re-education camps. A few days later, the first busload of American dependants left Kilometre Six for the airport.

Now we were barrelling along that same road past shophouses, soup stalls and billboards advertising Pepsi-Cola. Six kilometres from the city centre we turned left at one of those murals that extol the drudgery of peasants, and drove along a short stretch of smooth tarmac bordered by oversized freeway lamp-posts bending inwards like respectful serfs. An arched entrance bearing the words 'Lao People's Democratic Republic' beckoned. Cautious Khen looked for someone to report to. But thanks to the awe in which people held Kilometre Six, no guards were considered necessary. Unhindered, we entered a neat but graceless barracks of brick bungalows set out in small streets and bordered by severely pruned gardens. The gymnasium of the former American school, where Crown Prince Vongsavang had read out the king's abdication announcement, looked smaller than I had imagined, the red and gold hammer-and-sickle flag of the party hanging limp from a pole outside. How history had magnified all these things. It was clear nobody of great importance lived in this legendary place anymore. We walked past volleyball courts and a satellite dish on a lawn, and stopped to inspect the sole wooden structure in the compound, which turned out to be a large sauna. Khen stopped several times to ask directions. Eventually we came to a two-storey scale model of the former US embassy in Saigon, one of those strange American diplomatic structures with concrete lattice-work shielding the windows from rocket attack, and lots of air conditioners. Inside, it was musty and dark, with parquet floors and narrow corridors.

We found Sisana in an upstairs office which had louvres instead of panes in the windows. He was a nugget of a man, short with a boxer's stance and hard eyes. A German correspondent who had met him in 1979 noted Sisana's almost European features—he said he'd been told in Bangkok that the minister's grandfather had been a Corsican living on the Mekong. This historian–poet–bureaucrat wore a dark-grey flannel safari suit with epaulettes and two gold pens in the pocket, as if denoting his rank. He smoked Marlboros, the spoils of victory, holding them between his fingers like a chillum, the ash pointing up between his knuckles. His laugh was terrifyingly earthy, and he was a bit of a name-dropper.

'This was Kaysone's bedroom,' Sisana said, referring to the late Pathet Lao leader, and gesturing to the four corners of his office. Then realising he may have divulged a state secret, he added, 'But Kaysone had several houses.' Inviting us to sit on a brown vinyl sofa under an oil painting of That Luang, he made small talk while a heroic proletarian served coffee, one of those clean, deep brews you could only find in the offices of senior leaders.

'Why should anyone want to interview me, a humble historian?' Sisana asked himself aloud, feigning modesty. I'd encountered similar defensive artifice among Afghan warlords and Vietnamese communists, people whose world is a dangerous place in which even a simple encounter with a writer might pose a hidden threat. The glint in Sisana's eye told me he was a hard-boiled type who could be moved to poetry only by the concept of class struggle. A few months earlier, he had celebrated his seventy-third birthday in the usual rousing manner. Before becoming a freedom fighter, he had been a musician, playing and composing songs for the *khene*, the Lao bamboo harmonica. But while his compositions were musically traditional, they were lyrically revolutionary. His first song was 'Repression of the Aggressors', which today serves as the theme tune for the news on Lao National Radio. There followed more songs in praise of the motherland, including 'The Projection of the Lao Combatants', 'Triumph of Highway Number Nine', 'Walk Forward', 'Love of Laos', 'Victory of Nambak', 'The Success of Xieng Khouang', 'Twenty Years of Revolution' and—in what might have been a momentary lapse into bourgeois romanticism—'To Think of a Love'. He had even penned the national anthem, a crusty piece of revolutionary bravado:

From the beginning, the Lao people
have brilliantly represented their motherland,
with all their energies, all their spirits and hearts,
and as a single force, they have progressed united and determined,
honouring dignity and proclaiming their right to be their own masters.
All Lao ethnic groups are equal,
never again will they allow imperialists and traitors to harm them.
The people united will safeguard the independence
and freedom of the Lao nation.'
They are determined to fight and win, to lead the nation to prosperity.

For a man punished for an anti-Soviet tirade, Sisana seemed to have mastered bombastic Bolshevik poppycock. I told him I was curious about the fact that before 1975 the Pathet Lao had given no indication that they intended to abolish the monarchy.

• 'That's right,' he said. 'Our party appointed the king as advisor to President Souphanouvong. In a small country it's unnecessary to say, "We won't use the king." So we tried our best to use the king.'

'So the party didn't believe that the monarchy was necessarily a bad thing?'

'Generally the people did not like the king.'

'But it was an ancient institution.'

'Yes, but the Kingdom of Lan Xang only held power in the north. Champassak was different. There, Boun Oum was given rights but was considered only as a prince. The southern provinces came under the French protectorate. There was a declaration of independence in 1949, but the north remained a monarchy. Generally speaking, the Lao people—especially Luang Prabang people—didn't like the king.'

'Why not?'

'Because the administration had no justification.'

'Economically or socially?'

'Mainly economically. The king had teak plots in Paklai. No-one else could touch them.'

'Did he log them or just keep them?'

'They belonged to the king. No-one else could cut them without paying money to the king, like paying taxes. The villages were divided into guilds—weavers, entertainers. The village of entertainment should provide beautiful female entertainers just for the king.'

'Like a feudal system?'

'Yes.'

'But if the king had co-operated with the new regime, maybe today you'd still have a figurehead monarch?'

'Yes. At that time the Soviet Union built two statues of Sisavangvong. One is outside Wat Seemuang. The other is in Luang Prabang. And we still keep those two statues.'

'Because Sisavangvong was a good leader?'

'It's not that. It's the party's policy that what we have, we preserve.'

'But not the monarchy itself. The party forced the king to abdicate.'

'I don't know if that's the case or not, because before the first plenary session of the Congress of People's Deputies was opened, on 2 December 1975, Souphanouvong had a personal meeting with the king and tried to explain to him how the political situation would be. He tried to persuade the king to accept the new system of government.'

'Savang Vatthana was never really king,' Sisana said, dismissing the issue. 'The prince did not automatically assume the throne upon the death of his father. There should be a ceremony. The reason this did not occur was that at the time Sisavangvong died, there was still fighting in the country, from province to province, and it became worse later on. He was waiting until there was calm in the whole country.'

'What was the actual event which led to the arrest of the king?' I asked.

'The reason the liberation government arrested the king and his son was because his son, Vongsavang, with the French government and several other governments, tried to fight against the liberation government. The second reason was that we knew the crown prince wanted to send his father into exile. We knew of that plan, and that was why we arrested them, and stopped their plan in advance.'

As he spoke Sisana showed increasing signs of impatience with my line of questioning. He would look at Khen as if to say, 'What is this? Why is he asking that question?', and then Khen would look at me the same way.

Princess Mahneelai had told me that when party leader Kaysone referred to the death of the king, he did not mention her husband. Now seemed the moment when the riddle might be answered.

'The queen died before the king,' Sisana said, confident of that. 'But I'm not quite sure whether the prince died before his father or not.'

All three were dead, that much was new. Yet it seemed odd that such simple facts of Lao history as the dates of their deaths were unknown to the country's leading historian. What about the reports published in the West that the crown prince had been killed during an escape bid?

Sisana vetoed the idea.

'There was no escape because guards kept close watch on the people sent to seminar…There were several escape attempts by former high officers, but they were caught.'

To be fair to him, being official historian in a secret state was not an easy job.

'Writing is not difficult, but it depends on the politics,' he admitted, waving off the haze from his Marlboro. 'It's for the sake of the party. We used to have a dispute with China. So should we write about that? I don't. We may have a dispute with the Thai. Should we write about it? It depends on the future situation. That's the crucial point which I consider difficult. Writing is not difficult.'

George Santayana's remark, 'Those who do not remember the past are condemned to repeat it', came to mind. But Sisana had not forgotten the past. He knew very well that in March 1979 the Lao government had sided with Vietnam in its war against China, asking Chinese road construction gangs to leave the country and protesting against Chinese troop deployments on their common border. He knew about party insiders like Dr Khamsengkeo Sengsthith, a senior official in the Health Ministry, who in December 1981 defected to China and said the Vietnamese were using chemical weapons against Laos' Hmong tribes; and Khampeng Boupha, who was arrested in the summer of 1979 for conspiring with the Chinese. But relations with China were good now, so as a historian it was his duty to overlook the inconvenient past. Communist historians preferred to talk about the future, which was always bright and certain.

'Is the old system of monarchy finished for ever?' I asked. 'In 1975, did Laos move irrevocably into a new era?'

'Yes,' Sisana said, stubbing out a Marlboro.

'And Marxism?'

He nodded. At last, a question he was expecting.

'We agree Marxist–Leninist theory is good,' he said. 'But our government is still learning all progressive theories from other countries. The success of a theory depends more on the person who implements it than on the theory itself. The person who studies Marxist–Leninist theory should know the level of his own country's development. If you base your decisions only on the texts, you will die. In the beginning of liberation, we didn't have much experience, so we had to do it according to the way of the existing socialist countries. We wanted to become a socialist country quickly. Lenin wrote that even an underdeveloped country, under the leadership of a Marxist party and with the help of other socialist countries, can become a socialist country.

'Now the world situation has changed and the Soviet Union is destroyed. Some other socialist systems have been destroyed. So Laos has to be independent. Also, in Laos the economy is based on the natural economy. We don't produce any goods for export. We have only family production for family consumption. The Lao system is neither socialist nor capitalist. Whether it becomes socialist or capitalist, it should be based on turning this natural economy into an industrial economy. Once we get industries we can export. To become a balanced economy, we have to create several economic sectors, including government, joint-venture and private. We also need to open the door to foreign investment.'

The leftist leadership had not only opened the door, but prised off the nameplate, removing the hammer and sickle from the national crest. Apostasy, surely?

'In 1986, at the fourth plenary session of the party, we saw that we could not go to socialism. So we have to establish democracy. Once we set up the People's Democracy, there was no need for us to use hammers and sickles, which would create misunderstanding of our policy.'

The building in which we sat had been the venue for Politburo meetings until Kaysone's death in 1992. When our meeting was over, Sisana escorted us downstairs, stopping briefly to show us scores of gold-painted busts of the late leader made in North Korea for distribution around Laos to mark the revolution's twentieth anniversary. The mute conference of imported Kaysones said it all about communism's failed experiment in Laos, and its similarities with another obscure Stalinist basket case. Another building, which had housed the leader's office, would be opened soon as a museum. The attempt to create a lasting niche for Kaysone in the hearts and minds of the Lao hobbled on. In the meantime, his family, of course, was doing well.

On a visit to Vientiane earlier that year I'd met one of Kaysone's sons, Saysomphone, a former governor of Savannakhet, after, he became Minister of Finance, having ousted Souphanouvong's son Khamsai from the job. He was softly spoken and reasonably direct—until I attempted to garner some biographical detail, notoriously difficult to come by in Laos.

'How old are you?' I asked. 'Where were you born and how did your upbringing as the son of a great revolutionary affect your childhood? Did you have to move about a lot? Was it an unusual childhood?'

A murmur rose from the assembled acolytes. The translator shifted uncomfortably in his chair. Saysomphone laughed and adjusted his Omega watch, then mumbled something to the translator.

'The minister graduated from the Moscow Institute of Economics in 1983. He then became a teacher of economics in Laos. In 1987 he was appointed to Savannakhet as assistant to the governor. In 1991 he became deputy governor. In 1993 he became governor. Recently he was appointed Minister of Finance.'

Saysomphone continued to smile as he watched the translator. I fancied he was waiting for him to deliver a punch line. It never came. Perhaps being the youngest member of the party central committee was a sensitive issue if you were the son of Kaysone.

'You avoid mentioning your youth,' I said. 'You don't like to talk about your past?'

He laughed again.

'The minister likes sport,' came the translated reply. 'Football. As governor of Savannakhet he participated in football with others.'

A few weeks after my meeting with Sisana, I was one of a party of foreign correspondents permitted to visit Kaysone's office at Kilometre Six. The tour began in the former chapel of the American compound with a video of the great leader dancing the *lamvong*, the graceful Lao national dance that resembles slow-motion martial arts. His bungalow consisted of three small rooms, including a screened-in porch where his appointments were written on a whiteboard in English. A pile of audio cassettes on his desk suggested that, like Richard Nixon, he recorded important conversations. There was a lacquer painting of Ho Chi Minh talking to Kaysone, and a book by Ho was placed prominently on the desk. But a wall clock bore the logo of Tiger Beer, there was a Parker pen and a Russian desk calendar, a book called *Getting on in English*, an exercise bike and dozens of empty Johnnie Walker scotch bottles. A cabinet contained several Buddha images, and some incense sticks had been lit on an ancestor altar. Evidently the revolutionary leader had found religion.

I asked our guide what the cause of Kaysone's death had been.

'Health problems,' he said.

The communist experiment in Laos had been about as coherent as the contents of its leader's study. Beginning in June 1976 the currency unit known as the *kip* was withdrawn and replaced, withdrawn and replaced again, each time hugely devalued. Eventually this practice destroyed all wealth in the country. A catastrophic drought in 1977 forced the government to appeal for international aid to avert a famine. Attempts to forcibly collectivise agriculture began the following year, but were suspended at the end of 1979 after encountering mass resistance. Regular closures of the border with Thailand took a further economic toll on landlocked Laos, and the Thai embargo on strategic goods—including bicycles and fuel—was in effect a blockade. Pathet Lao troops began selling their units' fuel allocations to supplement inadequate salaries.

The old royal capital also proved particularly troublesome for the new government. Thousands of people reportedly took to the streets of Luang Prabang to protest against attempts to remove the talisman of Lao nationhood, the *pra bang*, from the royal palace. They were also outraged that Buddhist monks were compelled to give sermons endorsing the new government's policies. All monks had to study Marxism–Leninism, the religious hierarchy, the *sangkha*, was disbanded, and the ceremonial fans carried by senior monks were smashed as part of the general levelling. Addressing a training course for Buddhist teachers on 17 October 1976, Politburo member Phoumi Vongvichit said, '[T]he Lord Buddha tried to abolish class distinctions. In this way the Lord Buddha became involved in revolutionary politics. Monks should mix current politics with Buddhist politics when they give sermons… The policy of the party and government is merely to request Buddhist monks to give sermons to teach the people and to encourage them to understand that all policies and lines of the party and government are in line with the teachings of the Lord Buddha.' The monks were forbidden to accept donations of food and forced to labour in the fields, thus breaking their religious vows. But after a while the obsession with Marxist purity was abandoned. As a result, you still see old monks in Laos unlike in Cambodia, where most of them were exterminated.

Vientiane was beginning to strike me as a city of amnesiac misfits, unable to say where they'd come from and unsure where they were going. It was as if the revolution had thrown them all in the air and left them floating. A few had landed on their feet, and I'd managed to cadge a lunch date with one of them.

Souphaxay Souphanouvong, a son of the Red Prince, was that rare beast: a Lao citizen with both a royal and a revolutionary pedigree. The venue for our meeting was L'Opera, a converted warehouse whose Neapolitan cuisine, comprehensive wine list and espresso machine had led the revival of Vientiane's cafe society. Souphaxay did not call himself a prince. It was twenty years since his late father had formally renounced the family's heritage and assumed the presidency of the revolutionary republic. I arrived to find him seated alone at a window, a mobile phone at his elbow, smoking a Benson & Hedges and glancing now and then at the Nam Phou fountain outside. We had not met before, but I think I would have recognised him anywhere. He had inherited not only his father's stocky build, moustache and smile, but his brisk, confident mannerisms—the Souphanouvong swagger. He wore a fawn safari suit with epaulettes, and two rings—a huge sapphire on his left hand, and on his right, a signet with the letter 'S' formed in diamonds. He looked as if he could stand up in a hurricane. At an age when his father had been a revolutionary, Souphaxay was working at the Committee for Planning and Co-operation, the organisation which controlled foreign investment in Laos, and was involved in a power struggle with conservatives in the lead-up to the party congress.

'They tend to believe that you can solve problems by decree. This is not pragmatic,' he said, referring to the hardliners.

What had it been like, I wondered, to grow up in a cave?

Life in hiding in the caves of Viengxai, under constant threat from United States B-52 bombers, had been no different from the lives of other cave-dwelling children, said Souphaxay. Neither he nor his siblings had been told they were princes or communists. After the war, when their father became president and they moved to Vientiane, the family's role in Lao history had become clearer. Souphaxay could remember nursing his uncle, the neutralist prime minister Souvanna Phouma who, with his political career abruptly ended and his immediate family living in exile in Paris, was dying slowly of heart disease. He recalled the two old men, his father and uncle, arguing to the end about politics, as the patrician Souvanna Phouma taught his communist half-brother to play bridge. The Red Prince was still president at the time, but having suffered a stroke on his way to a non-aligned summit in Harare in 1983, his strength too was failing. In his latter years, Souphaxay said, his father would reminisce not about the Pathet Lao's victorious struggle, but about the early days of Lao nationalism after World War II, when the Lao Issara had briefly toppled the monarchy.

Now it was the party's authority that was waning, as its role in society was taken over by the military. The authoritarian nationalism that prevailed elsewhere in South-East Asia was seeping into Laos. The black Russian limousines that once scuttled along Vientiane streets with party chiefs hidden behind their dark-tinted windows had been replaced by Toyota Crowns with even darker windows carrying military officers. Six of the nine Politburo members were current or former generals. Army-owned trading companies were the biggest and most powerful in the country. Foremost among these was the Mountainous Areas Development Company based at Lak Sao in Bolikhamsai province. The village had been transformed into a go-ahead town of 12 000 people with a modern hospital, schools and an airport. Headed by General Chang Sayavong, the company kept people busy in agriculture, forestry, building, infrastructure, handicrafts processing, tourism and, allegedly, cattle smuggling. One of Chang's pet projects was a zoo staffed by foreign experts, which was constantly replenished with wild animals fleeing his company's logging activities. The rapacious exploitation of natural resources had been going on for decades. In the mid 1970s, the wife of a United States Aid and International Development official, Judy Rantala, observed elephants hauling teak logs at Ban Houeysai, part of the collusion between 'enterprising and unscrupulous foreign merchants' and 'greedy government officials who granted them permission to log…The labourers were paid pitiful wages and forests were irretrievably denuded. Millions of dollars were being realised from these valuable teak harvests, but neither the Lao people nor the Lao economy benefited.'

Some of the forests Rantala mentioned belonged to the king, whose youngest son, Sauryavong Savang, was Director of Forestry in the Department of Crown Properties. The opium trade, too, had royal connections. During the 1960s it was said to be controlled in northern Laos by General Ouane Rathikoun, the joint Chief of Staff of the Royal Lao Army. But according to their enemies, the Pathet Lao also engaged in the trade. Just before the arrival of the Japanese in 1945, Phoumi Vongvichit, later a Politburo member, allegedly made off with the entire opium crop of Xam Nua province, which had been stored in the provincial headquarters building.

A document circulating within the Lao exile community at the time of my lunch with Souphaxay suggested a death-bed renunciation by the Red Prince of his lifelong commitment to Marxist orthodoxy. (The first sentence is understood to refer to Souphanouvong's Vietnamese wife, Nguyen Thi Ky Nam, or Viengkham, to use her Lao name, whom many saw as a tool of the Vietnamese.) In full it read:

> Because of my worship of women's beauty, I was a deaf and blind person in my youth. Now I reflect on this and I recognise my mistakes. I would have never thought that Vietnam was capable of committing so many brutal crimes against our country and our people. In the past, we had agreed that once the war was over, Vietnamese would stay in Vietnam and Laotians would stay in Laos, although the two nations would continue their friendship as brotherly countries. I don't know when they will cremate my body, but the crimes I have committed against our country will not disappear with the cessation of my breath and my cremation. Before I could not say anything. Now I wish to leave something behind, and I urge all the children of Laos of all ethnic groups and genders to unify, and to resolve to wash clean the crimes I have committed against our country and our people. I realise

now that I have not been a decent and patriotic person regarding our country; it has only dawned on me when my bones are about to be boiled. All comrades, who are still healthy and strong, when you hear my call, please change and reform your thoughts so that you may guard our nation and the national treasure of our people, of which the most important is your life. Dear brothers and sisters, all the children of Laos, those in foreign lands in particular, are the true patriots. They are far-sighted and intelligent. Their love for our country surpasses all. You must not let Laos die. My children, especially those still in Laos, you must reform yourselves and embrace a new way of thinking, particularly the thinking of all Laotian children in foreign lands, so that you all will be fruitful and helpful to our country and our people. I believe that if you all understand the situation as I do now, we shall remain immortal. Before I die, I urge you all to do as requested and, for this, I am sure Laos will always be Laos.

This text had been sent to the exile newspaper *Sieng Lao Seri*. According to overseas Lao, it had been reprinted in the *Vientiane Times*, but the editor, Somsanouk Mixay, told me he'd never heard of it. I suppose it's not uncommon for old men to blame all their mistakes on sex, but this recantation seemed to me a crude forgery. Souphaxay agreed, saying his father had never expressed any such doubts.

'Did he regret his role in the abolition of the monarchy? It was never an issue we spoke about. He simply believed that it was an anachronism,' he said.

On 9 January 1995, the Red Prince died of a heart attack. He was cremated on That Luang esplanade in Vientiane. The monks, by order, accorded him full Buddhist rites as they had done for Kaysone in November 1992. The pallbearers wore the traditional *sampot*, but the red flag of the party was also flown. A witness told me that as the flames began to consume the coffin, a black limousine pulled up and a hysterical woman leapt out. She rushed to the pyre as if to throw herself on it in an ultimate act of wifely devotion. The woman was Viengkham Souphanouvong. Bodyguards bundled her back into the car, which drove off at high speed. Rumours had it that Souphanouvong's body was not even in the coffin, but had been cremated several days earlier.

The Red Prince and his wife had helped deliver Laos to the short-lived religion of Marxism–Leninism, and the rather more enduring legacy of Stalin, but their children seemed not to have been born with collectivised genes. Partly thanks to their father's power and the opportunities it provided, they had been well educated and given senior positions. As long as the system rewarded them, they supported it. Now, with their father and mentor gone, they had to survive on their own in the political fray. At the 1996 party congress, Khamphoui Keoboualapha, the leading reformer and Souphaxay's boss, was dumped from the Politburo. Souphaxay's brother Khamsai had earlier been dropped from his post as Finance Minister and dumped from the party's central committee.

In Laos, politics was family business to be inherited, and sometimes squandered. Those without family connections survived any way they could.

11

Competitive Spirits

Everywhere in the capital, signs of the new free-market policies of the Lao People's Revolutionary Party were to be seen. The government claimed to have changed not just its policies, but its outlook, launching a philosophy of *chintanakan mai*, Lao for 'new thinking'. A proliferation of small traders had enlivened Vientiane's mundane business district, and new imported cars were creating tiny traffic jams. Importantly in such a devout country, the *laissez-faire* policies were approved not only by the party, but also by the church.

It was *Ok Phansaa*, literally 'the end of the rain', which marked the conclusion of the Buddhist Lent, and across the country thousands of monks were filing out of their pagodas, and embarking on pilgrimages to far-flung temples and shrines. They had confessed their evil thoughts and deeds to their superiors and accepted new mats, robes and alms bowls from devotees. Some went door-to-door, ousting *phi*, or spirits, believed to have taken shelter in homes during the rainy season. These spirits, having been evicted, appeared to have flooded into the streets, infecting them with a heady licentiousness. In communist Laos, 'the party' meant a secretive, paranoid political organisation. But in free-market Laos, it meant a lucrative industry, and Vientiane had embarked on a sweaty bacchanal. Young Buddhist novices with freshly shaved heads could be seen along Quai Fa Ngum accepting free cigarettes from the

'555' girls and buying Bugs Bunny gas-filled balloons. Hawkers of lotus, incense and sticky rice in bamboo cylinders did good business as huge crowds blocked the street alongside the Quai, crowding its temporary taverns and surrounding the many stages on which rock bands played. My diplomat host, Felicity, had invited me down to the Mekong to witness a highlight of the festival, the *Lai Houey Fai*, or boats of fire ceremony. The Japanese, who celebrate a similar festival, say the boats represent the footsteps of Lord Buddha on the Yamuna River in northern India, leading the souls of the dead back to heaven. The Lao festival is more straightforward. Its purpose is to dispose of bad luck by putting it in tiny boats carrying lighted candles and releasing them onto the river in their thousands, transforming the Mekong into a Milky Way.

Soon we were swept up in the noisy human wave, rampant youths linking arms and jostling us as we held aloft our fragile *houey fai*, once made of dried banana leaves, but now fashioned from fluorescent polystyrene. There were so many faces passing, and on every face was a different reaction to the sight of the two *felang* carrying the holy boats while the Lao partied. At a small wharf, a handful of people were preparing to cast off their flame-bearing craft. Small boys glistened like otters in the water as they guided the lanterns away from the shore. My first problem was that I carried no matches, but a smartly dressed man in his forties proffered his lighter, and my candle of hope sputtered to life. I looked at that taper like a five-year-old counting his candles at a birthday party, and carefully handed my *houey fai* to one of the boy–otters, as if handing him my destiny. He took the lantern and placed it in the water. It rocked unsteadily, then seemed to catch a current and began surging towards midstream with the confident instincts of a hatchling turtle. All my troubles were heading for Cambodia, and my future seemed assured until, about five metres from the bank, my vessel was snatched up by another of the river boys, who began using it to relight the candle of a different boat he was fostering.

There was a certain inevitability about what happened next. The ten-year-old Mekong pirate tilted my craft at a dangerously sharp angle to relight his own candle, in the process setting fire to my boat. Replaced on the water, it flared briefly, then faded to a smoulder. A third boy took pity and doused it with a desultory splash of water. My bad luck wasn't going anywhere.

For the Lao the Mekong is a barrier between brash, aggressive Thailand and submissive, gentle Laos, but the festival of *Ok Phansaa* seemed to belie all that. Another manifestation of the general rowdiness came in the form of the annual longboat races on the Mekong. Instead of the flickering lights of *houey fai*, the river was clogged with gladiatorial rowing crews, fifty or more men and women to a craft, all competing for the title of fastest *pirogue*. New teams kept filing down to the river, marching in formation, dressed in team colours and shouting war cries accompanied by pounding drums and clashing cymbals. There was the Marlboro boat, the Pepsodent boat and the Lao Beer boat, and in the sparkling water they resembled speeding serpents. The girls on the Lux boat passed, grunting like tennis players, and as the final race ended, firecrackers exploded and a momentous, primal roar hailed the victory of the Thanalaeng warehouse rowers. People were cheering and hoisting trophies, tossing each other in the air, while the marquees sagged and the plastic tables toppled over.

Among the defeated was a team of *felang* women, whose penance involved preparing food as the victorious Lao women belted out nautical songs and passed the *lau lao*. Among the confluence of languages I heard a familiar twang. It belonged to Sou. Soumieng Deajpanyanan was a young expatriate Lao who had fled the country with her family during the revolution. Her late grandfather had been a trader in food and precious stones from China who married a Thai woman during his commercial forays into South-East Asia. From Thailand, the family business extended into Laos in the days when both countries were bulwarks of capitalism. In the family tradition of mixing business with pleasure. Sou's father married a Lao girl and they moved into a shophouse in Vientiane's Morning Market. Somsak Ma did not progress beyond the third grade at school, but he taught himself how to raise pigs and market their meat. Laos, he found, was a country crying out for quality pork. When there was no more room under his mattress for the money he made selling it, he began buying land. Somsak noticed that people liked to eat his pork with rice, so he began growing rice too. Seeing that they liked a drink as well, he bought a whisky distillery.

Soumieng was the eldest of Somsak's five children. She was sent to a Chinese school where portraits of the king of Laos hung alongside those of Sun Yat Sen, nemesis of the Manchu dynasty and father of the Chinese republic. The shophouse was a hive of activity during the week, and at weekends the family would move out to their farm, which boasted not only pigs but a small tiger, a sun bear and many other animals. It was well known among the hill tribes that captured exotic animals were best taken to Somsak at the Morning Market. Did they usually end up in Chinese medicines? Possibly, but several were donated to the zoo in Udon Thani in Thailand. The Ma family had plenty of servants, which left Sou free to indulge her great love—pond fishing. Most Lao families that can afford it have a pond beside or even underneath their house—a combined fish market, refrigerator and recreation facility. In Vientiane, the cloying aroma of home-caught fish being barbecued wafts through the streets.

'That's a very Lao thing,' Sou told me later at the two-storey bungalow that doubled as the office for the Gateway Enterprise Company, a joint venture building the first modern shopping centre in Vientiane.

Lao exiles often congregate on the Thai side of the Mekong, peering at their lost homeland through binoculars, unable to return for fear of government reprisals. But Sou was made of sterner stuff. A longing for her roots—and a liking for the new economic policies—had brought her back as manager of the project on the outskirts of the capital. At thirty-three, she had the brilliant black hair and compressed build of a typical Lao woman. Politely sensuous, she had an earthy laugh and chewed her consonants ferociously.

'I'm fifth-generation Chinese,' she said, still looking Lao to me. 'Chinese is funny. It doesn't matter how many generations your family has lived in a country, or whether your grandmother is part Thai, or even if you haven't a lot of Chinese blood in you. At the end of the day, you're still Chinese.'

'So you're Chinese. Not Lao? Not Australian?'

'I'm all of the above,' she said, letting out a belly laugh. 'When I introduce myself here, I usually say I'm Australian. In Australia, I'd say I'm Lao.'

Growing up in Vientiane in the 1960s, Sou was oblivious to politics. Around November each year, the king would allow his people to feast their eyes upon him at the festival of That Luang. Sleepy children would be shaken from their beds before dawn and dressed in their best clothes for a glimpse of the emperor of Lan Xang.

'My mother kept telling me not to stare at him,' said Sou. 'You were supposed to show respect. But he was just this big guy who looked older than in the picture at school. He also looked as if he wasn't very smart. He didn't have the authority of being a king. He looked really weak. That's what I thought. He was weak and old.'

If a ten-year-old found the kingly pomp inadequate, I wondered, how could the rest of the population be impressed?

'We didn't know anything about the king's son or the rest of his family,' Sou recalled. 'Or even his wife. I can't remember what his wife looked like. I think the only reason we remember him is because when you went to the movies you had to stand up for the national anthem. And they always showed a picture of the king.'

In the Kingdom of Thailand, just a few kilometres from where we were sitting, people were still standing to attention before images of their monarch projected from fly-spotted monochrome slides onto cinema screens. The Bangkok newspapers were full of pictures of the royal family doing good works, and businesses competed to take out the largest advertisements in praise of royalty. But in Laos, the only good king was a dead one, and even then possibly not.

When a coalition of leftists, royalists and neutralists took office in 1974, the children at Sou's Chinese school farewelled their Taiwanese teachers, who were politically unacceptable to the Pathet Lao. They were replaced by teachers from mainland China, who wrote in a Maoist-approved Mandarin script and led their classes in revolutionary songs about the Red Sun of the East. It was not unheard of for the children to rise at 3 a.m. and walk kilometres to the Patuxai—Vientiane's Arc de Triomphe—to prepare for mass parades. Communist insistence wore down a jaded aristocracy, most of whom had their escape routes well planned. One day in 1975 Sou overheard her parents arguing about whether to stay in Laos or leave. Her mother, Chou, wanted to take the children across to Thailand, but Somsak was against the idea.

'That's the first time I realised there was a war going on. I was really upset that we had to leave. I didn't want to go. All my friends were here. And I really had no idea why we had to leave. The history taught in the Chinese school didn't relate to the present, and Asian parents don't like to tell their kids about troublesome things. I think kids should know what's going on. At least let them know, "Yes, we do have a war here."'

The family stayed long enough to see the establishment of the Lao People's Democratic Republic, but fled across the river to Thailand a few days later. By that time Somsak was the largest pork producer in Laos, supplying the entire Vientiane market and exporting to Udon Thani and Nong Khai. The family had substantial holdings in property and industry. They left it all behind.

In Thailand, where the family stayed for three months, Sou began adjusting to a life without servants. She started doing the laundry and cooking. When the family reached Australia, both parents got jobs, leaving Sou to look after her four younger brothers. Letters received from old school friends still in Laos painted a picture of revolutionary change. The first Pathet Lao government was determined to challenge the comfortable old ways—including the antiquated and oppressive culture of good manners. Communist semioticians saw language as the key to thought and attitudinal change, so they embarked on an ambitious campaign to rid the language of vestiges of the feudal past. The four forms of saying 'yes', each denoting a different level of respect, were abolished in favour of the proletarian *jaow*, or yeah. The humble form *doi kanoi* 'at your service' or 'yes, my lord', with which children had for centuries addressed their elders, was no longer to be used. In New Lao, 'yeah' would suffice for all occasions and for all people. Decades later, Lao like Sou who returned to their homeland found they no longer spoke the same language as their compatriots.

'They told me, "In the old days, we used to have lords and servants and slaves—caste structure. That's why people would say 'my lord' and 'your highness'. From now on, we are brothers and sisters, uncles and aunts, nieces and nephews. There isn't a caste structure anymore." In fact, it was the wife of a very high official who pulled me aside and said, "Sou, don't say *doi kanoi* anymore. You should say *jaow*." I found it really weird that they could suddenly change the Lao we had known our whole lives into a different kind of Lao.'

In Lao homes, however, people never stopped saying *doi kanoi*. As the ardour of the revolution faded, traditional ways slowly reasserted themselves. Later I learnt that there were still places in Laos where the use of *doi kanoi* was officially encouraged—in some prisons.

Laos lost one in ten of its people in the exodus which followed the Pathet Lao victory. Those who left were mainly those with wealth and education. But no matter how privileged they had been before leaving, returning Lao had to overcome the stigma of having run away.

'The people who stayed never miss an opportunity to tell you how bad it was in the old days,' Sou recalled, exasperated. 'They're like war veterans remembering their terrible battles. They look at people coming back from abroad and they say, "You had a good, comfortable life. You educated your children. Look at us. We didn't even have high schools to go to. No travel. No opportunity." You suspect their motives for telling such stories; that they might want money or something. But generally they're just letting you know who's who, asserting their self-respect. And, of course, those who were loyal are bitter that the system wasn't able to reward them.'

Confiscated land and buildings helped ease the pain of those who stayed: a windfall of houses, cars and valuables. Among the booty inherited by the People's Democratic Republic was the Ma family's pig farm. The government had no idea how to run it, so eventually it invited Somsak Ma to return to Laos and resume pig farming. It would be a joint venture. Vientiane municipality would provide the land, which actually belonged to Somsak, and Somsak would put up the capital.

'Dad really wanted to do it,' said Sou, 'despite the bad terms. But when he asked the head monk in Sydney, the monk said, "You're sixty-five years old and you've killed enough animals for one life. So no more." After that he decided not to come.'

His daughter had returned, but gutsy as she was, the obstacles to reclaiming the family's lands had subdued even her competitive spirit.

'It's gone,' she told me. 'Let's forget about it. I know that if I go back and start putting in claims for my land it's a very long and complicated procedure. I mean they're not giving land back on a silver plate. I'd end up really angry and frustrated, with a bad feeling about the country. And I might not do the business I want to do because of that. So I'd rather just let it go. I know a couple of families who've done it, and we get a lot of Lao coming back with the intention of reclaiming their land. But my advice to them is, don't bother. Leave it. What's gone is gone. The day you decided to leave this country, you let it go.'

12

Casualties

In April 1976, the Pathet Lao newspaper *Sieng Pasason* reported a ceremony in Luang Prabang at which King Savang Vatthana handed over his palace to the state for use as a national museum. The previous month the British ambassador had been denied access to the palace and had noted anger among the townsfolk at the treatment of the king.

Officially, the seventy-year-old king was still 'supreme advisor' to the president, but since giving up the throne Savang Vatthana had taken no part in politics. Forced to move to a small villa near the Mekong, his main concerns—to maintain Wat Xieng Thong and the orchard at Pak Xuang—were frustrated by the loss of his property and royal stipend, and the need to obtain permission to travel outside Luang Prabang, which in his case was not given. The king and his immediate family remained in the royal capital under house arrest for fifteen months. In March 1977, residents of the old royal capital were surprised by a sudden revival of the organised street protests they had not seen since 1975. This time, the slogans were against the king, who was decried as a leech and exploiter. Officials of the new regime—the same people organising the demonstrations—went to the king's new home, and advised him he was no longer safe in his former capital. They proposed moving him and his immediate family to Houaphan province for their own safety.

The most detailed account ever published of the circumstances surrounding the removal of the royal family from Luang Prabang appeared in the Vietnamese army newspaper, *Quan Doi Nhan Dan*, in January 1984, almost seven years after the event. Savang Vatthana, the paper said, had almost escaped to Thailand during a revolt which was only crushed after heavy fighting. 'Reactionary forces directed from abroad' had tried on several occasions to arrange the king's escape, most daringly in March 1977, when 'pirates' attacked Luang Prabang with the aim of taking the king to a helicopter in a nearby town and then to Thailand, where supporters wanted him to lead a government-in-exile. It took four hours for government troops to fight off the rebels. 'Thus ended the last days of the king of Laos in Luang Prabang,' the report concluded. The Soviet newsagency Tass reported on 16 March 1977 that a plot to overthrow the government had been organised by Prince Souphantharangsi, the king's brother and secretary-general of the royal palace, with the support of the king, the crown prince and members of the King's Council. As a result, it said, the king had been sent to a 're-education centre'. The government made no formal announcement of what had happened to the king. A diplomat who was based in Vientiane at the time told me: 'We heard it first from one of our local staff in the embassy, the daughter-in-law of Souphantharangsi. She'd had a phone call from Luang Prabang on 12 March, saying that on that morning they'd taken away the king and his family, including her father-in-law and several other senior officials. Ministers we met socially gave the impression that the king had outlived any useful purpose, but they insisted they had no intention of executing him. They'd say, "We want to cure the patient, not kill him."' By late March, Deputy Foreign Minister Nouphan Sithphasai was telling people in Vientiane that the king was 'in a safe place, a long way from the Mekong'. Since his abdication, the minister said, the king had been allowed to work and was given Pathet Lao personnel to help him. However, he had proven unco-operative. His brother had been in contact with the rebels, who had attacked the airfield at Luang Prabang a few days after the king was taken away. The government now regarded the king as a security risk.

During those early months of 1977, the king's former right-hand man, deposed prime minister Souvanna Phouma, with his penchant for good cigars and bow ties, was still a fixture on the Vientiane cocktail circuit. Since the revolution he had tried to help the new government wherever possible, most notably in February 1977 when he had been dispatched to Luang Prabang to urge the former king and crown prince to go to Vientiane for a meeting of the Supreme People's Assembly, the rubber-stamp parliament that replaced the National Assembly. Three months later, Souvanna recalled the trip at a dinner hosted by the British ambassador. The king, he said, had rebuffed his entreaties, more or less telling him to mind his own business. According to a fellow dinner guest, 'Souvanna said that shortly afterwards, the king had made contact with the rebels by radio, asking them to rescue him.'

'Fairytales!' cried Boun Kham, taking a last slurp of his *feu*, or noodle soup, wiping his mouth with a napkin and placing his chopsticks across the top of his bowl. Snatching up a translation of the offending article, he read impassively, picking his teeth, then frowned deeply and shook his head.

'"Thus ended the last days of the king of Laos in Luang Prabang,"' he snorted. 'Fairytales!'

I had to admit that during my term in Hanoi, the army newspaper had impressed me more by its accuracy in reflecting the party line than by its regard for the facts. 'Look at this,' Boun Kham continued. 'It says nothing about what happened to the king. Nothing about Viengxai. They know everything, but say nothing.'

'There was no big rescue attempt,' Boun Kham said, sighing. 'His family told the king many times to leave Laos, but he refused! His youngest son, Sauryavong, swam across the Mekong to Thailand in

November 1975...His father told him it's okay to leave. But he himself would not leave. He wanted to stay with his people.'

According to the Vietnamese report, the Lao army had besieged the old royal palace. But why the palace? The king no longer lived there, and no-one I'd spoken to could remember any fighting there. Boun Kham turned up his nose, smelling a conspiracy.

'There was some shooting across the Mekong. Behind Chompet temple. But it's nothing! Some shooting in the air. By the Pathet Lao soldiers themselves. They wanted to make people think somebody was coming. Some Thai soldiers or something. That night, an army truck goes to the king's house, and Savang Vatthana and Queen Khamphoui are put in the truck. The same truck gets the crown prince and his younger brother Sisavang, and the king's brother Souphantharangsi, and the chief of protocol, Thongsouk, and the chef du cabinet, Manivong Khammao, and also Bovone Vatthana, the king's half-brother. When they are all together, the truck takes them to the airport, and they fly—two helicopters—to Viengxai.'

'Did they resist?'

'Of course they cannot! The Pathet Lao have guns. When a man has a gun, you cannot do anything.'

Not all of those taken to Viengxai were high-ranking family members. The king's second son, Sisavang, was a farmer who tended the garden at Pak Xuang and was not in the direct line of succession. Others who could stake a claim to the throne were overlooked. Mahneelai's son Soulivong was second in the line of succession, but he was left behind, put to work planting rice and cutting bamboo like the rest of the population of Luang Prabang. The Pathet Lao were familiar with guerilla warfare, not the intricacies of royal lineage. I tried to imagine the scene as the Pathet Lao troops took them away. Did they excoriate and lambast them as they made their accusations that the king's brother had made contact with the rebels—or was that charge for public consumption only? Whatever the circumstances, it seemed clear to me from all I had heard about him that the king would have remained calm. But the crown prince? How would he have coped with the insolence of sullen, bayonet-wielding Pathet Lao soldiers?

When the army truck had deposited the king, queen and princes at Luang Prabang airport, they were led to the two Russian-built helicopters, which took off through the smoke haze of the slash and burn agriculture practised in the surrounding hills. The helicopter flew high over the Plain of Jars, then over the rugged Annamite Range, setting down again amid the limestone karsts of Viengxai. The former stronghold of the Lao leftists had by then become one of the largest prison camps in South-East Asia, and these members of the region's oldest ruling family were its newest inmates.

Boun Kham had disappeared into the coffee shop's kitchen. He thought nothing of marching into restaurants big and small, inspecting the standard of hygiene and ordering the staff around. He would even send them off to the markets to buy fresh produce. The benefit of this audacity was the splendid range of Lao cuisine to which we were treated: green papaya salad with cabbage, dried pork skin and sour eggplant—a mango version of which we ate with chilli and small crabs caught in the rice paddies—and *laap*, a delicate envelope usually filled with minced meat and chilli, but sometimes with eggplant, onions, mint and peanuts. Then again, we could subsist quite comfortably on sticky rice, rolled into balls between our palms, dipped in chilli paste and *padaek*, fermented fish paste, all washed down with Lao beer. With Boun Kham around, even the humble *feu* could become ambrosia. His expertise proved invaluable as we criss-crossed the capital in our quest to trace the true history of Laos, despite his constant insistence that the food was better in the old days.

Straddling the seat of his Honda Dream motor scooter, with me clinging like a monkey to his back, Boun Kham had picked up an old scent and was shedding the decades. As we rolled down Lan Xang Avenue, past the Patuxai, he gave a running commentary.

'You like Patuxai? Like Arc de Triomphe, no. Arch is stolen, you know? The Americans gave Laos concrete for the airport, but we build arch instead!' he said with a rare giggle. 'Here they had student demonstrations. Stupid! Some students even came from Thailand. They said they didn't want to live under the dictatorship. They went back later. Sure! They got a degree in dictators. Look! Vienglatry! It's an old nightclub, only used to be on Rue Circulaire. That time we call it "Green Latrine".'

Where I saw a shabby, soporific town, Boun saw history. Building by building, he reconstructed the city, veering right to favour his good eye. The old Pathet Lao compound had been near the post office opposite the Morning Market, and what was now the Asian Pavilion Hotel had been the notorious Constellation, a nest of hard-drinking journos. One building, however, had not changed. From Samsenthai Road we could see it, crouching behind barbed wire and bristling with antennae: the American embassy.

Not wishing to be seen outside those particular gates, Boun Kham dropped me at That Dam, the Black Stupa, a short stroll away. Inside the embassy's cipher-locked doors, portraits of the president and secretary of state decorated the walls. The building had the look of a 1940s radio studio, its rooms soundproofed with particle-board panels. A map on one wall pinpointed sites of interest to US and Lao investigators searching for remains of American soldiers missing in action, mostly pilots lost on secret bombing missions over Laos in the 1960s and 1970s.

A hard-edged Texan, Jack Dibrell, commanded the Missing In Action detachment in which William Gadoury had the very American title of 'Casualty Resolution Specialist'. Dibrell introduced Gadoury as the 'institutional memory' of the MIA search in Laos, a man who'd been on the case since the early 1980s. Of the hundreds of US pilots shot down over Laos, only one was officially listed as a prisoner of war. His name was Charles Shelton, shot down in 1965. Intelligence reports said he was dead, but thirty years after the event his file was being kept open for what the MIA team called 'symbolic reasons'. Gadoury said the task force had located the initials 'CS' scratched on the wall of a cave near Ban Nathen, a few kilometres north of Viengxai.

'It was 1994, but two witnesses remembered that he'd died of ill health and they took us to where he'd been buried. We dug up the whole side of a hill. These guys were certain of the location to within 10–20 metres, and they seemed credible. But lots of years had gone by.'

Another pilot shot down over Viengxai a month after Shelton was Colonel David Hrdlicka. On their first visit to the north in the early 1990s, the MIA team met a Lao guard who remembered an American.

'He called him "Mr David",' Gadoury recalled. 'Hrdlicka, we assume, but he couldn't remember the surname. He said the prisoner had become sick and died. They stayed in the caves most of the time. They had no fire, so they couldn't boil water, and they just got sick.'

Gadoury had been surprised to learn that the American prisoners held near Viengxai had not always been manacled. When he asked Lao officials if they had not feared the prisoners might escape, their response was, 'Escape to where?' A couple of years later, Gadoury had returned, accompanied by Senators John Kerry and Christopher Smith. Armed with flashlights, they entered the caves where the Americans had been held.

'We went up a spiral staircase at the rear of the lower chamber. This led to a large auditorium-sized room, complete with a stage. At one time I'm sure it would have been the meeting and entertainment hall.'

The hunt for MIAs is replete with many ironies. The Pathet Lao won the war, but unable to effectively manage the country's economy, they were forced to curry favour with the United States. Co-operation in the search for the remains of Americans who died secretly bombing Laos is the price they pay for victory. A new generation of young Americans is nowadays sent to the jungles of Indochina, this time to find the bones or teeth that will identify their dead predecessors. Sometimes they accidentally die trying to find them. But the ultimate irony is that the remains often cannot be found because American bombing long ago destroyed all trace of them. Bones shipped out to Hawaii in coffins bearing the American flag are sometimes returned to Laos without ceremony, after scientific analysis determines that they are not those of Americans.

'In David's case we had two witnesses to his burial,' said Gadoury, 'the guy who buried him, and the village chief who watched. They took us to where they recall it happened, a place called Ban Bac, also in the karsts around Viengxai. When we excavated the site we saw evidence that the area had been bombed, and were unable to locate a grave site or any remains.'

The task force had even scaled the terrible heights of Phou Pha Ti, thought to be impregnable until it was overrun by the Vietnamese.

'You can't walk up that mountain,' said Gadoury. 'You need to be lowered down from a helicopter on top. We spoke to the military commander—Colonel Muk from Vietnam—who'd led the sapper team that overran the place. We got him up there and he pointed to the spot where the Americans were killed. We searched for them but didn't come up with anything.'

The talk around Vientiane was that the whole MIA show would be wound up in two or three years, but pressure in the US to obtain the 'fullest possible accounting' was huge, and Gadoury estimated it would take up to six years to excavate all the sites that had been identified.

In late 1995, the *Vientiane Times* reported the reopening of flights to the northern town of Xam Nua, close to Viengxai. The airport in the provincial capital had been closed for five years due to unspecified damage. By a stroke of luck I had secured a ticket on one of the first flights in, although the price of providence was the requirement that I be accompanied by government minder Khen. Independent advice for this trip would be essential, and I thought I knew where to find it. A short walk from the presidential palace were the offices of Lao Survey and Exploration, a company set up by a laconic geologist who'd had trouble with the law in his native Western Australia. Located in a stately villa on Samsenthai Road, the business was doing well, helped by strong demand from foreign resource and hydro companies needing detailed topographical maps of the country. Harold Christensen was pottering around his office when I arrived, surrounded by dozens of maps held down at the corners by rock samples. Told of my travel plans, he selected the appropriate map, and was soon minutely scrutinising it at close range through impossibly thick bifocals. We were searching for valleys and villages of the Hmong ethnic minority, most of whose members had supported the royalists and Americans during the war.

'It's a bit difficult,' said Harold. 'The valleys stay put but the villages keep shifting.'

'Slash and burn,' he replied when I asked why. 'They're a bit like you. Only settle down for a year or two at a time. I once had to go to Samarkan...' He pointed at a measles of dots on the map. 'It's not far, but because of this bloody mountain range you have to go all the way up here to get to it. Well, between Ban Dong and Samarkan, there are about fifty villages on the map, but I reckon we passed two.'

What a country! Not even cartographers could pin it down. But if its maps were ambiguous, could the history of Laos ever be accurately portrayed? Deciding that the more maps I could get the better, I moved on to the Service Géographique National. Miraculously, four years after the Soviet Union collapsed, the USSR survived here on a map pinned to a wall in Vientiane, a dead empire preserved in the aspic of Lao inertia. Presenting a list of reference numbers for the official charts of Xam Nua and Viengxai, I was astounded when the woman behind the counter emerged in no time with all five of the maps I had requested, each of them marked 'En secret'.

'You can have all the maps under the sun,' her expression seemed to say, 'for all the difference it makes.' I waited in vain for an official to rush into the room, horrified at the ease with which I had obtained the maps of these once secret areas. Instead, the woman handed me an invoice and pointed towards a hole in the wall marked 'Caisse', where sat a plump, grandmotherly lady who did needlepoint with one hand and counted out my change with the other.

Sunset was the cue for the motley bunch of traders, aiders, miners and misfits who constituted the expatriate community in Laos to gravitate to Nam Phou circle, the boozy heart of the new Vientiane. Here, the ornamental fountain was dry, but the *bia sot*—fresh beer—came in jugs. Speculators and dam builders swapped stories of Lao corruption and incompetence, while pilots and de-miners competed with tales of derring-do. A pilot who flew chartered helicopters told of being accompanied on every flight by a Defence Ministry official who directed him away from 'sensitive' areas. In some villages his company employed people for the sole purpose of shooing excited children away from the tail rotor-blades of their choppers. Another fellow had been working on a hydro project on the Ma River, which flowed into Vietnam and met the sea near Thanh Hoa. He told me an American aid project in the area had been badly delayed because some sites were so littered with unexploded bombs that they were no-go areas. Half the aid promised for irrigation and opium substitution had been spent on mine clearance, and the money had run out before the projects were completed. With the pilot was an American woman who had taught in Laos before the revolution. Returning in 1993 to the

Lycée Vientiane to resume work after a gap of eighteen years, she was astonished to find the curtains in the schoolmaster's office unchanged since 1975.

The revolutionary fervour of the early years of the Lao People's Democractic Republic had faded, like the schoolmaster's curtains, replaced by a dogged determination to hold onto power. Old soldiers like Boun Kham lived on the fringes of society, the resources and years invested in their training and education squandered. Mistrusted by the state, they acted furtively, haunted by fear of the arbitrary power that had smashed their lives and might one day do so again. Yet they refused to kowtow, maintaining their opinions, if not living them. On the eve of my departure for Viengxai, Boun had gathered together a few old-timers, victims of the regime, to brief me ahead of my journey. The venue was the Champa Lan Xang, a village theme park-cum-restaurant on the outskirts of Vientiane that bore an uncanny resemblance to a labour camp.

Boun Kham's pals were a mixed bag. There was Ounheuanne, a middle-aged man from Xam Nua who'd risen to a senior position in the Vientiane military police under the old regime, and Anou, a shy man in his forties who now worked for a private company. And there was Michael, a Brit who said he was a businessman being held over a barrel by the bribe-seeking deputy prime minister. He was pale, and slightly fevered.

'My impression is that people in the government know they haven't got long left,' he told me, 'and are just stuffing their pockets as fast as they can.'

Urged on by Boun, Ounheuanne told how in 1975 he'd been 'invited to have new ideas' on a fact-finding mission to Xam Nua— presumably arranged to show him how police should operate in a people's state. Sixteen years later he was allowed to return to his wife and family in Vientiane. He had spent those years in re-education and labour camps at many different locations. It looked to have done him no harm, but then he was one of the survivors. He wore single *baci* strings on each wrist, and a chunky silver watch.

'We built a lot of roads and houses in the villages,' he said, 'but we never complained. We always tried to win the confidence of the local people and make them realise that we were good men. Anywhere, anyplace, we could survive like that. They would bring us extra food, or herbal medicines, and sometimes we would sit down and have a drink with them. That's how we survived.'

Numerous officials of the old regime had been hijacked in a similar way. Some were told they were going on government business to China, and were surprised on landing to find local officials speaking Lao.

'*Sabaidee!*' they would greet their hosts. 'You speak excellent Lao.'

'Of course,' came the reply. 'We're Lao.'

'Ah, so what are you doing in China?'

'We're not in China.'

'We're not?'

'No. Welcome to Viengxai!'

In May 1979, former prime minister Souvanna Phouma told the *New York Times* that between 10 000 and 15 000 officials and military personnel who had served in his government had been detained, although other estimates put the number much higher.

'We tried to keep healthy in the mind,' continued Ounheuanne, who was now in his sixties. 'I used to run up and down the hills in the morning, and chop wood. They gave you weekends free. You could travel around the province and see people, stay overnight in friends' houses. Some men took local wives, especially those whose real wives had fled overseas or forgotten them. That was actually encouraged by the regime—to take a wife from Long Ma.'

Long Ma, he explained, meant 'the valley of the River Ma', on whose banks stood Sop Hao, site of the most notorious prison in Laos.

Anou sat quietly, saying little. As a student he'd been involved in the demonstrations against the monarchy outside the palace in Luang Prabang in 1975, and apparently regretted it. When the king came to Vientiane for the That Luang festival that same year, he had been welcomed by students shouting, 'Long live the king!' The welcome had been organised by the Pathet Lao, but a few weeks later, they changed their line.

'Then we were shouting, "Down with the monarchy! Out with the king!"' Anou recalled. 'After the revolution Luang Prabang people could see that they had been mistaken. We were very comfortable with the king, even if he was not very good at running the country. We knew him, but we didn't know what would come after. We were afraid of tomorrow.'

Anou's education continued after the revolution, but in the late 1970s he left Luang Prabang for Vientiane. After the abdication and the founding of the Lao People's Democratic Republic, he said, there had been a wave of arrests and forced deportations of Luang Prabang residents to the countryside. Among the first targets were all those who had been working at the court at the time of the revolution. They were rounded up and sent to camps all over the country.

'Big potatoes go to the south or to Xam Nua,' said Boun Kham. 'Some place where the language is different, and the people are different, so you look different. You can't talk to anyone. Easier to watch what you're doing.'

'They sent the entire military police academy, 750 men. Arrested them in July 1975 and sent them to Xieng Khouang without charging them.' Ounheuanne chimed in. 'Anyway, it's better now. The party only has 60000 members, you know. And with all this foreign investment, things must change.'

Michael disagreed. There had been little relaxation in political control in return for better relations with the West, he observed. A new generation of political prisoners now occupied the camps, people detained since the fall of the Soviet Union, when hopes for reform had flared briefly in Laos. •

Since Anou had been in Luang Prabang in 1975, I thought he might know something about the fate of the king. I wished I hadn't asked. He looked from face to face, breathing deeply, before answering: 'Most people never knew they had taken Savang Vatthana. You say it happened in 1977. That is correct. But most people don't ask about it. Most people don't talk about it.'

There was something about the silence of the others that seemed to presage a dreadful revelation.

'But I know…' Anou said, struggling with his words. 'I know, and I cried when the king was taken. I cried because my father was taken with him.'

Gone was the smouldering politics. Everyone looked like they'd had enough. But Anou continued.

'Once, my father was able to write to me,' he said. 'The letter was carried by a pilot who had flown some Pathet Lao officials to Viengxai. He pleaded with me to send medicine. He had a problem with his toilet. Some infection. He said there was not enough food and life was very hard there. My family immediately sent him several packages of food and medicine and clothing. But we never knew whether he received those things, and we never heard from him again.'

No wonder the government feared the losers. There were still scores to settle. Ounheuanne reached inside his jacket and took out a photograph. He handed it to me. 'This was taken in Viengxai,' he said.

The photograph showed two elderly people, a man and a woman. I knew who they were, but had never seen them looking so wretched and bedraggled. Savang Vatthana and Queen Khamphoui were kneeling on the ground in the Lao style, legs tucked behind them and to one side, with their hands clasped in prayer. There was a rudimentary flower arrangement, a poor man's *baci* bowl, in front of them, and some battered oil drums behind them. The queen's hair was dishevelled, and the king wore a plain black tunic. Gone was their regal dignity, replaced by distress and fear. This single image, passed hand to hand across the Lao diaspora and dissident networks, represented the agony of an entire people.

Boun Kham had his motorcycle with him, and invited me home that last evening in Vientiane to meet his family. We rode along Tha Deua Road, turning left into an alleyway and coming to a halt at a stilt house with a thatched roof. Boun Kham's family—his mother, wife Laoly and baby daughter Noi—greeted us warmly. His first wife had deserted him during his long years of internment, and Laoly—who was much younger—was now the family's main breadwinner, working a small patch of land on the banks of the Mekong and selling her produce in the market. Boun, who had graduated as a pilot and navigator from the French air academy near Marseilles and flew missions over Indochina for both the French and Americans, was too old to be rehabilitated and unwilling to demean himself by doing manual work.

Laoly soon had me seated with a cup of green tea on the comfy thatch floor, watching Thai television, as a wall clock flashed the syllables 'Wel' and 'Come' in gaudy lights. The old woman, lying in a cot under a mosquito net, smiled at me, and beautiful three-year-old Noi found me an exciting novelty. Rolling around on the floor with a brightly painted plastic duck, she showed me her book of the Roman alphabet, and we ran through the names of various things in English and Lao. Boun was teaching her English, and he laughed when his wife told him how the little girl had cried, 'Mummy, I'm here,' when Laoly had returned to the house that afternoon. Teaching his daughter a foreign language was a form of disobedience for the old rebel. At fifty-seven, he was still a handsome man, scrubbed clean, lean, and well built. Nobody could return what had been taken away—his rank, or his first wife. But he had his consolations, and they were in the thatched stilt house with us that balmy evening.

13

Exodus

Khamphan Thammakhanty could barely believe his eyes. After farewelling his wife at Vientiane's Wattay airport, he had been herded onto a rickety Dakota aircraft and flown to the Plain of Jars. From the air, he could make out the puncture lines of craters caused by American strategic bombers marching in strange procession across the desolate plain. After a brief stopover at an isolated airstrip, where hundreds more prisoners were staying temporarily in barracks buildings, the senior prisoners from Chinaimo were ordered onto a helicopter that took them across the Annamite Range to another airstrip squeezed between the haunting limestone karsts of Viengxai. There, they were transferred onto trucks that clambered over bone-crunching roads for many hours until reaching a vast natural fortress. Ringed by mountains on all sides, the camp near Muang Et, just a few kilometres short of the Vietnamese border in northern Houaphan province, teemed with hundreds of newly arrived prisoners busy in the task of building their own shelter.

'They wanted to ensure remnants of the capitalists and royalists were neutralised, and were trying to empty the cities of former government officials, and military and police officers to ensure security for the announcement of the new Lao People's Democratic Republic on 2 December 1975,' recalled a former director in the Planning Ministry, who had made the same trip.

For 600 years, Lao people prostrated themselves before the king. But in 1975, the Kingdom of the Million Elephants and the White Parasol collapsed under the twin pressures of the Vietnam and Cold Wars. For Savang Vatthana, the last King of Laos, the fall from grace would be steep.

Pictured: (top) ministers in the royal government farewell the king as he departs Vientiane, March 1961; (middle) President Kennedy farewells the King, at the White House, February 1963; and (right) with Queen Khamphoui.

A life both glamorous and tragic: At the time of her marriage to Crown Prince Vongsavang in 1964, Princess Mahneela was in line to become the next queen of Laos. But in 1977, when a leftist government arrested most members of the royal family, including the crown prince, she was left behind. Eighteen years later she had still not been officially informed about the fate of her husband.

The Mekong River viewed from Luang Prabang at its junction with the Khan River. Before a Lao prince could assume the throne, he was required to cross the Mekong from Luang Prabang, on the east bank, to a Buddhist monastery on the western side. There he would spend days deep in meditation preparing to shoulder the heavy responsibilities that lay ahead of him.

The dawdling streets of Luang Prabang, a gentle town of mouldering villas and 35,000 inhabitants, are dotted with parasols. But in the 1960s and 1970s, the timeless rhythms and traditions of the royal capital were buffeted by the overthrow of the monarchy.

(Left) Born the son of a Mekong River salt trader, Khamphan Thammakhanty rose to become a senior intelligence officer in the Royal Lao Army. Despite his humble background, he was posted to the royal capital and was deeply involved in efforts to prevent a leftist takeover of the entire country.

(Top) By 1975, with the royal government collapsing, Khamphan Thammakhanty was advised by his superiors to volunteer for re-education under the leftist Pathet Lao. Within weeks, he would be transferred to the communist gulag in north-eastern Houaphan province, where he would spend fourteen years in detention without trial. Upon his release in 1989, he was issued with a Lao passport.

Funeral stupa of King Sisavangvong, Luang Prabang, northern Laos. After the leftist seizure of power in 1975, the authorities banned the annual commemoration of the king's death. By 1995, relatives and residents of the former royal capital were once again marking the anniversary at the town's That Luang temple. A parachute abandoned by a downed American pilot provides shade for those paying their respects.

Buddhist novice, Luang Prabang. The Lao Loum, or people of the Mekong River plain, account for about two-thirds of the five million citizens of the Lao People's Democratic Republic. The overwhelming majority of Lao Loum follow Theravada Buddhism. At least once in his life, a Lao man or boy is expected to shave his head, don orange robes and live the life of a Buddhist monk for a few months.

For centuries before French colonial rule began in 1893, Lao kings inhabited modest palaces built of bamboo and timber. But in 1904, as a symbol of the alliance between Paris and Luang Prabang, the French administration began construction of a grand brick palace on the banks of the Mekong in a blend of Lao and French architectural styles.

Sixteen months after the leftist takeover of Laos in 1975, the king, queen, crown prince and other members of the court were arrested and interned in north-eastern Houaphan province. In the Pathet Lao stronghold of Viengxai ('City of Victory') they stayed first at the Number One Re-education Guesthouse, now a hotel (shown above), before being moved to a smaller house, and eventually to a remote prison camp.

Huge stone jars litter the Plain of Jars, northern Laos. The origins and purpose of the 2000-year-old jars are shrouded in mystery. Some jars were destroyed by United States bombing of Laos during the Vietnam War. The existence of a military airbase nearby meant the site was out of bounds to Westerners. Now, tourists are permitted to visit the area. Local guide Sousath Phetrasy (left) pictured with author.

The canopy of vegetation had already made them invisible from the air. One more wet season and they would probably be fully camouflaged by nature. Ruins of two brick buildings believed to have served as a dwelling for members of the Lao royal family after their arrest in March 1977. Viengxai, Houaphan province, north-eastern Laos.

(Top) The only known photo of King Savang Vatthana and Queen Khamphoui after 1975, believed to have been taken at Viengxai, northern Laos, in 1977.

(Middle) Khamphan with his wife, Singpheng, at their home in Portland, Oregon, March 2003.

(Bottom) Khamphan Thammakhanty (back row, third from left) with other re-education camp prisoners, Muang Et, Houaphan province, 1975.

Day in, day out, through the second half of 1975, truckload after truckload of new prisoners arrived at Muang Et from all over the country supervised by armed guards from the Lao Theung and Hmong ethnic groups. Former bureaucrats and army officers from the lowlands—the soldiers still wearing their royal army uniforms—laboured side by side to build the new camp. Known as Camp Six, located between Muang Et and Na Kham villages, it had been run as a prison by the Pathet Lao since 1969, and the vast site was littered with weathered bamboo barracks dating back to that time. In the bustling, improvised settlement, royalists mixed freely with Pathet Lao cadres who had been arrested and interned for breaches of party discipline. Even at that early stage, a few wondered how long they might be there. However, most maintained the cheerful mask the Lao wear in times of difficulty. Some had even brought cameras, and old friends reunited in this strange, bleak landscape posed like tourists for group photos.

Muang Et served as a staging post on what, for many prisoners, would be a long and tragic odyssey. Gradually, when the camp was built and the internees had been screened, they were assigned security classifications and distributed among a string of similar camps across the remote northeast. The totalitarian nature of the regime would ensure a steady flow of new prisoners, which continues until the present day, although at nothing like the rate of the early years.

Usually, a revolution is followed by terror. The Lao PDR's unique contribution to the history of the gulag was its ability to set one up even before it seized power. On 21 July 1975, the *Vientiane Post* reported that more than one hundred military personnel from the rank of lieutenant to general had been involved in re-education 'seminars'. 'They have had their eyes opened,' it said. 'This has given them greater confidence in the provisional government and taken away the fear they may have harboured of the patriotic forces. All fear and distrust have disappeared thanks to the direct and meaningful exchange of views.'

After taking power, the Pathet Lao also targeted social undesirables for reform. Vientiane's prostitutes, drug addicts, gamblers and lost children were rounded up and sent to two islands recently formed in the rising reservoir of the Nam Ngum dam, Don Thao and Don Nang—literally, Gentlemen's Island and Ladies' Island. Sisana Sisane, then Minister for Information and Culture, was quoted as saying the round-ups would 'teach the city dwellers how to follow the revolutionary line'. But many would die. Soon the numbers of seminarists had reached tens of thousands, and dozens of camps had sprung up across the country. In a speech on 6 January 1977, Politburo member Phoumi Vongvichit said, 'Those former bosses who never worked with their own hands must learn how to do so, because under the socialist system everyone must engage in both mental and physical labour. Some persons have asked me when they will be allowed to return home. I cannot answer this question, nor fix a definite time for their return. It is like asking a doctor how long he is going to keep his patient.'

The infrastructure of repression was established first, and the veneer of a judicial process added later as an afterthought. The first many internees saw of a court official was when he or she came to deliver their release papers, five, ten or fifteen years after their incarceration. The system made a mockery of the Pathet Lao's solemn pledge, contained in the Vientiane Accords, not to pursue a vendetta against its opponents after the ceasefire. Having set it up to deal with the royalists, the new rulers found the system equally useful in dealing with rivals for power and malcontents within their own ranks. Of the thousands of Lao students sent abroad to study socialism in Eastern bloc countries after the revolution, many ended up being punished for perceived misbehaviour on their return home. Dozens of students who went to Vietnam were accused of stirring up trouble by complaining about conditions there, and ended up in the camps in Houaphan province.

The camps, like upland villages, sometimes shifted location. The reasons given varied, from exhaustion of local food supplies to the need to build roads and bridges in different parts of the province. Security is also believed to have been a factor, ensuring that inmates never became too familiar with their surroundings, or too friendly with local villagers. Prisoners were also transferred between camps as the sifting process was refined. About a year after arriving at Muang Et, Khamphan and a group of other senior military men were transferred to a construction camp near Xam T'ai, close to the border of Houaphan and Xieng Khouang provinces.

The routine at Xam T'ai began with the ringing of the camp bell at 5.30 every morning. Before dawn, prisoners would be at work, cleaning the camp and cutting grass around its perimeter. Breakfast, like lunch, was a meagre portion of rice, after which the internees were assigned their work for the day, usually construction, agriculture and food preparation, or repair and maintenance of buildings and machinery. There were no books issued for re-education purposes, and the speaking of foreign languages like French or English was prohibited as traitorous. Lectures were organised, but these were not so much educative as critical. Every week, meetings would be held in which prisoners would be asked to confess where they had erred politically. A recurrent theme in the lectures was that the regime considered the inmates to be prisoners of war, and therefore they had no civil or political rights under Lao law.

'Most of us kept our mouths shut,' recalled a one-time inmate of Xam T'ai, formerly a senior bureaucrat in Vientiane, 'but some tried to co-operate with the camp leaders.'

There was a weekly meeting covering the duties of citizens of the new Lao People's Democratic Republic, and a monthly get-together with the camp commandant. This was the most unpleasant of all the seminars. The commandant would accuse his captives of not deserving the state's protection.

'He would tell us we were not true Lao. We spoke English and French, and thought about the past too much,' the former inmate recalled. 'He would analyse the performance of the camp as a whole in meeting construction targets.'

The oppressive regime of life at Xam T'ai was made bearable by a few liberties introduced gradually by the authorities. Prisoners were permitted to play football and volleyball, set up theatre groups, and occasionally write letters to their families. They could also receive letters and mercy packages from their relatives, although inevitably, with the Lao economy beginning to crumble, not all the aid got through. Some prisoners, whose families had taken the party's advice and moved to heroic Houaphan province to be nearer their detained relatives, received visitors, and eventually some families were even permitted to move into the camps. The prevailing atmosphere, however, was one of fear and mistrust. Drivers who supplied the camp network carried rumours that proliferated in the hothouse atmosphere. Sometimes they spoke of unrest in some of the camps, even rebellions, but most prisoners feared the drivers were spies and agents provocateur, and would not act on such information. For Khamphan, an officer trained in psychological warfare, these techniques were textbook material. His specialist training and the discipline of the army proved useful in surviving the rigours of internment. Unlike many captives, he did not come down with malaria in the first wet season in detention, seemingly possessing some immunity to it. He participated in work duties outside the camp, and tried to maintain a positive mental outlook. The year he spent at Xam T'ai occupied in road and camp construction duties was harsh, but bearable.

In Vientiane, Singpheng and the wives of other senior officials were being press-ganged into sweeping streets and cutting grass, tasks designed to humiliate and take revenge under the guise of acquainting them more fully with the new social order. Leaders of the party and their families enjoyed the fruits of power, and were spared uplifting proletarian duties. As he began his third year in detention, with no prospect of imminent release, Khamphan drafted a letter to his wife. In it, he asked her to send him a fishing net. Then, referring to their separation, he suggested she consider going to live with his brother.

'Maybe it will be a long time before we see each other,' he wrote. 'If you cannot come to Houaphan province, then you should move in with my younger brother. He will look after you and the children.'

Khamphan's younger brother lived in France. His coded message was a signal that his family should flee Laos. Not long after receiving the message, Singpheng, her son, Pong, and daughter, Chan, gathered a few possessions and made their way to an arranged point on the banks of the Mekong River, opposite Nong Khai. Under cover of darkness, they boarded a boat used by a paid people smuggler, and fled their homeland for the refugee camps of Thailand. It would be the start of a new and better life for the family, but for Khamphan it meant deepening isolation. On the morning of 12 October 1977 as he prepared to join a labour gang heading out of the camp, he was told by the guards to go back, and report to the camp's assembly hall where a meeting was to be held.

'You have to work here in the camp today. You stay,' the guards said.

On arrival at the hall, he saw other prisoners whose faces he recognised from before the revolution. There were no fewer than six brigadier generals of the now defunct Royal Lao Armed Forces, and a number of other senior officers and police. At 9 a.m., the appointed time for the meeting to commence, the hall was surrounded by Pathet Lao guards. An officer of the Viengxai command, Lieutenant Colonel Sri Bounheuang, began to address the meeting, urging increased efforts to prepare for the celebration of the new national day that December. Suddenly, he interrupted his speech, drawing a revolver and pointing it at his captive audience.

'Don't move,' the lieutenant colonel shouted, 'otherwise I won't guarantee your security.'

Simultaneously, the guards outside the hall raised their weapons. One by one, the prisoners were ordered to their knees and bound with their hands behind their backs.

'Don't be afraid,' one of the guards told a prisoner. 'The high authorities want to take you to the [people's] court. If you are not guilty you may be sent back to Xam T'ai.'

In the new Laos, 'guilt' could be a dreadful word. The People's Courts were star chambers that mocked the concept of a fair trial. You were guilty until proven innocent, and the verdicts were often lethal. To be accused of anything was to be convicted. A few minutes later, more prisoners were marched in single file towards the meeting hall. Most were senior military figures in the old regime, among them the last Chief of the Royal Lao Armed Forces, Lieutenant General Bounpone Makthepharak, but there were also senior politicians, including the jovial and charismatic Hmong leader Touby Lyfoung and parliamentarian Issara Sasorith. One of the new arrivals had his hands tied so firmly to his neck that he could barely breathe, prompting one of the guards to joke: 'Comrade, I see you are still afraid of dying.' Together, the two groups were led away, and were then joined by a third. They were forced onto a convoy of trucks that moved out of the camp heading north. Among the prisoners left behind, rumours flew about the sensational events.

'They were supposed to have been planning a coup,' said one former inmate. 'The guards said one of them, Pheng Phongsavan, the former Minister of Interior who had signed the Vientiane Accords on behalf of the Vientiane side, had a gun, and that others had been in contact with the American-backed Hmong rebels. But there did not seem to be any evidence for the story. Nobody in the camp knew anything about a rebellion.'

Seven camps located in Houaphan province near the Vietnamese border constituted the core of the seminar system. Khamphan Thammakhanty would eventually spend time in four of them.

Part Three

Viengxai

14

Children of the Revolution

Houaphan province was the cradle of the Lao revolution. Here the Pathet Lao burrowed underground to survive American bombardment. Some 25 000 rebels spent the best part of a decade living in dank caves in a subterranean society boasting theatres, hospitals, factories and sporting facilities. It was an experience they never forgot. Here, too, might lie answers to the fate of the last king.

A cold wind lashed the dirt airstrip at the provincial capital, Xam Nua, halfway between Luang Prabang and Hanoi, buffeting the thatched shacks whose backyards formed the runway. A cratered, single-lane road led into town, past stilt houses, grazing turkeys and toppled fuel tanks labelled in Russian. Hunkered down in a shallow valley on the northern arm of the Xam River, the town was only 35 kilometres from the Vietnamese border. Its marketplace clung to the river, while the featureless streets that formed its rudimentary grid soon abandoned civic ambition to the hills. All but two of the elegant homes the French had built before the war had been reduced to rubble by long-range bombing by American B–52 'flying fortresses'—but Xam Nua was a fortress too, and the French villas had been replaced by austere structures, some of which consisted of nothing more than sheets of pressed metal. It was so quiet that the sound of a passing jeep would outlast the clouds of dust and diesel fumes in its wake.

The Foreign Ministry's Mr Khen had tagged along with me from Vientiane. Nothing official, I should understand; just in case a visiting *felang ki nok* needed help with local dialects and hotel bookings. The Lao phrase means 'foreign bird shit', deriving from the ancient truth that when a bird defecates, the person with the biggest nose is most likely to catch some. Khen's job was to ensure that the 'big nose' foreigner in his care didn't get too much of it on his proboscis. The assignment had been cause for celebration for Khen, a mark of the ministry's trust and esteem. A brilliant career beckoned. So, with a few friends from work, he had embarked on a bender the previous evening.

'Too many bottoms up. Four people, two bottles of cognac,' he explained that morning, between bouts of vomiting and bad arithmetic on the plane.

At the Dok Mai Deng guesthouse the timber floors were unvarnished and the ceilings low. You didn't get much for a dollar-fifty a night in those days, but the bed looked good to Khen, even in broad daylight. He was sick as a parrot, but with work to be done, I was unyielding. Smiling ruefully, he suggested that we present ourselves before the local authorities. They resided in a sombre structure overlooking the Xam River, surrounded by shining black Russian sedans and weather-beaten jeeps. The staff wore fur hats and the bookshelves bulged with the latest works of that bestselling North Korean philosopher despot Kim Jong-Il. The governor was out of town, but we were promised a meeting with one of his deputies. Asked what the people of this chilly, spartan outpost did to amuse themselves, the governor's aide replied, 'Football and chatting.'

Houaphan province had changed hands many times since the defeat of the Vietnamese armies by a people called the Ai Lao in 1337. Early Vietnamese accounts referred to Laos as a lethal desert, and the emperors of Hue had difficulty persuading their troops to fight in a region believed to be teeming with ghosts and debilitating diseases. But fight they did, regaining and losing control of Houaphan sporadically until the 1830s, when Thai armies helped the king of Luang Prabang take it back from the Vietnamese. The area slumbered under French colonial control until 1953, when the communist Viet Minh forced French and royalist forces to vacate the province. The Pathet Lao were then allowed to set up their government in Xam Nua, while the Vietnamese used it as a base for thrusts into the Plain of Jars and South Vietnam. Kaysone Phomvihan, the half-Vietnamese Pathet Lao leader, stayed in Houaphan while his comrades were in Vientiane participating in a series of coalition governments. Later, when US bombing forced him into the caves at Viengxai, he would travel frequently by truck to Hanoi for meetings with Ho Chi Minh, Vo Nguyen Giap and the other Viet Minh leaders. In their 'liberated zone' the Pathet Lao ran a parallel government and disseminated propaganda via Sisana Sisane's radio station, staking their claim to national leadership. After the revolution they signed a treaty with Vietnam that would bind Laos' fortunes to those of its larger neighbour for the next twenty-five years. Several secret protocols in the agreement provided for close military co-operation and set the location of the common border.

The people of Xam Nua are predominantly T'ai, and their colourful tribal dress is all that enlivens the dour capital. Carrying babies in slings, Hmong and T'ai women browsed at meat and vegetable stalls, pausing to snack on marinated squirrel brain or invest in lottery tickets. A dog stiffened by rigor mortis lay in the road until a man picked it up, balanced it across the bar of his bike and cycled off. There was one beggar, an elderly man who said he'd lost his foot in the war against the French and had been dependent upon the generosity of others for half a century since. Several stalls proffered large jars of pink chloroquine tablets for malaria and bubble packs of Fansidar for the more lethal cerebral malaria. At the state-run store, a spry woman in a blue cardigan sat among plastic bowls, batteries, sheet metal, screwdrivers and nuts and bolts—everything except customers. Next door, a shop run by the Trade Ministry sold garments from Oudomsai, but again there were no buyers, the normal state of affairs according to the man in charge.

Khen, meanwhile, had found a cure for his hangover. Fertilised chicken egg—the only egg that's crunchy even after it's been shelled—was the guaranteed local remedy for morning after heebie-jeebies. Swallowing the solid, grey-green oval whole, he insisted it was delectable, burping loudly and flexing his muscles as proof. Eating out in Xam Nua put a new twist on the term 'bring your own'. Here, it meant bring your own food. Local restaurateurs were so under-capitalised that they dared not invest in ingredients. Fortunately, we heard about this before dinner, and were able to scour the market well ahead of time, depositing a carp-like fish, some pumpkin and a chicken with the proprietor of Joy's Café, promising to return later to eat them.

Xam Nua was such a strange place and yet, loitering in the market, I felt less conspicuous than I would walking along the main streets of Saigon or Hanoi. Although outsiders rarely visited, locals seemed utterly uninterested in those few who did. So unnatural was their lack of curiosity that I concluded that interest in foreigners must be officially discouraged. In the communist enclaves of South-East Asia, dealing with outsiders was the business of ominously named institutions like Houaphan Province's Committee for Planning and Co-operation. In the committee's stark concrete headquarters, its chairman, Chan Dee Onlat Bounmee, sat at his desk clutching at his paperwork as a stiff breeze tried to blow it out the window. He was a small man whose neatness was disturbed only by crooked teeth that frequently flashed a riotous smile. His attitude to information was as refreshing as the wind that funnelled through his office. The committee, he said, was in charge of assessing proposals for foreign investment in the province. Unfortunately, although there had been a number of inquiries from foreign companies, no actual monetary inflows had been approved, initiated or recorded. There was no foreign investment in Houaphan province.

'We'll welcome it,' said Mr Chan Dee, his optimism as irrepressible as his teeth. 'Tourists as well. But we have no decent hotels, and our roads are very bad.'

Twenty years of socialist rhetoric had failed to deliver the goods. The average life expectancy in Laos was only 52 years, and about one child in five died before reaching age five. Xam Nua's only hospital was a dirty, dangerous place which showed how little progress had been made. The iron bed frames were covered not with mattresses, but pieces of plywood, and the wind howled through paneless windows. There were mosquito nets, but they were useless—most of the patients already had malaria. With no apparent staff to call on, families nursed their own sick. The carer for one young patient was an ageing T'ai woman whose hunched body was draped in a black tunic and embroidered blue *sin*. She wore large silver earrings in elongated lobes, and had walked forty kilometres from Long Ma carrying her sick grandchild in a sling. As the bronchial cries of the child and other babies stabbed the air, a father sat quietly in a corner of the room feeding sticky rice to his son.

If you tire of seeing monks in Laos, go to Xam Nua. I hadn't encountered a *bonze* since arriving, although the drab streets would have benefited from their dazzling orange robes. Although Buddhism dominates the lowland areas, one in three Lao are not adherents, preferring to follow the animist tradition of the remote highlands. What little Buddhism had reached remote Xam Nua had been all but snuffed out during the war. Two battle-scarred *stupas*, one of them leaning alarmingly, stood in the centre of the town. The deeply carved doors of Wat Phosai, the town's only functioning temple, were about all that had survived the bombardment. One of the monks, Maha Thong Phone, said he had arrived in 1978, and renovation of the temple had begun the following year. The government had provided the labour—work gangs formed from the ranks of re-education camp prisoners.

'The carvers were very good,' the monk recalled. 'They'd obviously worked on *wats* before. I think they were from Vientiane and Luang Prabang. There were some very skilled people in the camps.'

Not many plumbers, unfortunately. Returning to the Dok Mai Deng at the end of a long, wind-chafed day, I was greeted by the cheerful owner who insisted on forcing five flasks of boiling water on me. When I returned four of them—I required only one to make tea—he began scratching his armpits so vigorously that I thought the place must be infested with lice. It was, in fact, a kind of pantomime about what to do with the water. Soon I was happily mixing the contents of the flasks into a bucket of cold water, and ladling it over myself by candlelight, there being no electricity or hot running water. My spirits rose another notch when the town's generator kicked in, illuminating the hotel with an ethereal yellow light that oscillated slightly. Two decades since leading Laos to liberation, Xam Nua was still getting only three hours electricity a day, from 6.30 to 9.30 in the evenings.

Come dinnertime, I found Khen seated at the bottom of the stairs, putting on a pair of leather slippers, ideal footwear for people who get drunk a lot, he explained, there being no need to fiddle with laces. In the bracing night air we walked along streets dimly lit by household light bulbs. Here and there, flashlight beams played on the road as a few people moved about in the gloaming. The market was completely deserted now, and rats foraged among the vegetable waste around the market. But at Joy's Cafe, the atmosphere was cheerful. We arrived to find the cook preparing our meal, hammering garlic cloves with a mallet and frying them with the skins on. At one table a group of local men who'd already eaten sat picking their teeth, engrossed in the Chinese television serial *Dragon*

Sword. Joss sticks smouldered on a Buddhist altar, and the tables were set with vinyl tablecloths and blue plastic toilet-roll dispensers. Cartons of imported fish sauce, Ovaltine, Johnnie Walker Red Label and Orange Crush formed false walls. Khen almost squealed for joy when the beer came. It was Lao beer, flown all the way from Vientiane and sold here at double the price. Houaphan province had been too busy liberating Laos to build its own brewery.

Dinner came in the form of a stew containing our *panai*, or carp, a watery chicken curry, sticky rice and steamed pumpkin. But as we were about to begin, Khen jumped up to greet a suave, dark-haired stranger who sauntered in, hands dug deep into the pockets of a light-grey suit, and his shirt buttoned to the neck. There was something about the way he walked, like the star of a Lao *Casablanca*, that suggested this man was somehow important in Xam Nua.

'Please allow me to introduce Mr Lamphan,' said Khen, who was suddenly gulping for air like a landed fish. 'Mr Lamphan is the representative of the local authority. He will accompany us during our visit to Houaphan province.'

Masking my disappointment was made all the more difficult by Khen's euphoria. The last thing I needed was another minder to block and obfuscate. The two of them would have much to discuss as we toured the province: the relativity of civil-service pay scales between Vientiane and Houaphan; famous Pathet Lao leaders they had worked for; beer. If they tired of conversation they could take turns watching me. Lamphan had been informed by the provincial headquarters of our arrival and had come to discuss our itinerary. A former organiser of the Youth Union, he had been born in Xam Nua and was a veteran of government service. It seemed to have imbued him with a kind of confident shiftiness. His thick black hair was swept back off a dual-purpose face that bore a fixed grin—while his eyes kept careful watch on the room.

Through Khen, I explained my purpose: to collect material for stories about the twentieth anniversary of Pathet Lao power.

Lamphan nodded that it was no problem. I proposed we begin with a day in the countryside, followed by a day in Xam Nua to meet officials. A good plan, Lamphan said. As to the day in the countryside, I suggested we start by driving early in the morning to Viengxai, then continue along Route Six to the village of Sop Hao, at the junction of the Ma and Hao rivers. Khen's translation faltered, and he asked me to repeat what I had said. When I had done so, he paused, smiling a congealed smile. Lamphan took advantage of the delay to begin eating Khen's dinner, doing so in a serious, professional way that suggested he was practised at helping himself to other people's food. But when Khen finally stammered out a constipated translation of my suggested itinerary, Lamphan stopped eating and stared directly at me. His gaze was like an x-ray, capable of determining whether my suggestion was the product of naivety or intelligence. Holding my nerve, I returned his gaze with a smile of pure innocence, hoping not to betray the inside information, obtained through Boun Kham's contacts, on which my request was based.

The arrival of five well-dressed Asians and a red-bearded European in mountain gear saved me. As the newcomers took their seats at a reserved table, nodding politely in our direction, Lamphan was distracted, and whispered something out of the corner of his mouth to Khen. The European in the group called for drinks in fluent Lao, then, having made sure his guests were settled, stood up and approached our table.

'Hi!' he said, with an open smile and an American accent. 'I'm Tom Love. What brings you to Xam Nua?'

Tom had been working for the aid group Food for the Hungry in Houaphan since the early 1990s. Others, like the Quakers and Mennonites, had come and gone, he said, but only the 'Foodies' had endured, working on small irrigation and hydroelectric projects in remote villages. The invitation, or rather the order, to work in the revolutionary province had come from President Nouhak himself.

'When we came, he made a speech saying that since the revolution, nothing had happened in this area. We were *assigned* to work here. We didn't have a choice!'

So far, Food for the Hungry had built thirty weirs costing $7000 each. Tom's guests were journalists from Seoul inspecting a South Korean-funded project in Xieng Kho district on the River Ma.

'Xieng Kho was the first liberated district in Laos,' Tom said, mainly for the benefit of Lamphan and Khen, I gathered. 'You're a true patriot if you're from here.'

Called back to his table, he took up his flashlight—standard equipment for living in Xam Nua—and joined in a feast of *nok sect* and *nok peet*—sparrows and rice birds—along with chicken claws in soup, beans with chicken liver and deep-fried pork ribs.

Continuing to watch the foreigners' table, Lamphan told me there was a fuel shortage in Xam Nua so it might be difficult to venture outside the town. Houaphan, he explained, was dependent on Vietnam for salt and petrol. Petrol from Vietnam was yellow in colour, while that used in Vientiane, which was from Thailand, was red. The only storage facility in Houaphan, at Nathen, was moribund, so fuel had to be trucked in from Vietnam as needed. During the rainy season the road would get cut, but even in the dry season it was difficult to estimate the need correctly, which led to frequent shortages.

'Before the airport was fixed we could go two to three months without a flight from Vientiane, and then only Antonovs could land at Viengxai, or helicopters at Xam Nua,' he said, affecting the common touch. 'Cups and saucers cost twice here what they do in Vientiane. A bottle of beer costs 850 *kip* in Vientiane, here it's 2000! In Xam T'ai and Xieng Kho they get two rice crops a year. Here in Xam Nua we get one. Electricity is too expensive. I have three lights, an iron and a TV and it costs me 4000 *kip* a month. In Vientiane, Khen has a refrigerator, fan, hot water and TV and he pays 2500 *kip*.'

Still, as an official, Lamphan was much better off than most people. I told him I knew I could trust him to come through with the petrol, and I wouldn't mind paying a little extra if necessary. With one last calculating look, he disappeared into the night, ostensibly in search of fuel. Tom, meanwhile, had finished dinner and waved goodbye to his Korean friends. Seizing my moment, I thanked Khen for his sterling efforts that day and suggested he take a well-earned break for the rest of the evening. As I expected, he took the bait, scampering out the door. Freed from his eavesdropping, I wanted to know what the aid worker could tell me about the re-education camps. Just outside Xam Nua town, a large detention facility had at one time held a transient population of about 300 prisoners awaiting processing through the seminar camp system. By May 1988, it held only civil criminals or government officials facing disciplinary charges. Were any re-education camps still operating?

'This province is very sensitive and cautious about outside involvement,' Tom said, by way of preamble, wringing his lumberjack hands. 'One of our best Lao workers was a man from Vientiane who was very good at motivating villagers to contribute to projects. You know, he'd go around telling the Lao to help themselves, how the old days when they could live off Soviet aid were gone. But by the time word of his speeches reached the provincial headquarters, those talks of his had become anti-Soviet propaganda, and we were told in no uncertain terms that our man was no longer welcome in the province.'

Tom had been too busy building weirs to notice much else, but he did tell an interesting story about a royalist army officer who'd spent sixteen years in detention. In 1991, there was still a functioning re-education camp on the main road between Viengxai and Sop Hao. It consisted of a dozen or so buildings and held about nine prisoners, the numbers having been reduced greatly over the years. Not wanting to get involved, Tom had been careful not to stop there, but one day the local crew he was travelling with decided to pause for lunch in the village.

'After a while, we noticed this guy nearby, who obviously was not a villager. He was just too sophisticated, you know, he spoke English. Turns out he'd been there for sixteen years. We got talking to this guy, who had worked with the Americans during the war. He took us to his house and it was incredible. He had built himself this fully functioning bar, with bar stools and army memorabilia on the walls. But he didn't want to speak in English in case there were any misunderstandings. You know, they all think I'm CIA or something. So we spoke in Lao. One year later, another of our trucks was passing through that camp when this guy runs out onto the road, waves down the truck, sticks his beaming face inside the cabin and yells, "Guess what? In two weeks, I'm going to Chicago!" They had finally decided to let him go.'

Returning to the Dok Mai Deng, I settled down to enter some notes in my laptop. I'd been at it only a few minutes when the faint blue screen suddenly flickered and died, along with the room light. It was 9.37 p.m., lights out in Xam Nua. On the street outside the only illumination was provided by flashlights groping about like blind men's sticks. I finished my notetaking on paper by candlelight.

In Xam Nua, the dawn is red. At 6.30 a.m., the Ministry of Culture loudspeakers mounted on lamp-posts began their ritual scourging of the population, bellowing distorted music and messages. Fiery streaks darted across the sky as the sun came up over the mountains, and the greyness of the main street was highlighted by the impossibly pink tracksuit of a lone jogger.

The lure of making a few dollars had apparently outweighed Lamphan's concerns about the threat posed to national security by taking me to Sop Hao. He arrived in a jungle-green Russian jeep for which he'd scrounged a tankful of petrol from local households. Crossing the bridge, we headed north-east past the airport, the sun flashing on crowds of yellow flowers and signs allotting firewood rights to individual villages. Black pigs with coarse hair were everywhere, the sows so heavily pregnant that their stomachs scraped the ground. Each pig wore a yoke-like wooden collar up to a metre long, designed to stop it slipping through vegetable garden fences. Khen said the bigger the collar, the 'naughtier' the pig. The road descended into a broad valley dotted with dozens of limestone karsts. During the war, motorists were forced to drive without headlights at night, lest they attract the unwelcome attention of American reconnaissance planes and bombers. Forward Air Guides (FAGs)—often Lao with local knowledge—would drop flares at the sight of any road traffic, illuminating the area sufficiently for a strike. When a flare went up, motorists would slam on the brakes and run to the foxholes dug in beside the road. Gaping holes in the karsts formed the entrances to caves up to several kilometres deep in which schools, hospitals and prisons had been built. Before the battle of Dien Bien Phu, Vietnamese army units had moved into the Xam Nua area and begun reinforcing and enlarging the natural caves for themselves and their Lao comrades. Initial construction ended in 1963, but the caves were constantly being improved and enlarged. Throughout the war, as Xam Nua was pounded into dust, the caves formed the secure heart of the 'liberated zone', and after the war the party seriously considered moving the capital of Laos from exposed Vientiane to the cave country around impregnable Viengxai. A quarter of a century after the event, Lamphan knew the number of people killed by American bombing at each locality: a family of eight blown up here, a hospital blown up there.

A small airfield and some barracks painted ochre and green announced that we had reached Viengxai, the 'City of Victory'. Officially it was a mere district capital, but its role in the Pathet Lao's legend gave it disproportionate status and power. Lamphan prided himself on having influence in Viengxai as well as Xam

Nua. Being important in the provincial capital, he pointed out, didn't necessarily carry weight here. The first monument you see in the town makes its affiliations pretty clear. On a raised plinth, a soldier, a worker and a peasant hoist their hammers, sickles and rifles in the air. Under their feet rests a bomb inscribed with the letters 'USA'. All the town's buildings, which were constructed with the help of Cuban, North Korean, Russian and Vietnamese fraternal work brigades and seminar labour, looked decayed. The yellow two-storey building housing the district headquarters appeared quite grand from a distance, set at the end of an open square. But upon closer inspection it was revealed to be decrepit, with broken windows, collapsed ceilings and plants sprouting between the terracotta roof tiles. A man in jungle greens, one eye clouded by cataracts, sat listlessly on the front steps beside a veteran in a Pathet Lao uniform and floppy cap. The interior was decorated with a bust of Lenin, a portrait of Ho Chi Minh and a set of antlers.

Our host was a genial, owlish man who introduced himself as Pengsone Lovankham, chairman of the local Kaysone Museum project. Like everywhere else in Laos, there were ambitious plans to build something that didn't look like eventuating any time soon. In this case, the grand scheme involved turning gloomy Viengxai into a permanent revolutionary memorial for the delight of tourists. First, however, a survey was required to determine transport, infrastructure and accommodation needs.

'Houaphan is a historic province for Lao people,' Pengsone said. 'There are many caves where the different leaders hid during the war. We would like to show other people.'

Unlike Khen and Lamphan, Pengsone was old enough to have personally experienced much of the area's history. During the war he had trained in propaganda at Sisana Sisane's Ministry of Information and Culture, and had met Souphanouvong many times between 1963 and 1973 when the Red Prince and his family had been living in the caves. He proved to be the ideal guide, accompanying us the short distance to Souphanouvong's cave. The first thing we saw at the cave site was a large cream and lemon-coloured villa built for the prince after the Paris peace accords ended US bombing in 1973. The building, and a garden of poinsettias and pomelo trees, had been laid out around a former bomb crater transformed into what Pengsone called a 'peace pond'. The president's car had a little cave of its own in the base of a nearby cliff, and a path led from the villa to this subterranean garage, where a group of villagers hacked away at the undergrowth with machetes. The jungle seemed determined to strangle the revolution's history. An area cleared by the villagers revealed a *stupa* Souphanouvong had built to entomb the ashes of his eldest son, Arya, who'd been assassinated in 1973. The assassins, local men, were executed by firing squad on the square in Viengxai. Arya's Vietnamese mother, Viengkham, had spared two others accused of involvement, sending them to a labour camp instead.

The cave entrance was perched about 10 metres above the ground and was protected by a concrete bunker. We waited for a generator to provide light inside the cave, but when it failed Pengsone fetched a hissing gas lantern and began leading us through a series of rooms created by wooden partitions. Small signs in Lao, French and English identified Souphanouvong's office, a living room and bedrooms for his ten children. One room in particular stood out, the only one formed of metal rather than timber walls, and the only one with a false ceiling. It was accessed through a riveted metal doorway similar to those on ships and submarines, and contained what looked like an electric pump. Pengsone described this as the emergency room, into which oxygen could be pumped in the event of a gas or chemical weapons attack. As Souphanouvong's son, Souphaxay, had told me, the cave was damp, but it was lighter and airier than I'd expected, and all openings were screened off to prevent bats and birds getting in. The kitchen, with an open hearth and a meat safe, was outside on a natural patio overlooking the ravine, protective cliffs towering hundreds of metres above. Not all the caves were so comfortable; some were used as prisons. The Pha Deng camp was one such cave prison. Located two kilometres east of Viengxai township, it was bordered by steep cliffs on one side and a deep valley on the other. According to the US Central Intelligence Agency, 'harsh conditions inside the camp led to a number of cases of insanity'.

There was little in the bare rock surfaces to give any sense of the real life of Souphanouvong; the place was as cold and hard as the official portrait of a one-dimensional revolutionary. Marxism–Leninism had helped resolve his many grievances: the slight of being given a position lower than his half-brother Souvanna Phouma in the colonial civil service; the injustice of being born into the lower echelons of the royal family, destined to play a secondary role to the intellectually inferior sons of the king. Souphanouvong had good personal and political reasons for despising a system of governance by birthright, even as he used the advantages it offered him. In the 1930s, while working as an engineer in the Vietnamese beach resort of Nha Trang, he'd met Nguyen Thi Ky Nam, better known as Viengkham, an innkeeper's daughter who shared his detestation of colonial rule and belief in socialist ideas. The motto of the bride's family was 'Jointly, the family finds happiness; unified, it reaches prosperity'. But Souphanouvong subjugated the unity of his family to the solidarity of the revolutionary struggle. In 1957, he signed an agreement with Souvanna Phouma ending the civil war and committing the Pathet Lao to participation in the first coalition government. The communist rank and file were dismayed, thinking the struggle against Vientiane had ended in a miserable compromise. But in a speech to Pathet Lao cadres and soldiers, Souphanouvong explained that although national liberation could not be accomplished immediately, the Central Committee of the Lao People's Party was not relaxing its revolutionary effort in any way: 'The purpose of the revolution and the goal of our struggle is to liberate totally our homeland by expelling the imperialist aggressors; to bring about peace, independence, freedom and national unity; to progress until the overthrow of the puppet regime, the abolition of the monarchy, and the establishment of a genuine democratic regime in its place.' Royal hobnobbing still had its place, however. In March 1974, Cambodia's Prince Sihanouk was the Souphanouvongs' guest at Viengxai. A joint communiqué denouncing American imperialism was issued, and Madame Souphanouvong hosted a banquet for the Cambodian royals.

Moving from the cave out onto the sunlit terrace, I decided to hit on Pengsone for an interview. To my shock and surprise, he agreed, and soon was recalling in eloquent terms the days of revolutionary struggle. Almost as an aside, he mentioned that after the war, in Vientiane, he had served as the Red Prince's barber.

'Was he the kind of man who shared confidences with his barber?' I wondered.

'No, not really,' said Pengsone. 'He'd joke around, or discuss what a man should do in order to be respected. How he should work hard.'

'Souphanouvong was a prince, a member of the royal family. Did he ever give the impression of being different from other people in that way?'

'No, never,' said Pengsone without hesitating. 'He was just like ordinary people.'

'There were other members of the royal family up here, too, but they were prisoners,' I ventured. 'Were they kept here in this general area as well? Was the old king, Savang Vatthana, here?'

Khen almost choked and died translating the difficult question. I was resigned to a pro forma plea of ignorance, but my ears pricked up when I heard the words 'Long Ma' in Pengsone's Lao reply.

'They were in seminar in the Long Ma area,' he said.

Such a precise location, provided by such a qualified official, was unprecedented. First, there had been Sisana Sisane's admission that the three senior royal family members had died. Now, confirmation that they had been held near the Ma River. I dared to hope for a breakthrough.

'Did Savang Vatthana die there?' I asked, holding my breath for the answer.

But Pengsone seemed already to be having second thoughts about his candour.

'I don't know,' he said, reverting to the archetypal response of the Lao historian.

Returning to the market, we ate a lunch of boiled chicken, small fish, green vegetables and rice. I was given the prized chicken head, its expression frozen at the moment of slaughter. Including the beer, lunch for the four of us cost about three dollars. Although prices were thrown down, the only stalls doing any business in the almost deserted marketplace sold the ubiquitous lottery tickets. State-run lotteries, rather than dreams of socialist utopia, gave hope to the Lao people.

After lunch, we set off again, heading north from Viengxai to link up with National Highway Six—the road to Sop Hao, 'the lips of the Hao River', as Ounheuanne had put it, 'where it meets the River Ma, close to Vietnam'. Reaching the junction, Lamphan turned the jeep east in our agreed direction, and the landscape gradually underwent a transformation. Brooding peaks gave way to broad terraced valleys. At Ban Ban Hai there were fields of sugar cane, and at Ban Nam Mau only the second *wat* I'd seen in Houaphan. The road followed the Keng River, a shallow dreaming stream of wide sandbanks on which buffalo lazed. River sand was being sold at the roadside in several places, while boys carried long-barrelled hunting rifles and machetes. Women struggled along with babies suspended in slings from their foreheads, and men with limbs missing—veterans of the many wars—hobbled along in jungle greens. Also in green were the Vietnamese road gangs, distinctive in their pith helmets. They were heading for Xam Nua, leaving a line of concrete power poles neatly dotted behind them every 30 metres or so. The authorities were promising that Xam Nua would soon have power 24 hours a day, supplied by the Russian-designed Hoa Binh hydroelectric dam in neighbouring Vietnam. This, in a country embarking on massive hydroelectricity projects of its own. The Vietnamese had secured the deal by offering to build the power line free of charge. Only the electricity consumed would be paid for. But Laos would pay a higher price for Vietnamese power than Thailand paid for electricity generated in Laos.

After ninety minutes we crossed from Viengxai into Xieng Kho district, and the Nam Keng became the Nam Hao.

'Now we enter the hot zone,' said Lamphan, and within minutes the temperature seemed to rise. There was also more light as the river valley opened out, with palm trees clustered in groves and a vista of blue mountains way in the distance.

'Pears won't grow here, but coconuts do,' Lamphan said, enjoying the chance to exhibit his local knowledge. 'They don't have frost here like in Xam Nua.'

The road, however, was getting worse, dwindling at one point to a narrow dirt walking track traversing badly eroded rice terraces. Small dams provided local hydroelectricity to run rice mills, and the rice was stored in what looked like houses, but were really granaries. It was sobering to remember the subsistence level at which the overwhelming majority of Lao people lived, so removed from—yet so affected by—politics.

A sprinkling of rudimentary huts finally announced Sop Hao. The village was large and well ordered, with dozens of stilt houses and even a couple of small shops. First stop, as always, was a meeting with the local government representative, who turned out to be on a posting from Xam Nua. He was staying in a lodge for officials, the thatched walls of which boasted postcards from Hanoi. But no sooner had we arrived than the official, vigorously supported by Khen and Lamphan, suggested we should leave soon in order to return to Xam Nua before nightfall.

'Why not stay the night?' I suggested cheerfully.

The idea mortified them.

'Here? You want to stay in village Sop Hao?' said Lamphan incredulously, triggering a round of nervous laughter from his cohorts. 'Why do you want to stay here?'

It was a fair question, difficult to answer too.

'Well, I'm interested in the history of the Lao revolution,' I managed.

They laughed again, assuring me there was no history here.

'But the camps,' I said finally. 'There were re-education camps here. They were part of the revolution. People here would remember the time of seminar.'

Khen assured me nobody in the area would remember anything. That was my opening.

'Well, that's easy to prove,' I said, relentlessly cheerful. 'Let's ask.'

The village shopkeeper was minding his own business in his bamboo-thatch stall when our party descended on him. Boua Sy didn't get up. He was fifty, had been born in Sop Hao, and opened his little shop by the main road in 1987. It was the time of the so-called New Economic Mechanism, which allowed private business activities for the first time since the revolution, the command economy having performed abysmally. By the mid 1990s, small businesses like this one were flourishing all over Laos, and the shopkeeper had adorned his shack in the spirit of the times, lining the walls with pages from an old copy of the *Far Eastern Economic Review.*

'It's just for decoration,' said Boua Sy, who neither spoke nor read the language of the publication.

The shop displayed the usual array of biscuits and soft drinks, but an ornate black leather cash box caught my eye. It must have been from the French colonial time. Confirming my guess, Boua Sy said a passing aid worker had offered him 1500 *kip* for it, but he'd refused to sell. Or hadn't needed to. The advent of shops was the best thing to happen in Sop Hao in recent memory. There were, of course, fluctuations in profitability. Turnover depended on the size of the harvest. The arrival of electricity from the Hoa Binh dam on the Black River, just across the border in Vietnam, was another welcome development.

My intention had been to relax my interviewee by discussing everyday matters before raising more sensitive issues. This shopkeeper's story about a man who stayed where he was born, immovable in the face of upheaval, was as much a part of history as the fate of any king, and no less significant. Yet harassed by my minders, I took refuge in it for longer than I should have. Around us, a small crowd had gathered. They were gawking at the shopkeeper, gawking at me and my entourage, and following the interpreted conversation with bemused smiles. As we spoke, Boua Sy cast glances at his audience, clearly uncomfortable with all the attention. My strategy of warming up to the difficult questions had gone disastrously wrong.

'Were there ever any seminar camps around Sop Hao?' I asked suddenly, feeling like a doomed idiot.

'Never heard of them,' said Boua Sy.

Was it widely known that the king died in the vicinity?

He didn't know what I meant by 'king'.

Frankly, had a complete stranger accompanied by translators and minders from the government wandered into my village and started interrogating me about state secrets, I wouldn't have said anything either. Boua Sy's unruffled demeanour had been replaced by tense looks and sly smiles. I could have sworn Khen was winking at the poor man. With all avenues of serious inquiry evaporating, we ended up talking about fishing. They were catching whoppers in the Ma River, apparently. I could hear the river, a short distance away, tumbling towards Vietnam. If only it could speak, the river would have told us we had reached the Ground Zero of Lao history.

On a mid-October evening in 1977, not far from where we were standing in village Sop Hao, three military trucks rolled to a halt after a two-day journey from Xam T'ai. Tied up in the back of the trucks were twenty-five senior officials of the Royal Lao Army and government. Offloaded with their hands still tethered, they were frogmarched to a canoe moored at the riverbank, and paddled across the Ma River in relays under close armed guard. Among them was Khamphan Thammakhanty, the intelligence officer whose medal had been found lying outside his daughter's workplace in Vientiane two years earlier. The operation to transfer the prisoners across the river took hours, but eventually all of them were assembled several kilometres downstream near village Nakaa T'ai, just a kilometre from the Vietnamese border. The prisoners—all men who had already spent months or years in detention—thought their final hour might be approaching. After two days without food, the former generals, ministers of state and ambassadors to China and Australia were herded into a public hall in the middle of the village and individually tied to the supporting beams of the bamboo structure. They slept unfed that first night, plagued by clouds of malarial mosquitoes and unable to swat them. The following day, the guards gave them some rice, but the comfort of the food was soon shattered by the arrival of a senior official, who recognised one of the prisoners, the retired general Ouane Rathikoun, a former joint Chief of Staff of the Royal Lao Armed Forces. The two men had known one another during the war, but had not been friends.

'When we were together at the Plain of Jars,' said the Pathet Lao officer Inpanya, clearly savouring a moment of revenge, 'you used to tease me that I was running after the Vietnamese. "Eating their shit," you said. Now it's my turn to say to you, American lackeys, you also eat shit, right?'

Such crossing of paths is not uncommon in a country as small and intimate as Laos. Although Khamphan didn't know it, the man in overall charge of the seminar camp system throughout the 1980s was none other than General Saisompheng, the Pathet Lao representative at the bi-monthly joint security conferences in Luang Prabang, that Khamphan had attended after the city was neutralised in 1973.

For a fortnight after arriving at Nakaa T'ai, the prisoners underwent intense interrogation. They were accused of helping plan coups against the revolutionary government, of attempting to escape to Thailand, or knowing the location of a secret underground prison in Vientiane where Vietnamese POWs were held. Then, towards the end of October, they were again rounded up and marched three kilometres north through the jungle, past the present-day village of Nakaa Nua, until they reached a small clearing ringed by mountains. Standing in the clearing were about a dozen barracks buildings constructed in anticipation of the prisoners' arrival. The barracks were built from bamboo and sawn wood, with gabled roofs of grass thatch and bamboo beams. Unlike most Lao village habitations, they were not built on stilts, but directly on the ground in the style of the Hmong ethnic minority, indicating that local Hmong may have been employed to build them. The camp was fenced by sharpened poles and overlooked by two watchtowers five metres high. The rudimentary settlement included a small rice field, and straddled a stream that sometimes flowed into the Nam Ma. Sop Hao village was only two kilometres to the south-east across the Ma River, but there was no vehicular access to the camp, which could only be reached by walking trails. It was called Camp Number One, the highest security detention facility in all Laos, and it was ready to welcome its first 'guests'.

Unlike labour camp internees, who enjoyed a degree of freedom of movement, the inmates of Camp Number One were confined to barracks seven days a week. The camp guard consisted of a platoon of twenty Pathet Lao troops drawn mainly from the Lao Theung, or Khmu ethnic minority of the upland areas, whose fierce loyalty to the regime was the legacy of the intense American bombardment of their homelands. Most of them were filled with contempt for their prisoners, all of whom had in some way co-operated with American operations in Laos. Seventeen men in that first group of prisoners were senior military or police officers, six were leading politicians or diplomats, and two were Pathet Lao officers who had defected to the royalist side. They included the last Chief of the Royal Lao Armed Forces, Lieutenant General Bounpone Makthepharak; the Minister of the Interior, Pheng Phongsavan, who had signed the Vientiane Accords that agreed a ceasefire on behalf of the Lao government; and Prince Sinxay-Sana, a brigadier general and cousin of both President Souphanouvong and the former prime minister, Souvanna Phouma. Their elite connections were of no use to them now. Holding high rank or position only made things worse.

On arrival, the prisoners were informed that failing to scrupulously obey the orders of the guards was a crime punishable by death. Prisoners were prohibited from whispering among themselves, and were required to respond promptly and loudly to morning and evening roll calls. The barracks in which they were confined had dirt floors, and to sleep, the prisoners lay down beside one another on woven, split-bamboo mats spread over wooden planks. There was a single window fitted with steel bars in each barracks, and a doorway. Denied physical exercise and reading materials, most prisoners spent their days lying quietly in the darkness. The guards selected five inmates to form a small work team that would take care of the other prisoners' basic needs. Khamphan was one of the five. He was appointed cook and head of his barracks, and given an assistant, another colonel, Amkhar Khantha-Mixay. Two former policemen, Phoumi and Bao Thong, and Phimpha, an army driver, collected firewood and did other odd jobs. Despite their egalitarian principles, some subliminal consciousness of class saw the Pathet Lao assign these manual tasks to those of lowest birth and education in the camp.

'The guards were always asking me, "You didn't finish high school? How did you become such a big man in the government?",' Khamphan would later recall. 'So I told them, "I am like you. I survive on my wits. I succeed because I am a good fighter." I tried to convince them that I was like them. And partly it worked.'

While the generals and senior politicians rotted in their barracks, the five prisoners selected as part of the work team got sunshine, fresh air and physical activity. They were entitled to bathe every day, although they never saw a cake of soap.

'The work kept us fit, and took our minds off our problems. I became strong and it helped me,' Khamphan said, 'but the other prisoners had nothing to do but worry and think.'

In the concentration camps of Nazi Germany, as the eminent Viennese psychologist and Auschwitz survivor Dr Viktor Frankl observed, 'those who knew that there was a task waiting for them to fulfill were most apt to survive'. At Camp Number One working prisoners able to move around in the open, like their predecessors at Auschwitz, were soothed by 'glimpses of the healing beauties of nature'. The sight of a tree or a sunset could keep a person alive, at least for a few more days. Together with Amkhar, Khamphan took to the task of feeding the camp with enthusiasm and inventiveness, but from the outset he faced impossible odds. The glutinous Lao staple, sticky rice, was never provided to prisoners in the camps. They were given broken rice from Vietnam, the inferior grains normally milled into rice flour or left for the rats. The individual ration of 400 grams of cooked rice a day in Camp Number One was a third of what they had been given in other camps. Supplemented only rarely by the slaughter of a pig or a hen, it was basically a starvation diet. Even the guards did not eat well, but they were at least free to poach wildlife or visit Sop Hao village across the river for bowls of *feu* when off duty. One night, a guard shot a tiger that had ventured out of the jungle to drink from a water hole near the camp.

There were no uniforms in Camp Number One. Prisoners wore the clothes they had arrived in, which over the years deteriorated into rags. In late October, a consignment of supplies and personal effects arrived from the camp they had left behind at Xam T'ai. Clothes, flashlights and other items were fallen upon enthusiastically. In Khamphan's case, the prize item was the satchel he had taken with him on the day he left Vientiane. That night, in the dark of the barracks, he reached inside the bag and felt the $270 in banknotes still secreted in the bag's lining. There was nothing to spend it on; but one day it might save his life.

In early November, another small ray of sunshine brightened the prisoners' bleak outlook. New blankets and mosquito nets were distributed. They dared to hope that the hardships of the first few weeks might be over, and that life would begin to resemble that of the other camps. Some even suggested that an amnesty might be under negotiation. However, in mid November the real reason for the gifts was revealed. One night, the usual coughing and snoring in the barracks was broken by a commotion in the compound outside. Unable to see what was happening in the darkness, the prisoners waited until morning, when peering through the cracks in their hut walls they saw a new group of eleven prisoners being herded into a smaller, previously vacant compound across the rivulet. The new arrivals were standing around the small bamboo hut that stood in the middle of the compound. The prisoners inside Khamphan's darkened barracks recognised and identified the new arrivals one by one.

'My god! It's Prince Sisavang,' Khamphan whispered in disbelief, recognising his old friend, the king's second son, from Luang Prabang days. The group included three brothers of the king; the palace secretary-general, Prince Souphantharangsi; the palace director of protocol, Prince Thongsouk; and Bovone Vatthana, a former provincial governor. Touby Lyfoung, the ebullient and rotund leader of the Hmong ethnic minority, was also among them. Amid much shouting by the camp guards, they were being organised into a work team.

The new arrivals comprised the cream of the ruling elite under the old regime. But the most important prisoners of all had still to arrive.

Khen and I had argued in the jeep on the way back to Xam Nua. Displaying obvious irritation with my line of questioning throughout the day, he suggested that if I wanted to know what had happened to the king, I should ask his family.

'I have,' I said. 'They don't know.'

'So ask those Lao living overseas,' he said peevishly. 'I'm sure they'll give you a good story.'

'I don't want a good story, Khen. I want the truth.'

He laughed, and that made me angry.

'What's the point of asking the family of someone who's been kidnapped, or someone who's been murdered, what happened to them?' I challenged him. 'If you want to know, ask the kidnapper. Ask the murderer.'

'So, that's it!' he shouted, reflecting my own anger and irritation. 'You accuse the Lao government of being murderers! Murderers and kidnappers, you say. Well, I hope you have evidence of that. Can you prove it, eh? Can you?'

I realised I had overstepped the mark and would score poorly when Khen wrote his report. We drove on, plunged into a black and moody silence, absolved at least of the need to shout to be heard above the whining Russian engine.

Next morning, at the provincial headquarters in Xam Nua, Khen and I did a passable impersonation of two people who had not argued the previous day. We were greeted by deputy governor Cheu Ying Vang, a Hmong from Ban Houakhang,[1] a village we had passed on the way to Viengxai. As usual, there was a phalanx of note-takers, fixers, photographers and minders sitting on the fringes of our meeting. The deputy governor was pudgy, with fat, hairy forearms, and the whole room was the brighter for his lovely flower-embroidered shirt. He personified the fact that not all Hmong had thrown in their lot with the Americans. In response to my questioning about seminars and kings, Cheu said there were still four people in detention, all of whom had been convicted by a court. One had married a local girl. The king, he acknowledged, had died in Houaphan, but the issue 'belonged to Vientiane'.

'We just implement their policy,' he said.

The province was considering a foreign proposal to develop a tourist resort in the Long Ma area, where Pengsone had said the king had been interned. In principle, he was in favour of it, Cheu said, although transport would be a problem. At the end of our meeting, the deputy governor leant over and asked a favour.

'Some overseas Lao have the wrong idea,' he said, applying his charm like ointment. 'They think Vietnam dominates Laos. Here, you have seen the truth with your own eyes. You should explain to them that we are really independent.'

It was Saturday afternoon, and boys and girls promenaded on the main street of Xam Nua, stopping to observe a mural painter who was daubing a concrete billboard with flowers to mark the approaching anniversary of the revolution. His work was attracting the sort of attention accorded to the slab in *2001: A Space Odyssey*. A curious boy scratched it. A woman sniffed it. By 4 p.m., shadows enveloped the town, the sun touching only the mountain tops around it. The loudspeakers started up with a cough, a burst of static and a flood of advice, the words 'doll–aar' and 'Ameri–caa' interspersed with distorted music from *khene* bamboo pipes. A rooster crowed and a woman threw slops onto the street. The flag of the Lao People's Revolutionary Party stood in the lobby of the Dok Mai Deng, waiting to be unfurled on 2 December. From the window of my packing crate of a room I saw the deputy governor returning home in the gubernatorial Toyota, one of the few modern vehicles in the town. With no electricity to run my laptop, I was listening on my portable shortwave radio to the BBC reporting on the strife in far-off Bosnia. Was it the European focus that was so comforting, I wondered, or the economy of language and reverence for fact? It was a relief to know that independent reporting existed somewhere, and that I'd soon be leaving the claustrophobic atmosphere of Xam Nua.

At 5 a.m. the next day, loud music began blaring near the hotel. It transpired that two young townsfolk were to be married that morning, and preparations for the party had begun in the house adjoining the Dok Mai Deng. The green parachute of a long-lost American airman was put up, creating a canopy under which several dozen chickens were being slaughtered. By ten, the rice wine was flowing, and a *baci* bowl decorated with poinsettias and marigolds anchored many lengths of holy string held by relatives and friends. A despondent bride and groom stood together as a shaman shouted mantras and rice was thrown. Earlier, the young man had gone to the house of his bride and bartered for her symbolically. Later the newlyweds would be confined to their bedroom amid much bawdy sign language. In the lobby of the guesthouse, Khen was getting into the spirit of things, knocking back *lau lao* with a girl of thirteen. Lamphan joined in while three small boys and I looked on, disgusted.

At the airport, a Yuen-12 light plane operated by Lao Aviation squeezed between a gap in the hills and raised dust as it hit the runway. My passport was checked and I walked down to the landing strip, past a small open-air meat market which had sprung up for the benefit of travellers. On display were bunches of dead squirrels threaded together through their noses and selling at

800 *kip* a kilogram. One of the passengers bought a live bamboo rat, a beaver-like creature, for 2000 kip. The sharp-toothed rat was not a good traveller and would pose a threat to all on board. So, after pocketing her money, the vendor bashed the hapless animal in the mouth, breaking its prominent front teeth, before tossing it onto the grass for the buyer to pick up. It stumbled about, drunk with pain, blood spattering its furry face.

15

The Plain of Jars

Back in Vientiane, the street murals invoked the 'spirit of Xam Nua', but the people were still partying. Tens of thousands of them thronged the city's temples on the nights leading up to the full moon. Wat Seemuang was engulfed by a sweaty human sea, as families seeking merit carried silver *baci* bowls and swaying *phasat peung*—wax castles decorated with palm leaves, money and marigolds—in a procession around the six-pillared temple. The sky was full of fireworks, and acrid smoke mixed with the fragrance of incense and the pervasive odour of chicken and bananas grilling on charcoal braziers along the road. Under normal circumstances, Wat Seemuang would have been a quiet place to meet up again with Boun Kham. But given the crowds, I found it an odd choice for a rendezvous. Amid the thousands of people milling around the base of the statue of King Sisavangvong, I was lucky to see his billiard-ball head from metres away.

Boun was impressed and disgusted. Impressed that I'd made it to Sop Hao; disgusted that, other than getting official confirmation that the king had been held in Long Ma, I had seen and heard little which might throw much more light on the fate of the royal family.

'You must have seen the Vietnamese!' he shouted above the sound of nagging loudspeakers calling out the names of people who'd made donations to the *wat*, and noting exactly how much they'd given in dollars, baht and *kip*.

'Only the workers building the electricity line.'

'Aha!' he cried. 'They take off their uniform to work on the road. But their guns are never far away. Those Vietnamese you see, they are commandos. They occupy my country!'

Boun fiddled with his collar, as if to let out steam.

'You did good,' he said. 'But the communists are very clever. They know how to hide everything. But don't worry. Don't give up!'

'I *am* giving up,' I said, glaring at him. 'I never want to see Houaphan province again.'

'Take a break, guy,' he said, slipping into the US army-speak he used in lighter moments, and slapping me hard on the back. 'Go see That Luang.'

The celebration at Wat Seemuang was only the curtain-raiser to a much larger act of devotion two days later—the festival of That Luang. According to legend, the original *that*, or large *stupa*, was erected by the Indian Buddhist emperor Ashoka in the third century BC and contained relics of the Buddha. The great esplanade leading to the monument disappeared beneath vast crowds caught up in a fever of giving. Long lines of monks, carrying begging bowls in crocheted slings, accepted sticky rice, boiled eggs, candy bars and 100-*kip* notes, as the sounds of pounding drums and cascading xylophones punctured the air. Above the fray, crowned with a slouch hat, rose the statue of the city's founder King Setthathirath, who'd built the present *that*. The crowds were attempting the impossible feat of squeezing inside the confined space of the cloister, which already groaned with devotees, monks and flowers. Through it snaked a current of beautiful women, their necks swathed in gold chains and ornate sashes, their hands sweeping rhythmically as they danced the *lamvong*. Men beat bamboo staves on the ground in a warlike manner. One man of especial dignity preened and fussed over his antique tunic and emerald brooch of the Buddha and cooled himself with a courtly mauve hand fan. He fairly pranced about in the baggy pants known as *sampot*. This traditional costume was being worn by more men than at any time since the revolution. The government-controlled *Vientiane Times* newspaper saw the trend as perhaps a 'renaissance of interest and pride in Lao culture'. Yet it was a stunted renaissance, held back like the crowds at That Luang by the Lao People's Revolutionary Party. Extracting myself from the crush in the cloister, I returned to the esplanade to see a young boy buying a finch housed in a small bamboo cage. A new pet, I thought, until he opened the cage door and released it. Freeing birds was a traditional way of obtaining *boun*, or merit. The liberated finch escaped over the top of the national monument, remembering how to fly, just as the Lao had remembered how to live.

That Luang was part religious festival, part commercial hard sell, and part village fair. There were even freak exhibits—a four-horned buffalo and a white elephant, the latter of which was said to live under high security at the home of Mrs Kaysone, wife of the late party leader. Albino elephants had long been prized in Buddhist South-East Asia as talismans. Pregnant women would walk beneath them for good luck, and nations had been known to go to war over them. In *The Life and Lore of the Elephant*, Robert Delort wrote that whenever a white elephant was spotted in the forest, 'it was captured with the utmost care, ministered to by a host of attendants and adorned with exquisite jewellery. It was served luscious delicacies in the hope of prolonging its life and with any luck it lived to a ripe old age. Its death prompted consternation, grief and fear, from the king down to his humblest subject.' The Thai believe people of great merit can be reborn as white elephants to help society in times of trouble—unless you are a convicted criminal, in which case a white elephant is usually the one trained to carry out the death sentence by crushing you underfoot.

If Laos had ever truly been the land of 'one million elephants' it was, sadly, no longer. Logging and clearing for agriculture and development 'threatened the pachyderms' continued existence. Their hides were coveted for making shoes and bags, their teeth were used in medicines, and ivory poaching—which targeted only the tusks of bulls—had severely upset the male–female ratio. The government had established the Nakai Nam Theun National Biodiversity' Conservation Area, which stretched across Bolikamsai and Khammouane provinces east of Thakek. It was home to about 250 elephants, but even within the protected area, logging continued at a steady pace.

The days grew longer in Vientiane, city of stolen arches and white elephants. Even during the war it had been a soporific city, or so I'd been told, utterly out of touch with the war that slowly and inexorably was destroying the old order, supplanting it with a morbid legacy. More shrapnel than had been dropped on Hitler's Germany was lying around out there, much of it on the Plain of Jars, one place I had yet to see. Like Viengxai, it was a place of secrets, so I headed back to Lao Aviation and bought a return ticket to Phonsavan, capital of Xieng Khouang province.

From the air, the denuded landscape around Phonsavan resembled the pelt of a shorn camel. Bomb craters marched across the plateau, carving bizarre patterns in the farmlands, like crop circles. The American pilots had performed an unintended service, pock marking the landscape with thousands of depressions that gradually filled with water and became dams. On a bright, clear day, these small reservoirs reflected the sky and sun like a brilliant array of mirrors. Travelling alone, my intention was to see the famous jars, then head straight back to Vientiane. But emerging onto the tarmac at Phonsavan I was struck immediately by the clarity of the air and the stiff, bracing breeze off the mountains, such a relief from the heat of the lowlands. Around the corrugated iron shed that served as a terminal milled an odd assortment of races and nationalities—displaced, gold-toothed Tajiks in stale Soviet uniforms, burnt-cheeked Asiatic women in football socks and Lakers caps and men relieving themselves on piles of dirt. It was good to be back on the frontier, a sort of South-East Asian Ulan Bator, all stark and improvised and half-finished and changing. I was standing there at a thousand metres above sea level, admiring a flock of pelicans wheeling above me, when a MiG fighter jet screamed overhead, barrel-rolling on a dummy strafing run all the way to the horizon. When the deafening roar abated, the querulous sound of a young backpacker haggling with a taxi driver in the carpark replaced it.

'Five thousand? You must be kidding!' the young man howled in a plummy English accent. 'I mean, fair's fair. That's outrageous!'

The backpacker's outrage was heartfelt, genuine. He had long hair, grey drill trousers and a stained pullover that told me he'd been on the road for some time, like a well-spoken English tramp. We introduced ourselves, then someone called to him.

'Richard! Over here.'

The summons came from a lumpen-looking character who towered over a short Lao man beside a Russian jeep. Damien had met Richard on the plane, and had apparently negotiated a deal on a taxi. The driver, a local tour guide called Sousath, would eventually provide much more than just the use of his car.

Soon the four of us were bumping along the ramshackle streets towards the Dorg Khoune Hotel, where the lobby was decorated with rusting bombs and land mines, and the room key-rings were spent bullet casings. Apart from its ancient and massive stone jars, Xieng Khouang's main claim to fame was the amount of unexploded ordnance that littered the province. You could just see the car numberplates: 'Xieng Khouang—Explosive State'. Its capital was Phonsavan, an upstart village turned city whose predecessor, Old Xieng Khouang, had been destroyed during the war. Too impatient for style, its buildings rose rough and ready, with reinforcing rods protruding from their flat roofs, set to rise again as soon as funds permitted. The broad main street was the stage for a comic opera of overladen buses, dusty black Volgas and packed *tuk-tuks* groaning to and from Nong Het on the Vietnamese border. The town's cinema had been driven out of business by the recent arrival of videos, and satellite dishes that sucked down news and entertainment direct from the stratosphere. The city had received its first fax message the day before my arrival, and a new one-hour photo shop shone like a gold tooth in a mouthful of decay. Unfettered by a past, Phonsavan was headed for a future that its cantankerous *tuk-tuks* could not reach quickly enough. It was only a matter of time before all the land mines and bomblets were melted down for scrap or sold as souvenirs, and its people embraced their destiny. Only the dogs, dozing in the gasoline haze, seemed oblivious to the opportunities.

Sousath's 'bar'—the basement of his home, which he planned to turn into a restaurant—was the scene of a rendezvous that night. The host began the evening's entertainment by producing a bottle of rice wine, made to his own recipe from fermented sticky rice, honey and ginseng. Sousath wore a black mop top hairstyle and a bomber jacket over a football jersey sent by a relative abroad. Having lit a fire in our bellies, he proceeded to fire our imaginations with his other props: maps, photographs and stories. Xieng Khouang was one of the key battlegrounds in the Indochina war. Three major road arteries intersected in the province and the Ho Chi Minh trail was only a few hours drive away. The Hmong general Vang Pao, who with American support came to represent a greater threat to the Pathet Lao than the Royal Lao Army, had been based at the isolated mountain settlement of Long Cheng. America's support for Vang Pao was supposed to be a secret, but passengers on civilian flights to Luang Prabang were occasionally diverted to remote airstrips, where GIs wearing fatigues—but no identifying insignia— marshalled Hmong fighters and supplies and equipment with military efficiency. Boarding one such diverted plane at Long

Cheng, a soldier once announced to the startled passengers: 'You have not been here. You have not seen anything, and you will not talk about this to anyone!'

Vietnam's military mastermind, General Vo Nguyen Giap, had worked hard to ensure Viet Minh and Pathet Lao control of the plateau, allowing him to bear down on both Vientiane and Luang Prabang. Although his fate was being decided upon its rolling hills, King Savang Vatthana rarely ventured onto the plain, apart from a couple of visits to Long Cheng, designed to boost morale among Vang Pao's men. Time had softened the edges of the province's many bomb craters, the ugly depressions absorbed by wind, grass and rain. But danger still lurked in the earth in the form of 'bombies'—the lethal cargo of the cluster bombs that had failed to thwart Vietnam's ambitions.

Sousath and Richard hit it off right away, sharing an interest in the archaeological mysteries of the plain. Richard was doing postgraduate work at the School of Oriental Studies in London and had written a thesis on transport policy in landlocked states like Laos and Afghanistan. Excited by his subject, he would launch into theatrical dissertations about the history of the ancient stone jars of the plain, with Sousath chiming in.

'I heard about a village north of Old Xieng Khouang. Completely deserted!' Sousath told his enthralled audience, tossing back another rice wine. 'No Westerner has ever been there. Around this town, you've got hundreds of statues of dogs, made of stone. Everybody fled this town because the shaman, you know, the holy man, had a dream that a big bird would come from the sky and eat the village. So everybody moved to Old Xieng Khouang.'

In the event, it was not the village but the provincial capital of Old Xieng Khouang, comprising fifteen hundred buildings, that would be destroyed.

'Unbelievable,' said Richard, his adrenaline rising. 'Have you been there? To Dogville?'

'I've never been there,' said Sousath. He did, however, know Old Xieng Khouang and several jars sites. He also had a jeep and spare time. Richard and Damien wanted to explore immediately, but it was not until Sousath revealed some of his own history that I committed to the enterprise. 'My family name is Phetrasy,' he said. 'My father was Soth Phetrasy.'

'The Pathet Lao representative in Vientiane…during the war,' I said.

'Exactly! He was the one who decided whether to fight, or whether to shake hands.'

Sousath's father, Soth Phetrasy, had been the public face of the Pathet Lao, whose duty it was to liaise between Vientiane and Xam Nua during the civil war. The role was not unlike that of an ambassador to a foreign country, and the presence of his detachment in the capital, only 300 metres from the American embassy and guarded by a company of Pathet Lao troops, chafed many royalists. A short, stocky man, Soth was subjected to petty harassment by the royal government, and worn down by the constant threat of assassination by right-wingers egged on by their American advisors. However, he was invited to all the best parties, and was a guest of the king at the New Year celebrations in Luang Prabang in April 1975.

'He was in the communist style,' a Lao exile later told me. 'Not open. Watched everything. Said very little.'

Sousath had spent part of his childhood living in a compound in Vientiane guarded by one hundred Pathet Lao soldiers.

"I played volleyball with them. They were my friends," he said. 'No-one could touch us. But I had to go to school at the Lycée, and I fought with the French kids. The Pathet Lao always won. The French fought only with their fists. But I kicked!'

Mimicking the wince of a Frenchman holding his balls, he exploded in laughter.

'My family even had a cave in Viengxai. You know Viengxai? Here, look…'

He dug a photo album from the pile we'd been looking at and turned to a dim image of himself pointing to some rock graffiti.

'*Hasta la victoria siempre!*' Richard read aloud. 'Victory is coming, always.'

'That's my family's cave. You know who wrote that? Fidel Castro himself!'

Castro had visited Viengxai after the bombing stopped in 1973.

We left Sousath's that night having agreed over a final toast to engage his services. He would take us to visit the jars, Old Xieng Khouang, and Phou Khout, the site of a fortress built by the French in 1953 to defend the western approach to the Plain of Jars in the event that the Viet Minh took Luang Prabang. American bombing obliterated the fortress after it was taken by the Pathet Lao in the 1960s.

Over dinner at a restaurant in the town, I learnt more about my new companions. Richard was from Newbury outside London. A vegetarian, he nevertheless loved fishing for pike. He had a special interest in unexploded ordnance and the Black T'ai tribes, who had fled communism several times, moving from Dien Bien Phu to Xam Nua, Xieng Khouang and finally Thailand. He reminded me of a nineteenth-century English archaeologist transplanted into the information age, with dozens of obscure facts at his fingertips. He knew the going rate for old bombs—10 *kip* per kilogram—and when Sousath had mentioned the Han dynasty, he noted casually that they'd ruled around the time of Christ. Damien was a software engineer from Australia, who affected the look of a more primitive age. His ruddy face, golden earring and hirsute neck and forearms gave him a somewhat Neanderthal appearance, but he seemed an easygoing, adventurous type, and his hefty build might help if we got into a tight spot. We were finalising plans for the next day's travels when, from the street, a youth appeared and made straight for Damien, who seemed to know him.

'I met him walking in town this afternoon,' said Damien. 'He's going to take me to an opium den.'

The young Lao man smiled his assent and Richard did a double take.

Opium is nothing new in Laos, but successive generations insist on rediscovering it. For the Hmong tribes who left China in the early 1800s, it was the economic basis of their hopes for an independent homeland, and to this day many Hmong in Laos still depend for their living on opium poppy cultivation, which is not illegal. In some hill areas the number of people addicted to opium is greater than the number who can read. The French colonial administration was largely financed by it, with the opium harvest of northern Laos being sent to Luang Prabang's *bouillerie*, or boiler, while that of southern Laos went to Saigon. The processed product was sold to Ho traders travelling with mule trains from Yunnan in China. So vigorous was the industry during World War II that Luang Prabang became 'rotten' with silver, the currency in which the Ho paid, and many of the solid silver necklaces worn by Hmong women to denote status and store wealth date from that time. In the 1960s, the planes of the CIA airline, Air America, were used to transport opium to Saigon for processing into heroin and subsequent sale to US troops. The CIA claims it had no idea that the contraband was there. Yet drug revenues helped keep America's allies in the Indochina wars onside. For the Hmong resistance, opium meant weapons—6 kilos of the sticky paste was enough to purchase a light machine gun and ammunition; a rifle cost 2.5 kilos. Decades later, the impact of this high-stakes game was still apparent in Laos.

On a previous trip, I had visited the opium-growing areas on the slopes of Palavek Mountain, south of Long Cheng, in an area under direct military control called the Xaisomboun special zone. In the market at Palavek, the French were remembered for their baguettes, and the Americans for their turkeys. A live monkey could be purchased for about 50 cents, including the bangle round its neck.

The lofty peak of Palavek soared to 2000 metres from the valley floor, a big broken nose swathed in gossamer clouds. In the Phou Nyom escarpment, working elephants hauled logs, and motorists avoided blowing their car horns for fear of stampeding them. Boys shot game with rifles and slingshots, and men carried AK-47s. The local Hmong king was a toothless, nuggety old man who claimed to be 106 years old. His name was Nau Her Tor in Hmong, but he was better known as the Phia Luang. In the 1920s, King Sisavangvong had gifted him the area, but he had no time for the old king, saying that all the king did was lie around 'like a castrated pig'. The Phia Luang was one of the few Hmong leaders to side with the Pathet Lao, and had been rewarded with a Japanese jeep and the only brick house in the area. But the need to take sides, and to kill other Hmong, as well as other Lao, still clearly bothered him.

'People came to me and offered me money to fight on their side, but I've never wanted to take sides. I've always said, "I'm on the side of the winner, but I want to stay by myself and look after my people,"' the old man recalled. 'But they came and told me to kill the Pathet Lao. Because I refused, they killed my daughter, my princess, and they killed my people and shot me. So we had to take up muskets to defend ourselves. That's how I became a hero of the revolution. Not because I wanted to kill anybody, but because we had to defend ourselves.'

Now, the war was against opium. Opium traders had been coming to Palavek with packhorses to buy the local crop for a very long time. The dark-brown resin still served as a currency in the Hmong homelands, and was the only widely available painkiller. Nevertheless, high levels of addiction wasted the upland communities. One of the UN people showed me a poster painted by a Hmong girl featuring a sick man lying on a bed. 'My daddy is an opium addict,' read the caption. 'He is yellow, and he does no work. And he smells like a goat.'

'It's not the man eating the opium,' the Phia Luang said, 'but the opium eating the man.'

At his request, the United Nations Drug Control Program had built a new road to the mountain, making it more economic for Hmong to grow cash crops like coffee and chilli for the Vientiane market. Opium production had been cut from more than 5 tonnes a year to only 100 kilos. The Phia Luang's son, Sathor, had himself cultivated opium until the arrival of the UN project.

'It's very difficult work,' Sathor said. 'You have to grow it high in the mountains, and you have to leave the village and go and live in the opium fields. And there's a lot of weeding to be done, because grass grows very quickly among the poppies. Then when people get addicted, they lose their health. They can't work well and they start to steal because they have no money. There's no peace in the village.'

Now I was walking the dark streets of Phonsavan with Damien, towards the other end of the opium food chain, a chain that remained intact despite two decades of Pathet Lao rule. Our young Lao friend led us to a mud-floored house on the outskirts of town, where an elderly Hmong man lay on a double-bed base in a corner. Removing his shoes, Damien climbed onto the bed, and lay down on a grass mat beside him. The only light source, a small oil lamp standing on the bed base, shone on the old man's face, which was pale and almost entirely free of wrinkles. He was extremely thin, but not unhealthy, and wore a ponderously heavy gemstone ring. When he moved, it was with great economy, and in the warm light his face was suffused with a child-like innocence. He began preparing Damien's pipe as a matter of course, watching the opium intently, as a tranquil lover regards a treasured partner. Then, cupping the lamp over the bowl of the long bamboo pipe, he trained the flame onto the opium as Damien inhaled deeply several times, and then rolled onto his back to stare at the ceiling.

'You smoke?' Damien asked me, lifting his head briefly.

Suddenly, I felt dry-mouthed and inarticulate.

'Not me, no,' I replied, giggling nervously like a Lao.

The old man, meanwhile, had begun the intricate ritual of preparing another pipe. His eyes possessed an unearthly concentration and calm as he removed a small dark pellet from a plastic film canister and placed it in an ornate spoon, which he held over the flame of the lamp. As the opium began to boil, he stirred it with a silver needle, to which it started to stick. He kept turning the needle in the spoon, spinning the coagulating substance onto it. Then he grafted the resin onto the bowl of the pipe, and turned a lighter on it. As Damien began to suck with great inhalations, the old man scraped the bowl, turning the resin over as it bubbled and disappeared.

'It tastes sort of strange,' said Damien, holding his arms above his prostrate body. 'I mean smoking a joint is one thing. But this is a different sort of situation.'

I took the canister in which the opium was stored and breathed from it, expecting it to have a rich aroma, like hashish. But it smelt of nothing. Only when it burned in the pipe was there a slight fragrance of caramel. Beside the bed, the young man who had brought us to the place sat watching intently, like a dog at table. In an adjoining room lit by another oil lamp, an old woman sat at a table, staring fixedly at the lamp in front of her. She was drinking from a cup, raising it to her mouth with extraordinary slowness, and lowering it the same way, then slowly taking a bite of some kind of bread. She was either an opium addict, taking the drug as a tincture, or an opium widow. The atmosphere was as solemn as a temple.

When it came time for reckoning, Damien calculated what he owed at five hundred *kip*, or about 50 cents, per pipe. No sooner was the money handed over than the young Lao man who had brought us leapt onto the bed for his 'commission', a single pipe. When that was done, the old man began packing away his utensils with the same deft movements and mild smile with which he had conducted the dark, mysterious ritual.

A storm was brewing over the Plain of Jars that night, and the following morning we awoke to find strong winds carving patterns in the straw-coloured sea of grass. On a hill overlooking the main jars site, we surveyed the huge stone containers, scattered like pantry pots in a giant's kitchen. There was an Easter Island quality to the place, the legacy of an assertive and powerful culture existing on the plain centuries ago. 'We believe they were transported by elephants from Xam Nua to this area,' said Sousath. 'The elephants carried the rock, and the rock was shaved here. We don't know the purpose of the jars, but there are two stories: for keeping rice wine, and also as burial jars.'

Even had the jars been made purely for ceremonial purposes, it was hard to believe their obvious potential as storage containers had been ignored by subsequent generations. An old Khmu song, 'Call of the Khmu Soul', seemed to point to the existence of a popular eatery somewhere close by.

O soul spirit, return and drink
the beer of the great jar,
Eat the white egg, drink the strong beer,
Eat the fat pork, eat the hard head,
Eat the fatty brains.

The jars sat leaning at strange angles, spilling down the hill, across a flat and up the other side. There were about 300 of them, carved from stone and clothed in lichen. I'd read that all the jars had miraculously survived wartime carpet bombing, despite the fact that Pathet Lao guerillas had sometimes taken shelter inside them. Yet as we approached, several large bomb craters came into view with shattered jar fragments dug into their rims like broken teeth. 'How old are they?' mumbled Damien, bleary from his adventures the previous evening.

Sousath paused meaningfully.

'Actually, we don't know about the age,' he said, adding that early Chinese travellers had noted their existence several thousand years ago.

The rest of his story was drowned out by a MiG fighter jet flying low overhead, mocking the ancients as it swooped down onto the nearby airport runway. From where we stood, about twenty MiGs were clearly visible lined up beside the runway of the main military airbase in Laos. The proximity of the base meant the government had been reluctant to open the jars site to tourists, and Sousath claimed credit for having persuaded them to do so. In the early 1990s, surveying, fencing and mine clearance had begun, and hotel plans were approved. But five years later there were no hotels, only a handful of English-speaking guides, and still not many tourists.

In 1968, royalist troops supported by their American advisors had briefly occupied the site, before it was retaken by the Vietnamese. We had moved to the edge of a line of trenches dug by the lost armies. A snake was coiled up, hibernating, in one of the jars. Another, full to the brim with water, teemed with insects. Graffiti on another read 'BOMB USA', and its outer shell was dimpled by bullet holes. The whole area had once been a minefield.

'This area we're standing on here...' Damien started to say, but Sousath interrupted him.

'It's safe,' he said.

I was beginning to see Sousath in the way I imagine he saw himself: a bold explorer on the frontier of Laos. Sporting a denim photographer's vest, world-time watch and brown leather moccasins, he was like a Lao Indiana Jones. He claimed to have co-authored the government's tourism plan for Xieng Khouang province, and longed to meet Western scholars who could bankroll a big expedition that would keep him in *per diems* for a lifetime. Until then, his chubby, ageless face would continue to ambush foreigners at Phonsavan airport. In the new free market, Sousath survived on his wits, holding down jobs as a private detective, a disc jockey and an auditor. His stories were so good that you wanted them to be true.

'Some guard jars in the forest are still sealed,' he told us, eyes widening. 'Local people don't want to open them because they're afraid of spirits inside. They never touch them.'

The source of most of his information about the jars was a Frenchwoman he called 'Miss Coronee'. We thought she was one of his Western girlfriends until he said she'd been in Laos in the 1930s.

'Colani?' said Richard. 'Madeleine Colani. Of course! The French archaeologist. She worked in Indochina between the wars. There were those big digs—the Dong Son culture in Vietnam.'

Richard explained that Colani had worked the limestone karsts south of the Red River, before being drawn to Laos by the jars. She had found ancient crematoria, human remains and bronze and iron tools. Sousath had seen her photos from the thirties that showed the position of the jars unchanged.

We spent the afternoon poking around toppled forts, robbed *stupas* and a ghost town. Gradually, as the eye adjusted to the denuded landscape, it revealed its colours. Electric-green pines stood like trimmed manes on ridges of freshly ploughed brown earth; a steel-grey lake mirrored a leaden sky; a teak tree sprouted from an ancient jar, covered in avocado-green lichen. Red clay bricks tumbled like guts from *stupas*. The sixteenth-century That Phuan had been disembowelled by worms and thieves who burrowed in search of treasure. Grass held the facade together and taproots drove deep into the cracks. And everywhere, the lethal legacy of *that* war, all the more dangerous because it was invisible. We stepped carefully on a narrow trail up a shale hill to a crumbling French observation post. A foot misplaced could become a foot amputated by a buried bomblet. The bomblets, dropped in clusters of more than 600, infested villages, schools and farmland. Many people were still being killed and injured by simply lighting fires in the open, the heat triggering the buried explosives. Before its destruction, Old Xieng Khouang—now renamed Muang Khune—had boasted many grand buildings and monuments. It was, in fact, another royal capital, the seat of the Chao Noi Muang Phuan, the king of Xieng Khouang, who in the 1800s had been captured by the Vietnamese and executed in Hue. The ruined palace of the French legation resembled a Mediterranean villa, designed to catch the sun, with wide balconies and ornate balustrades. But the roof was missing, and doorless openings gaped at grand vistas—rice paddies on one side, mountains with high meadows on the other. Of the town's main temple, Wat Phia Wat, there was nothing left bar the foundations and a large stone Buddha that seemed to meditate on the ruins around it.

Helping to clear the province of the UXO threat were teams of foreign de-miners. Normally ex-army types, they had achieved cult-like status in the West—but not in Laos, if Sousath's attitude towards them was any indication. At Phonsavan's Sangah Restaurant that evening, he launched into a tirade against a table occupied by a de-mining team working around the town. The foreign experts, he claimed, were paid $200 a day, while Lao de-miners on $200 a month did the dangerous work.

'Give me $1 million, I can clear all the UXO in one month,' Sousath boasted.

It wasn't just de-miners who irritated him. On several occasions he'd acted as a guide for Americans revisiting old war sites. He'd helped the first American POW of the war, Lawrence Bailey, to return to Xam Nua, and claimed to have had contact with the teams searching for US servicemen missing in action. The Americans avoided offering rewards for soldiers' remains because whenever spurious rumours swept Laos that money was available, the embassy was besieged by unwelcome vendors of old bones. Sousath, it seemed, was one of those who had been spurned.

'They want the bones, but they won't pay money,' he said, grimacing. 'So they don't get bones.'

The old Pathet Lao fire was still in Sousath's belly. He had lived in East Germany for seven years, and thought of himself as a David defying a morally bankrupt Goliath. Communism had convinced him that there was only a limited amount of cash to go around, and only the morally pure should have it.

Damien, who had been distracted and withdrawn for most of the day, had gone off to the opium den and Richard was deep in discussion with the de-miners, when Sousath produced a bottle of whisky and suggested I join him for a nightcap. Moving to a table on the open terrace facing the street, we had settled down to watch the passing traffic and discuss our mutual interest in Lao history, when Sousath suddenly announced: 'My father could have been president of this country.' After his years as the Pathet Lao representative in Vientiane, Soth Phetrasy had joined the third and final coalition government of leftists and royalists in 1974, becoming Minister for Economy and Planning. But the following year, when the People's Revolutionary Party took power in its own right, he was conspicuous by his absence from the cabinet: The terror was calling him.

'He was sent to Xam Nua to oversee the cases of re-education,' Sousath said with a bitter smile. 'The Pathet Lao did not know who the people in the camps were. Only my father could tell them, because he spent many years in Vientiane mixing with the royal Lao government. So he told them, this one is okay, that one is a fascist.'

It was important work, yet a posting to Houaphan province was never a promotion. Was Soth being punished, I wondered? After all, proximity to decadent Westerners could contaminate even the most dependable cadre. A sobering stint in Viengxai was the only antidote.

'My father got nothing from the revolution,' Sousath said with a bitter intensity. 'After that they made him ambassador to Moscow. We lost everything because we believed. One day my father thought he was dying, and he called us to his bedside and said he would look after us like Souphanouvong looked after his children. I used to have to go to the hospital all the time because my father was there. At that time Souphanouvong was also in there, and he looked pathetic. You know in the communist system the individual is not important.'

Political struggles became personal ones in the hothouse atmosphere of the little revolution. Sousath's first marriage had ended after the son of a party leader was seen leaving the Phetrasy residence late one night while Sousath was away. When the party learned of these nocturnal activities, it sent the young man in question to Xam Nua for three years re-education. Sousath's wife fared worse, being sent to Don Nang, the women's island in Nam Ngum reservoir. She died there among what one visitor to the camps called the 'sad-eyed girls and listless young men'. There were, in fact, five prison islands in the Nam Ngum reservoir: for men, Thao Island (formerly known as Monkey Island); for women, Nang Island; and the mixed islands of Setthakit, Nampho and Thong, all of which opened for business in 1976. Publicly, the authorities maintained that all the islands were rehabilitation centres for social undesirables such as drug addicts, gamblers, hippies, juvenile delinquents and prostitutes, and used them as showcases through which foreign officials visiting Laos were escorted. In fact, according to the CIA's 1992 report, the island prisons were also home to hundreds of military personnel and officials of the old regime, as well as teachers, merchants and Lao employed by embassies in the capital, who were accused of spying for foreign governments. In all, several thousand people spent time there.

'I visited her once,' Sousath said, referring to his former wife. 'All the guards on the island were women. They hadn't seen a man for months. They looked like they could eat you!'

By the early 1990s, security on the island prisons had become so slack that male and female prisoners could be seen swimming to each other's islands. One such gallows romance even produced a marriage. Sousath himself was for several years restricted to the Xam Nua–Viengxai area after returning to Laos from his studies in

China, where he had misbehaved. The caves and camps of Viengxai were beginning to sound like one big reform school for the bratty offspring of the party leadership.

Carried away by Sousath's amazing life story, we had given the whisky quite a nudge, and I was emboldened to ask what he knew about Sop Hao, and what had happened to the king.

'Sop Hao? No, I don't know,' he said. 'But I know where the king stayed in Viengxai.'

'Where?'

'In my father's house.'

'What?'

'Why not? You want to go there? When my father was in Moscow, the house was empty. At that time the king came to Viengxai. So he stayed there with his family.'

'Do you still own the house?'

'No. Not really. My father lives in Vientiane, and anyway the house has fallen down. You can't live there now.'

Richard came over to us and drew up a chair.

'How would we get to Viengxai?' I asked Sousath.

'Easy, we drive there. I've been many times. Over the mountains. Takes about twelve, maybe thirteen, hours.'

'Over the Annamite Range?' cried Richard. 'Wow! Let's go!'

The nineteenth-century archaeologist in Richard was further excited when Sousath mentioned a Bronze Age site in the mountains, lost to science since the days of Madeleine Colani. The site at Hua Muang consisted of standing stones arranged in circles around large stone tables.

'Like your Stonehenge,' said Sousath, 'only smaller.'

We spent the rest of the evening raking over the details—money, available time and Sousath's commitments. I wondered how my return might be greeted by local officials, even if I was travelling as a tourist.

'Don't worry,' Sousath spruiked confidently. 'You'll be travelling with Sousath! I am your passport!'

16

The Re-education Guesthouse

Early the following day, Sousath's jeep creaked to a halt, raising the dust at a truck-stop junction northeast of Phonsavan. Damien was leaving us. He'd been slumped in the back of the truck with his parka zipped all the way up to his prominent nose, hood tightly drawn over his head, since leaving the provincial capital.

'What day is it?' he mumbled, agitated because he couldn't find his cigarette papers, then, realising it was sunny, stripping down to an Angkor Wat T-shirt and a bumbag large enough to hold a sizeable camera.

'Ten pipes last night,' he boasted with a huge yawn. 'An addict smokes fifty.'

'That's a lot of lying down,' replied Richard sniffily.

It had come to this, a parting of the ways at a destitute crossroads. We were at the intersection of two great colonial roads built by the French—Route Seven, connecting Luang Prabang with the Vietnamese border town of Nong Het, and Route Six, which traversed the mile-high Annamite chain to link the Plain of Jars to Xam Nua. Japanese troops had marched past this point entering Laos from northern Vietnam during World War II. It had been a strategic crossing during the American war too, when the settlement was known as Ban Ban. Damien planned to hitch his way across three rivers—the Khan, the Xuang and the Ou—all of which joined the Mekong near Luang Prabang. From Muang Noi he could take a riverboat down the Ou to the former royal capital. A Last Supper—really more of a Last Lunch—was celebrated with some baguettes and tinned mackerel taken by the roadside. We drank a few beers to mark the occasion, until a truck arrived heading Damien's way, and he dumped his backpack into the tray and awkwardly climbed in, donning his parka while holding a floppy baguette between his teeth.

'Reckon I oughta get outta here,' he said, a momentary twinkle enlivening his glazed eyes. Then he was gone, disappearing like a wisp of opium smoke.

Discarding Damien did not make our progress any easier. National Highway Six was a responsible road to the point where a Soviet-built bridge crosses the Neune River, but bucked like a bronco as it penetrated the wild realm beyond it. The first four hours passed without sighting another vehicle, then the daily Xam Nua-Phonsavan bus careered around a blind corner, almost pushing us off a precipice. At one point we piled out to take in the spectacular view across the towering peaks and thickly wooded valleys of the Annamite Range, whooping and hollering to hear our voices amplified and echoing in that awesome cathedral. Seeing a wartime foxhole dug into the bank of the road, I plunged in head-first, only to come face to face with a snake, prompting an ignominious exit. Along the road, thatched huts cascaded down hillsides and Hmong men toted antique long-barrelled guns, the sight of which prompted Sousath to reveal that he'd shot a tiger in Houaphan the previous year. Richard was appalled.

'Why not?' was Sousath's riposte. 'It tried to eat me.'

Eventually, the incessant groan and clatter of the truck silenced all conversation, and we lapsed into a grim silence, Sousath absorbed in his struggle with the road, Richard absorbed in his Walkman, and me absorbed in memories. Despite the regular bone-jarring potholes, I somehow managed to sleep, but was rudely awakened by Sousath's manic cries of 'Honey! Honey!' Braking hard, he produced a revolver and went tearing off on foot into the jungle.

'What the hell's he doing?' Richard shouted, lunging at the handbrake as the truck rolled back towards a cliff. 'Where'd he get that gun?'

In the forest above the road, a large golden-brown growth had attached itself to a hanging rock. Its surface rippled with the rhythmic motion of thousands of bees. Sousath was crashing through the undergrowth towards it, and, when he got within range, raised his pistol and fired.

'My God! He's shooting!' cried Richard.

'Won't the bees get angry?' I asked, confused to find Richard suddenly missing.

'I'm down here,' he replied, looking up from the ground onto which he'd fallen after the first of two gunshots rang out. 'I think they're getting ready to attack.'

It turned out that Sousath had actually been firing at a second hive which the bees had deserted, trying to dislodge it or cause a honey flow. He'd holed it, but the hive was dry. Still, he seemed to walk taller back to the car. Richard and I followed him cautiously, as if the path was a minefield. The de-miners in Phonsavan, who'd been clearing areas adjacent to the road, had expected to find up to eight hundred metal fragments of exploded ordnance per kilometre of Route Six. In the event, they uncovered five times as much.

Hearing the gunfire, a group of Hmong from a nearby village had gathered. They said these bees were bigger than average and produced excellent honey. But if angered, they would follow you for a kilometre or more through the jungle, and had killed many times. The only way to survive a mass attack, the Hmong said, was to cover yourself in honey and lie very still. Their village was a Gothic settlement in which everyone wore black. There was a primitive stone grinding wheel on open ground, and animal hides were strung up tightly like drums on vertical frames, forming primitive motifs against the sky. Chickens pecked at the earth between mud-floored houses with thatched roofs, while buffalo chewed and watched. There was a simple yet ingenious reticulated water system, consisting of elevated bamboo aqueducts connected to a common weir. A little girl, who couldn't have been more than three years old, worked alone at the weir, scrubbing pieces of black clothing from a pile taller than she was. The village looked settled — it had been there five years—but could easily be abandoned when the time came for the Hmong to move on. No-one knew when that would be. Some nomads lived by the motto, 'Seven times around the mountain'—a full cycle of shifting agriculture before the soil is exhausted by slash and burn. Others, like the Kha Tong Luang, moved on when the banana-leaf roofing of their huts turned yellow. A gnarled old woman approached us, proffering scratched pebbles of aquamarine. Sousath assayed them with an expert air, weighing them on a miniature set of brass scales belonging to the woman. But the scales were what caught my eye; they were freakishly small, precise in every detail and obviously very old. When Sousath had handed over some money for the stones, the old woman produced a smooth wooden wallet, like a small spectacles case, which had been carved to hold the scales.

It was almost sunset and we'd been on the road for about ten hours when Sousath turned off Route Six and found traces of the Americans. It was a road, wider than National Highway Six. Two years earlier, the road builders had ploughed through this remote district of Hua Muang, about seventy kilometres from Xam Nua. The idea had been to reduce opium cultivation among the desperately poor Hmong. But the project was not undertaken by the Lao government, nor even the fraternal Vietnamese. It was an American road, funded by American taxpayers. The American plan was to provide the Hmong with alternative crops and open up their remote areas to nearby markets, so the dependence on opium would diminish. Following a ridge for several kilometres, we eventually reached what looked like an overgrown cemetery, its headstones standing at different angles amid trees and low scrub. Approaching on foot, we saw large, jagged shards of a grey, flinty schist that had been carved centuries before to form a kind of sacred site. There were at least fifty shards in the one spot, and they sparkled, as if containing fine particles of metal. They were over two metres tall and a metre wide, but only a few centimetres thick, grouped around circular stone tables. They were warm to the touch, having absorbed the day's sun, and silhouetted after sunset seemed to confer in silent communion.

Madeleine Colani dubbed the stones menhirs, a term believed to be of Celtic origin that the French use to describe similar artefacts, particularly in Brittany. Her 1940 monograph, *Champs de Menhirs*, had never been published in English, let alone Lao. Anywhere else, this site—which Colani had been the first and only archaeologist to study seriously—would have been declared a protected historical monument. But in Laos, with its poverty and war, and the obscurantist ideology that followed the conflict, the burial grounds at Hua Muang, situated some 1200 metres above sea level, had been forgotten by the world. In the mid 1990s, when Japan offered the Lao Department of Museums a limited number of carbon-dating tests for their artefacts, the Lao submitted some human bone fragments excavated from under the standing stones. The results indicated that the site dated back to somewhere between 500 BC and 500 AD. Yet when the American aid officials inquired as to whether their road needed to be re-routed to avoid environmentally or culturally sensitive areas, they were told by their Lao counterparts that there weren't any such areas. We were looking at only a handful of the headstones dotted among the pine trees that stretched at least six kilometres along the ridge. There were supposedly other *hintang*, the Lao term for standing stones, elsewhere in Houaphan province, particularly above the Ham River

Valley, south-west of Xam Nua, although Colani was unaware of their existence.

'I've seen things like this before,' said Richard, staring hard at the shards, as if the intensity of his vision might burn their secret from them. 'They're quite a bit like the Standing Stones of Stenness in the Orkney Isles. That lot are 5000 years old. Norse influence. These are smaller.'

'Lao version,' said Sousath, nationalising his short complex.

Crossing the road, Richard climbed a hillock and found more stones there. The new road ploughed through the middle of the site, cutting the ridge only a few metres from the main cluster. The forest that protected the site had been cleared. One table had collapsed due to the road widening, and erosion in the next wet season would probably topple more stones. Some of those still standing were daubed with graffiti.

Richard was apoplectic.

'If you can't bomb it, put a road through it,' he fumed, the strain on the trans-Atlantic alliance obvious.

An old Lao Loum woman carrying a hoe appeared, walking home from her day's work in the gardens. She had heard of 'Madame *Felang*', as she referred to Madeleine Colani, and said the stones were spread out from the mountain of Phou Chalay to the Peun River. When we asked what the purpose of the stones had been, she laughed and said she didn't know. Women, she added, did not have the right to discuss such things. At a nearby house there was further evidence of the Hua Muang site's destruction. One of the stone tables was being used as a chopping board in the yard, and some of the shards served as steps and fence posts. We saw an old man supervising construction of a new kiosk to cater for the expected flood of tourists to the place. Po Lah was seventy-five and he too remembered the Frenchwoman who had visited the area when he was a teenager—but not, perhaps, as she would like to be remembered.

'She used to ride on an elephant,' said the old man. 'The local men would follow her all the way to Xam Nua. She wore no underwear. We could see right up her skirt!'

Unpacking our sticky rice and chilli *padaek*, we sat down on the floor of the half-finished kiosk for lunch. According to local folklore, a man called Hart Unh had erected the standing stones, using a diamond scythe to shape them. Colani had paid villagers to help her excavate the sites, and had moved some of the tables. Beneath them, in holes more than two metres deep, she found human remains. Po Lah said Mount Chalay, about two kilometres away, was the main stones site, and for a mere 3000 *kip* offered to take us there and other places where 'Madame' had not been. With the light fading, and still several hours drive to get to Xam Nua, we regretfully declined. As he shuffled on his way, the old man left a final piece of bad news for the American government. The Hmong had not switched to other crops, he said. They had moved closer to the road, but only to get their opium to market faster.

We wandered for the last time among the stones. On one of them, I read a scrawled name: Lamphan.

'Oh, shit!' I said.

'What?' asked Sousath. 'You know him?'

'I'm afraid I do...It seems I can't escape him.'

'Hmmnnn,' mused Sousath. 'Seems like you got important friends.'

The closer to Xam Nua we got, the more the road—and my state of mind—deteriorated. I wondered what the Foreign Ministry in Vientiane would think if they knew where I was. What would Lamphan think? And where would we stay? How to be inconspicuous in a town like Xam Nua? A few months of functioning in an atmosphere of all pervasive secrecy had made me pessimistic, almost timorous. The paranoia of one-party rule was contagious, and the potholes were bone-jarring. We'd been on the road since 6 a.m. It was dark and cold.

'How far now?' Richard asked repeatedly, like a child. 'We must be close.'

'*Baw*,' Sousath would reply. 'Another twenty kilometres or so.'

Eventually, we rounded a bend and saw the lights of Xam Nua glistening in the valley below. It was a sight that inspired more foreboding than relief. Soon we were passing along the wide, cheerless streets that I'd been so happy to leave so recently. The few feeble streetlamps glowered, and there was nobody around.

'Ghost Central!' Richard exclaimed, his voice uneven with the chill.

The Dok Mai Deng was shuttered—had they treated me too kindly?—but we found another small guesthouse on the same street and took three rooms. They gave us black coffee for dinner, supplemented by the sticky rice, *padaek* and some sausages Sousath had brought from Ban Ban. After dinner we briefly made plans for the following day. It was necessary to register our arrival in the province with the local authorities, but as it would be Sunday, the government offices would be closed. So we agreed simply to drive to Viengxai the next morning, visit Sousath's family cave, spend the night in Viengxai, and return to Xieng Khouang the following day. We were all exhausted, and turned in.

The following morning, Richard and I breakfasted on eggs and coffee at the Hin Restaurant, where I enjoyed an anonymity no longer available at Joy's, while Sousath was off seeing some friends. A small crowd of men and boys had formed outside the place, gawking at a multicoloured motorcycle belonging to a young Westerner called Colin, who'd ridden all the way from Vientiane. In Viengxai the previous day, Colin had been prevented from entering any of the caves for obscure bureaucratic reasons. Deciding to follow the road beyond Souphanouvong's cave to see where it went, he was flagged down after a few kilometres by villagers, and turned back.

'It was like a citizen's arrest,' he told us. 'There was no way I was going to get past them.'

It wasn't an isolated incident. The week before, the representative of an international travel guide had been turned away as well by officials who refused to show him the caves. Earlier, a British backpacker who'd made his own way to Viengxai had been arrested and held for a week, after trying to enter an unmarked cave whose entrance had been covered with iron sheeting. The Tourism Department's plan to showcase the heroic province of Houaphan was clearly having teething problems.

'You've got to wonder what they're hiding,' said Colin, who was betrothed to a Lao. The girl's family approved of the union, but they'd been waiting more than a year for the Interior Ministry to give its consent. Bureaucrats were demanding that the family host a *baci* ceremony for 600 of the ministry's staff and their families before they processed the paperwork.

As we were leaving the restaurant a Japanese four-wheel drive pulled up outside and a number of Asian men in suits disembarked. Among them was Lamphan. He hadn't seen me, so I looked for an escape route. There was none. My only advantage was surprise.

'Lamphan!' I yelled, exploding with fake joy.

He was confused at first to hear his name. Then he saw me, and a look of shock seized his face. 'What the hell are you doing here?' his incredulous features seemed to say, before recomposing into a smile as fake as mine. Hoping to confound him further, I unleashed a blizzard of chumminess, foreign words and local place names: Tourist…Viengxai…Go…Vientiane…Today. The language barrier was working in my favour.

'Vientiane?' he said uncertainly. 'You go to Vientiane today?'

'Vientiane,' I said, smiling and nodding. 'Viengxai. Vientiane.'

Nodding unhappily, Lamphan shot an embarrassed glance at his guests, who were beginning to scrape their feet. They were Vietnamese, and seemed suspicious of Lamphan's relationship with the foreigner. Finally, I let go of his hand, which I'd been pumping furiously, gave him a big '*sogdee*', and got the hell out of there.

'What was that all about?' asked Richard, following me up the road.

'You don't want to know,' I said, an awful taste in my mouth, and now well aware that I was running out of time. Within minutes we had found Sousath and were headed for Viengxai, and before long, its ominous landscape came into view.

'Oh, here we are,' said Sousath, ever the tourist guide, as he guided the jeep into the driveway of a compound lined with pines. 'Welcome to the Number One Re-education Guesthouse!'

On 26 April 1974, two helicopters landed at Viengxai, one of which carried King Savang Vatthana. Accompanying him were his cabinet, members of the National Political Consultative Council, Buddhist monks and members of the king's personal staff. They had flown from Luang Prabang at the invitation of the Red Prince, Souphanouvong, who welcomed them to the 'liberated zone' with the gentle admonition, 'You should visit your people and see how they live.'

It was indeed Savang Vatthana's first visit to the north-east as king. He reviewed Pathet Lao troops and visited Xam Nua during the week-long trip, toured the scenic limestone karsts, and was moved to comment that he regarded the population of the province as his children. The Paris peace accords had put a stop to American bombing, and reconstruction was under way in earnest. One of the first new buildings was a two-storey brick and stucco structure referred to as 'the king's palace at Viengxai', where the royal family and staff stayed during their visit. Savang Vatthana had been excited by the invitation, seeing the visit as a public affirmation of the unity of the nation under the crown, and as a way of gaining the trust of the Pathet Lao. But for the Pathet Lao, the trip had a different purpose. To them, it bestowed royal endorsement on all that had been done in the north-east, and reassured the rest of the country about their intentions. On both counts it was a great success. Villagers thronged Xam Nua, some of them walking for up to four days, carrying their children on their backs to see the king. Many Lao wanted to believe that the visit indicated a change of heart by Souphanouvong, who in 1957 had told his cadres that the purpose of the revolution was 'to progress until...the abolition of the monarchy'. But the ideologues of the party and their Vietnamese backers would remain implacable. It was to this same building—the Number One Guesthouse—that Savang Vatthana would return as a prisoner in March 1977. It stood with its back to the wall of a chalky bluff near the district military headquarters, an unlovely block of vicious angles and grim corridors. The windows were shattered, some boarded up, and it had been painted by committee in a patchwork of white, aqua and jaundiced yellow. The thinness of the paint, the paltriness of the stucco and the erosion of the bricks had spawned a multitude of blotches and eruptions that gave the entire structure a diseased air. It had that unmistakable combination, unique to Stalinist architecture: authoritarian lines marred by poverty and slovenly execution.

They showed us to our rooms. The plaster had fallen from the walls. The wood had fallen from the banisters. Nothing worked. Miserly light bulbs hung down on nooses, and red plastic chamber pots from China lurked beneath thin mattresses. In a vain effort to keep the savage winds out of the bedroom someone had tried to tape old newspapers over a shattered window, but the glue had evaporated and both the tape and the newspaper flapped uncontrollably. The newspaper looked familiar. It was a copy of *Nhan Dan (The People)*, the daily paper of the Vietnamese Communist Party. It was dated 11 July 1975, and the front page carried a photo of three men in a motorcade limo: Soviet party chief Leonid Brezhnev, his Vietnamese counterpart, Le Duan, and the former Vietnamese prime minister, Pham Van Dong.

'Nice place, eh?' Sousath said, fiddling with something under the bonnet of the jeep, when Richard and I presented for our caves tour. 'This was where political education was given to people from the old regime. They learnt all about Marxism here. Then we sent them into the villages to practise what we taught them. Over there was the seminar room, where the dining room is now.'

We went and looked. It was a long room with pillars supporting the ceiling and overhead fans. The tables were arranged in two long lines down either side of the room, and there were girlie calendars on the far wall. It looked like a reprobates' refectory.

'It's incredible,' said Richard. 'We're actually staying in a former gulag.'

The blaring horn of the jeep beckoned, and we headed off, only to be alarmed when our first stop was the home of a local policeman.

'Do we have to?' I whimpered. 'Can't we just visit your family cave in private?'

'We cannot!' Sousath barked. 'In Viengxai, you need permission for everything.'

The policeman turned out to be a reasonable chap. It was his day off, and he was just sitting down to a meal. Without much difficulty, he persuaded us to join him. Our last decent meal had been at the Sangah restaurant in Phonsavan. After lunch he took a large machete, walked us down to the base of a karst, and began hacking away at vines and creepers choking the path.

'This was the area of the Foreign Affairs caves,' said Sousath, waving a flashlight at the rock face. 'Here there used to be a kind of supermarket for all the Foreign Affairs staff. And here, here is Castro's graffiti.'

Beside the message from Fidel, who was said to have visited Viengxai when American planes were still bombing the area, were words of encouragement from communist delegations from France, the Soviet Union and Germany.

After taking the obligatory photos we climbed higher, and soon reached the gaping mouth of Cavern Phetrasy, where Sousath had lived from 1971 to 1973, after blotting his copybook in China. A Western diplomat who knew them remembered the Phetrasys as a strange family. In the 1970s, the diplomat had gone with Sousath's father to Wattay airport to meet Sousath on his return from abroad. It had been years since the boy had seen his parents, and there was speculation as to whether they would recognise each other. As it happened, they didn't. Now, as we moved around the family cave, Sousath glumly pointed out a drawing on one wall which he said was done by his sisters. In the living room, which featured a stone table and shelves, he brightened momentarily, standing behind the table and mimicking the actions of a cocktail waiter. But it seemed an old joke, dismal like the cave. The bedroom was a catacomb, with gutters cut into the floor for drainage.

'This would make a fantastic nightclub,' said Richard. 'What was it like sleeping in here?'

'At night, there was a lot of moisture,' replied Sousath. 'And when we slept, it was like being buried. You felt very tired.'

When the bombing stopped in 1973, the government built a house for Soth Phetrasy, but after living there briefly during his period as a re-education commissar, Sousath's father was sent to Moscow as ambassador. Sousath left for Vientiane in 1976, and the house remained vacant until 1977, when the former king, his queen and the crown prince moved in. Sousath stood at the mouth of the cave and pointed to a small, fenced slope directly opposite. There were some banana palms growing there, and the rest of the ground looked to be taken up by vegetable gardens. On the far side of the block were two brick buildings without roofs, obscured by vegetation. Lao officials in Vientiane at the time of the king's arrest had defended the government's treatment of him, while not allowing even family visits. Said one: 'Our government gave him a special allowance, double the minimum, as well as other benefits in his new position in his family life. In order to guarantee his security and permit him to make a lasting contribution to the national government of the Lao People's Democratic Republic, it was decided to invite him, his wife and his son Vongsavang to travel by air to a safe place. There the government has continued to give him special advantages for his material and political position: a solid house with running water, electricity and adequate comforts, a radio receiver and servants.'

Said another: 'A new stone or brick home was built especially for the royal family to provide a minimum standard of comfort in their exile.'

Other sources gave conflicting information as to who owned the houses—some said Soth Phetrasy, others Souphanouvong or Souvanna Phouma—but the description of the royal prison as a 'solid house' was not disputed. Another informant had been even more specific, referring to 'two brick houses'.

'The one on the right was the house,' said Sousath. 'The one on the left was a kitchen and guardhouse. When the king came back to Viengxai in 1977, he stayed first at the Number One Guesthouse. But after a short time, they moved him and his family here. The guards stayed in the second house and did the cooking. When I came back here for the first time in 1992, I saw the roof was missing. Somebody stole the wood.'

Before leaving, I photographed the two houses from our vantage point in the cave. The canopy of vegetation had already made them invisible from the air. One more wet season and they would probably be fully camouflaged by nature. As far as Sousath was concerned, that was as it should be. The royal family was best forgotten.

17

The Bamboo Palace

Although he had not the slightest culinary experience, cooking two meals a day for thirty-seven men with hardly any ingredients had its advantages for Khamphan Thammakhanty. Working in his outdoor kitchen, assisted by the inventive Amkhar, gave him a bird's-eye view of life inside a prison that, officially, did not exist.

In the week following their arrival, the new political prisoners had been engaged in building an outdoor structure similar to Khamphan's kitchen. At first, he assumed they would be settling permanently in the bamboo and timber thatched cottage in the smaller compound across the rivulet, about 30 metres from where he stood. However, on the afternoon of 24 November 1977, as he rested in his barracks after lunch, Khamphan heard a disturbance outside. Jumping to his feet, he saw the new arrivals being led into his own compound, where they were split into two groups. The first group was heading towards his barracks, the second to another dormitory in the same compound.

Suddenly, the door to Khamphan's barracks was flung open, and an old friend walked in. It was Prince Sisavang, the king's second son and manager of the royal farm at Pak Xuang, who had been one of Khamphan's drinking buddies in Luang Prabang. Following him was Ouane Rathikoun, a charismatic but corrupt former army chief and politician who was a big wheel in the opium trade under the old regime, and six other generals, all of whom had been with Khamphan in the camp at Xam T'ai until their arrest. Khamphan had not seen Sisavang since his own expulsion from Luang Prabang in 1975. Camp Number One was no place for the affable and engaging prince unburdened by high office, whose only crime was the accident of his birth. It was not a happy reunion. Everyone present knew that this was the heart of darkness. The rules of Camp Number One forbade prisoners from talking quietly to one another. In the barracks all remarks were required to be made in voices loud enough to be heard outside. Guards prowled around near the buildings listening for any breach of the rule. Worse, the atmosphere inside the barracks was one of mistrust. The majority of the thirty-seven prisoners were high-ranking officials from Vientiane and Luang Prabang, but mixed in with them were a handful of low-ranking individuals who, like the guards, originated from Houaphan province. A word out of place could be a death sentence, and so conversation died, and with it old friendships and sources of mutual support. Camp Number One, like the rest of the country under the Pathet Lao, became a microcosm of paranoia and repression.

In late November, as they settled awkwardly into their mean quarters on an early winter's night, another disturbance was heard outside. In the darkness, Khamphan could not make out what it was, but the following morning, the reason Prince Sisavang and the others had been shifted to new barracks became clear. Three new prisoners had arrived overnight, and had been allocated the smaller compound on the opposite side of the dry river bed. As Khamphan and the others peered out from their darkened dormitory around 7 a.m., they saw His Majesty King Savang Vatthana and his heir, Crown Prince Vongsavang. The king wore a light jacket and trousers, and the prince sported a long, untamed beard, like a *liusee*, or ascetic. Later, Queen Khamphoui emerged from the hut, and together, the royal family of the 600-year-old Kingdom of the Million Elephants and the White Parasol surveyed the thickly forested hills that surrounded their new realm.

Centuries of respect for the Lao monarchy had come to an end. The Pathet Lao would not bow and scrape before the American puppets. In Camp Number One, even the lowest corporal showed them his face. For hundreds of years before the French colonial period, the Lan Xang kings had inhabited bamboo and timber residences. Now fate and history had turned full circle, and the last king of Laos resided once more in a bamboo palace.

'We could not believe our eyes!' Khamphan would later write.

Standing beside him, Prince Sisavang gasped. He had not seen his parents and brother for seven or eight months since they had been taken to Viengxai, while he and the other family members and courtiers arrested in Luang Prabang had been jailed in a cave at Muang Liat, ten kilometres to the north-west of the town. Now, he could see them; but they could not see him. Although his skills as a farmer were sorely needed in the camp, the prince was not assigned work and remained permanently locked up inside the barracks. Whatever their former station in life, all the prisoners—except those assigned to the work team—would be allowed out only once a week. On Saturday, each prisoner was released for five or ten minutes, just enough time to walk accompanied by a guard to a ditch behind the barracks where rainwater formed a shallow pond. There, the prisoner would bathe, before being marched back to the barracks.

Camp Number One now boasted forty inmates from a wide cross-section of social backgrounds; from a salt trader's son and a Hmong ethnic minority leader, to the highest born princes of the land. According to declassified CIA intelligence, 'Camp 1 was intended by the LPDR to be a, "deathcamp" with no survivors of re-education.' If even the king had no rights as an individual, who in Laos was safe?

A 24-hour watch was maintained by sentries posted on the ground and in watchtowers overlooking the prison, which, unlike Xam T'ai and most other camps, was surrounded by a fence. The guards, unlike most Lao, were animists and prohibited religious observances of any kind. At Viengxai, the king and his family had been permitted to worship in detention, but at Sop Hao, there was no *Pimai* water festival, nor the *Ok Phansaa* and *baci* ceremonies so loved by the lowland Lao. Prevented by the regulations from speaking to the guards, the prisoners could never really get to know them.

The arrival of the king marked a new phase in the grinding routine of life at Camp Number One. Unlike most of the other prisoners, the king and his family were free to move around in their compound during the day. Savang Vatthana's passion for working the land, so apparent at the royal farm at Pak Xuang, quickly asserted itself. Having turned seventy that month, he was the oldest person in the prison, the average age being around 55. Despite that, he got to work immediately, assisted by the crown prince. Soon, a vegetable garden and grove of papaya trees were flourishing. The prince also helped Queen Khamphoui prepare meals for the family, who, like other prisoners, were restricted to a ration of 400 grams—or about two handfuls—of cooked rice a day per person. Although unable to speak directly to them, Khamphan kept a close watch on the first family as he busied himself in his kitchen. Every day he saw the crown prince leave his compound, and walk unguarded along the western side of the main compound, beneath the shadows of the watchtowers, to fetch the royal family's ration of rice and salt from the camp granary.

In the depths of that first winter in early 1978, a delegation from Vietnam arrived at Camp Number One. The Vietnamese did not control the day-to-day running of the camp, which rested with the Interior Ministry of the Lao PDR, but fraternal Vietnam maintained an interest and apparently exerted some influence. The visitors inspected both compounds, including the king's.

They seemed to be advising on security, looking inside the barracks with flashlights and checking if the fences were strong enough and that kind of thing. They saw everything,' Khamphan later recalled.

The Vietnamese were not impressed by Lao laxity. Several weeks after their visit, prisoners in the smaller of the two main barracks, including former Interior Minister Pheng Phongsavan, former army chief General Bounpone, Hmong leader Touby Lyfoung and four other high-ranking officials were put in shackles.

In early 1978, *Pimai*—the Lao New Year heralding the advent of spring—brought good and bad news. Since the arrival of the king several months earlier, the prisoners had longed to bolster his spirits by showing their continued respect, but there were few opportunities to do so. Eventually, Khamphan decided to act. At his suggestion, a precious can of sweetened condensed milk brought from Vientiane and kept by one prisoner was opened, and poured over a bowl of steaming rice. Prince Thongsouk, the former chief of protocol at the royal palace in Luang Prabang, was tasked with approaching the guards with the request to pass on the gift. At the risk of incurring the authorities' wrath, he handed the festive dish to one of the guards.

'Can you give this to those guys?' he asked, motioning towards the royal compound, disguising his humble purpose by referring to the royal family in the blunt language of the Pathet Lao.

Taking the bowl, the guard inspected it, then called out to the crown prince, who came to collect it. It was the only time the prisoners were able to enact a collective gesture of goodwill towards the royal family. A few days later, the gift was reciprocated with a basket of vegetables from the king's garden, passed on by the crown prince through the same guard. Then the camp commandant, Thao Ninh, announced that the daily rice ration would be drastically cut over the next three months due to a general food shortage, and the cordial exchanges ended. Meanwhile, the commandant's wife—who served as a bush doctor for the guards—informed the prisoners that the camp's stock of medicines would henceforth be used solely for the treatment of the camp staff, and would be allocated to prisoners in emergencies only. Fed on an inadequate diet and denied proper medical treatment, the health and mental wellbeing of most internees went into steep decline. Neither the International Committee of the Red Cross nor any other humanitarian agency was given access to the camp, nor were the prisoners permitted to write or receive letters. Those who wore spectacles, like the king's nephew, Manivong Khammao, had their glasses confiscated, and no reading materials of any kind were permitted. At Xam T'ai and some of the other camps, prisoners could play sport, and stage cultural performances. But in Camp Number One there were no sports, entertainment or cultural activities. The only approved relaxation was smoking—which kills you—but there was no tobacco. Instead, the prisoners dried vegetable leaves and smoked them in handmade pipes. Occasionally Khamphan would see the king sitting outside his hut, smoking a Vietnamese-style long pipe.

In the summer of 1978, the king and crown prince were ordered into the paddy field adjoining the camp to undertake the onerous work of righting fallen fences and planting rice. Throughout their incarceration, a strict separation between the royal family and the rest of the prisoners was maintained. They worked every day for two months in the middle of the day, when the five-man work team was resting. The following year, in 1979, the king and heir returned to the paddy field to work another season. A sharpening divide between China and Vietnam would lead to a brief border war that year, and in pro-Hanoi Laos the political atmosphere became strained. Lao leaders feared Beijing might stage a provocation, perhaps even kidnap the former king and use him as a pawn against the regime. That summer, the demeanour of the guards changed suddenly for the worse. After dinner every evening for several weeks they would push open the barracks doors, jeering and hurling abuse at the inmates for a quarter of an hour.

'Traitors! American lackeys!' they would bark. 'You brought the Americans to bomb our country. You are parasites! You never worked, just took money for yourselves. Victory to the people!'

Occasionally, special interrogators from Xam Nua would visit to question prisoners about this or that alleged escape plan or conspiracy. The royal family enjoyed no immunity from questioning. One day, Khamphan was washing rice near the office of the camp commandant, when he distinctly heard the king's raised voice.

'We don't know anything,' Savang Vatthana was saying, as if in response to repeated questioning. 'We only responded to your invitation to come over to Viengxai for our security. We want our people to live in peace and harmony without rancour.'

In less than a year, the harsh conditions in which the prisoners were held began to take a lethal toll. As cook, and aided by Amkhar, it was Khamphan's job to serve meals to the most wretched of all—the seven senior officials and officers held in rigid wooden leg stocks in their own barracks twenty-four hours a day. Shuffling in twice a day at 11 a.m. and 5 p.m., Khamphan found himself serving his former boss, General Bounpone. In 1975, the former army chief had been invited to visit Beijing, along with the senior Pathet Lao leader Phoumi Vongvichit. The visit was viewed with suspicion in Vietnam, which saw it as a Chinese attempt to interfere in a country under strong Vietnamese influence. As they returned home via Hanoi, the general was arrested by the Vietnamese, who transferred him to the custody of the Pathet Lao. His communist travelling partner, Phoumi Vongvichit, returned home to Vientiane, but the Lao army chief was sent to Houaphan province.

In Khamphan's own barracks three brothers of the king were quartered: the Princes Souphantharangsi, Bovone Vatthana, and Thongsouk. Khamphan had dined with Bovone when he was governor of Houa Khong province. He had warned Thongsouk about the growing threat posed by the Pathet Lao before his expulsion from Luang Prabang. Also in Khamphan's barracks was General Lee, the former intelligence chief, who had assured him there was nothing to fear by staying on in Laos. Lee, in particular among the prisoners, suffered from a deep sense of shame, as if he was personally responsible for the plight of all of them. What kind of intelligence chief was he, not to have foreseen the situation? The former ambassador to China, Liane Phavongviangkham, also sent to Camp Number One, blamed himself for his plight.

'I could have sought political asylum in France...had I known it in advance,' he said.

Slowly, it was becoming clear to everyone that detention in the camp was tantamount to a death sentence. The authorities also knew it, but took no action.

'It was difficult for us to believe that the purpose of keeping us in those conditions was to ensure our elimination, and the elimination of the entire royal family,' Khamphan would later recall.

Every prisoner reacted differently to the prospect of almost certain death. Some, like Prince Souk Bouavong, sensed it early.

'If we cannot quickly find a solution to our plight, we may all be leaving our bones here,' he told the others, hatching a plot to offer the guards a share of his hidden wealth. But the guards were not interested, sounding the death knell for future efforts to negotiate freedom.

General Ouane Rathikoun, once such a power in the land, was wasted by constant diarrhoea and plagued by an injured sense of chivalry.

'I never thought they could really destroy us in cold blood,' he told Khamphan. 'When Souphanouvong and his acolytes were held at Phonekheng in 1957 I even asked my family to bring them their favourite dishes every week.'

Three months after arriving in the camp, Khamphan had obtained permission to establish a vegetable garden in the main compound. Deputising Amkhar to take over the cooking, he introduced variety to the prisoners' diet, with lettuce, chilli and local vegetables. But it was too little, too late. In August 1978, a chilling cry that would eventually become familiar rose over Camp Number One for the first time. It was the prisoners in Khamphan's barracks raising their voices to alert the guards that one of them had died. It announced the death of the king's half-brother, Prince Bovone Vatthana. With his body terminally wasted from inactivity and malnutrition, Bovone's death seemed to trigger a spate of mortality. The king's son, the popular and ebullient Prince Sisavang, was next to go. As he lay dying of starvation, a snake had slithered into the barracks and occupied the space beneath his bunk. To the prisoners, it was a bad omen. A few days later, in his final hours, Sisavang beckoned Khamphan to his bunk side and begged him for a glass of rice wine. There had never been a drop of alcohol in the camp.

'But how can I get it? I cannot find it,' Khamphan sadly told his friend, who died before lunch. His food, bedding and clothes were quickly divided among the survivors.

Before year's end, another half-brother of the king, Prince Thongsouk, and Prince Souk Bouavong had both died, as had the former army chief Ouane Rathikoun and Bong Souvannavong, president of the now defunct Lao Unity Party. In the implacable new order of the Pathet Lao, Bong had been starved to death in a prison camp, even though his son Boutsa Bong was at that time highly placed in the new government. The grim task of burying the dead was given to the two former police sergeants, Phoumi and Bao Thong, who belonged to the five-man work team. They were ordered to wrap the bodies in cloth, tie them to bamboo staves and carry them to the improvised graveyard in a small valley two hundred metres north of the camp.

The New Year of 1979 brought a second winter and a new camp commandant, Kong Tong, whose reign at Camp Number One would set a new standard in depravity. As he worked in the cookhouse, Khamphan would often hear a strange, childlike sound coming from the smaller of the two barracks. It was Touby, the avuncular Hmong leader, singing nonsense songs he had composed during his long months in fetters.

He would sing, "Oh the new government is very good. They put us in prison,'" Khamphan would later recall.

One guard, emerging from the barracks after failing to stop the singing, pointed to his head, indicating that the Hmong leader had lost his mind. Eventually, a Hmong official in the new government was called from Xam Nua to talk sense into Touby, but still the singing continued. A few weeks later, as Khamphan and Amkhar prepared dinner in the cookhouse, they heard a rare and terrible sound. It was the unmistakable crack of a gunshot, multiplying while fading as it bounced off the surrounding hills. Alarmed, they rushed to the door of the kitchen shack and saw Touby lying on his back near the ditch where he had been having his Saturday bath. A crimson patch was spreading across his shirtfront, his blood welling from a wound in his chest. Standing a few metres away, a guard lowered his gun, and called to work team members Bao Thong, Phoumi and Phimpha to take the body away and bury it. Afraid of becoming involved, Khamphan and Amkhar returned to their work, and barely spoke of what they had seen. One by one—whether by starvation, illness or execution—the prisoners were being picked off. Finally, one of them decided to do something about it.

Nouphet Daoleuang and Ratana Banleung Chounlamany were brigadier generals who had been given the job of emptying the latrine from Khamphan's barracks. The latrine was a crudely cut-down half of an oil drum located at the end of the dormitory, which fouled the air day and night, and Khamphan had taken to using the cold ashes from his wood stove to cover its contents and smother its odours. One day, as the two prisoners wrestled the steel latrine out of the barracks, Nouphet dropped his hold on it and made a beeline for the nearest Pathet Lao guard, aiming to seize his rifle. It was a futile effort. Even had he managed to grab the gun and kill a few guards, the shooting would have alerted the camp's radio operator, whose mayday would have brought police and army reinforcements racing to crush the rebellion by a group of mainly sick and elderly men. In the event, the weakened Nouphet was not quick enough, and the guard's gun was raised to his head before he could take it. After that, both men—even Banleung, who was merely a bystander—were permanently confined, with the other prisoners taking turns to empty the latrine. Nouphet at least had the comfort of knowing he had tried.

Khamphan's survival strategy could not have been more different. He had no interest in rebellion, which he saw as doomed. His priorities were clear: first, to strictly obey all orders; second, to strive for perfection in every act, no matter how mundane; and third, to admit no negative thoughts, or memories of a better past, or hopes for a better future. The harder he worked, the better he slept. Like a horse that is blinkered and in harness, he shut out anything that might distract or handicap him, trusting no-one, opposing no-one and living completely in the moment.

'I decided to forget everything,' he recalled later, 'to forget about the life I had before. I don't think about my home, or my rank, or my wife or children. I stay quiet. I respect the regulations in the camp. I make friends with everybody, even with the police. I don't expect anything good to happen to me.'

In his brilliant essay on his time in the Nazi death camps, Dr Viktor Frankl speaks of the 'last human freedom' available to Hitler's doomed victims: the ability to determine one's attitude in the face of suffering and death. That attitude was not always what might be expected. Fond memories of a happier past might torment a man cut off from the source of such pleasures, especially his wife, children, home and career. The possibility of a sudden and undignified demise so traumatised some prisoners that their previous lives came to seem irrelevant or beyond redemption. 'Anything outside the barbed wire became remote, out of reach and, in a way, unreal,' Frankl says. All efforts focused on 'preserving one's own life and that of the other fellow' and the constant strain 'forced the prisoners' inner life down to a primitive level'. The struggle itself, however, could take on an existential significance that transcended the hopes of the individual. 'Once the meaning of suffering had been revealed to us, we refused to minimise or alleviate the camp's tortures by ignoring them or harbouring false illusions and entertaining artificial optimism,' Frankl wrote. 'It did not really matter what we expected from life, but rather what life expected from us.'

With the rest of the prisoners literally depending for their survival on the food he provided, Khamphan scoured the perimeter of the camp for vegetable remnants still growing in what had been farmland before the authorities had forced the peasants off the land to establish the camp. Resources given to him for the prisoners' benefit like seeds, and later some chickens, were carefully shepherded with a deep sense of responsibility to the others, and an eye to the reality that they may be there for a long time. By 1979, Khamphan's garden had become a mainstay of not only the prisoners' food supply, but the guards as well. But the lethal neglect of the new camp commandant, Kong Tong—under whom the occasional gift of a buffalo or pig, or can of fish or bully beef disappeared—undermined Khamphan's efforts to improve the prisoners' health. The ravages of camp life were becoming unbearable. Without proper maintenance, even the condition of the buildings had begun to deteriorate, and water poured through the thatched roofs during rainstorms.

In the claustrophobic confines of the prison, trouble was brewing. The politics of Khamphan's position as barracks boss were complex and difficult. In return for his 'privileges', he was expected to alert the authorities about conspiracies or escape plans. In the event, he says, he never did, because there never were any that he was aware of. In his charge were the *crème de la crème* of Lao society. He had served them with respect for a lifetime. Yet their failure to properly read the political situation had delivered him, his family and the entire Lao nation, to a terrible fate. Should any of them plot an escape or rebellion, he would be blamed for not informing the authorities in advance, and that could cost him his life. In the zero sum game of survival, the Pathet Lao were the only winners. Unavoidably, Khamphan was forced into the role of mediator between his fellow prisoners and the camp authorities, discouraging dangerous and unrealistic talk among the prisoners of escape or cutting deals in exchange for their freedom, while pressing successive camp commandants for more and better food. But as the pressures grew on them, the prisoners began turning on one another, and Khamphan was an obvious target. They resented his freedom to leave the stinking cell every day, resented their own dependency on him, and above all suspected him of being in league with the authorities. As a former intelligence officer he could be selling information, or just playing both sides of the camp. Why else had he been made head of the barracks and given outdoor duties? At every meal, the larger food helpings given to members of the work team starkly illustrated the divide between them and the rest of the inmates. Eventually, the confined prisoners rebelled, complaining to the guards that Khamphan was giving himself larger portions than anyone else. Although no action was taken against him by the authorities, the row deepened Khamphan's sense that it was now every man for himself.

In mid 1979, a new commandant, Bounyay, provided a respite from the corrosive neglect of Kong Tong's rule. Soon after arriving, the new boss sent a chicken and a bowl of fresh, fertilised chicken eggs to Khamphan with the suggestion that he breed poultry. By using all the hens' eggs for breeding, Amkhar managed to raise some forty chickens by the end of 1979. But they were planning for a future that would never come. In October 1979 one of two Pathet Lao defectors in Camp Number One, Major Sivilai, succumbed to typhoid and died. Those who survived, including immediate members of the royal family, were walking skeletons. One morning, Khamphan awoke to find the man who slept in the bunk next to his, politician Issara Sasorith, dead. The number of vacant bunks was multiplying. Khamphan began to pray.

'Everybody looked terrible. Our bodies became very weak, and very, very thin. People became very tired and were just sleeping all the time.' Khamphan later recalled.

By January 1980, nine more prisoners had died, and even Khamphan had begun to wonder if he would survive. The retired police director-general, Lith Lunammachak; the former commander of the Champassak military region, Major-General Phasouk Solatsaphak; the former Interior Minister Pheng Phongsavan; former deputy Veterans Affairs Minister Soukan Vilaisarn; Royal Lao Army officer, Captain Seri Xayakham; the king's nephew, Prince Manivong Khammao; and the former Defence Ministry spokesman Brigadier General Thongphan Knocksi were all buried without ceremony, or even cremation, because funeral pyres consumed scarce firewood. As the fourth anniversary of the Lao People's Democratic Republic approached, the new commandant, Bounyay, ordered that a buffalo be purchased and fattened for the prisoners to join in the celebration. But the gesture would have unexpected consequences. One afternoon in November 1979, as Khamphan was clearing up after lunch, he heard a ruckus coming from across the rivulet. A guard was arguing with the crown prince over the disappearance of the buffalo, that had been put in his care.

'You are very bad!' he was screaming. 'You were supposed to take care of the buffalo, but you let it go!'

'I tied it already before I went to eat,' the crown prince shot back. 'Why are you angry?'

Infuriated, the guard raised his rifle and a shot rang out over the camp. The bullet had flown over the crown prince's head. Now, both men were furious.

'Fire on me!' the prince roared at the guard with frightening intensity, ripping open his shirt and pointing contemptuously at his own chest. 'Fire on me, not in the air. I don't care!'

Ordered back to his compound, the crown prince was met by a distressed Queen Khamphoui, who attempted to calm her eldest son, telling him not to talk to the guards. But the incident seemed to have broken the heir's spirit.

'Why must we stay here?' Khamphan heard him howling at his mother. 'How long are we going to endure? I just want to get away from it all. The sooner the better.'

After the incident, the prince, then aged forty-eight, no longer collected the royal family's daily rations from the granary, and was rarely seen again outside his quarters. One morning in January 1980, prisoners in the camp were awoken by a woman's voice. It was Queen Khamphoui, calling out to the guards.

'*Chao Noi tai leo!*' she was calling. 'The crown prince is dead.'

Having gone to investigate, the guards returned to the main compound and ordered the work team to dispose of the body. Phoumi, Bao Thong and Phimpha wrapped the cadaver in a sheet, tied it to two bamboo poles, and covered it with a bedspread. Phimpha and Amkhar then carried the body through the scrub to the burial spot north of the camp. The royal cortege consisted of the three men, their gun-toting guards and, bringing up the rear, Khamphan carrying a shovel. The king and Queen Khamphoui attempted to accompany the body to the burial, but were ordered by the guards to remain behind. When the funeral march reached a large, spreading *kok kau* tree, Khamphan began digging. Watched over by armed guards, he and the others buried the prince in a shallow grave without a coffin on low ground near the west bank of the Houey Kar rivulet. When Khamphan tried to fashion a crude sign to mark the grave he was told by the guards not to bother. The guards wanted their lunch. After the death of the crown prince, Queen Khamphoui took on the daily task of collecting rice and salt from the granary.

During his three years in Camp Number One, Khamphan had only three dreams. In the first, he is in trouble: as he prays one night, an angry provincial governor interrupts him, telling him to be quiet, and not to do anything. In the second, he is enchanted: awaking beside a placid lake on which Prince Sisavang is boating. The happy prince is later joined by his family. In the third, he is frustrated: attempting to escape from the camp, he can find no way out.

One day in February 1980, as he rested in his bunk after lunch, Khamphan heard voices from the paddy field. Turning to look through a crack in the wall, he saw the king, then 72 and physically much reduced, bent over with a machete cutting grass. Standing the regulation several metres away, a guard was taunting him.

'Cut it very well. Just work,' the guard said.

It was the same guard who had shot and killed Touby Lyfoung. At that moment, Savang Vatthana raised himself from his labours, and faced the guard. It was only weeks since his son and heir had died.

'You know, in Luang Prabang, I also worked in the fields,' the king told the Kalashnikov-wielding Pathet Lao.

'Don't complain!' the guard shouted. 'Just work!'

After the confrontation, the king was not seen again outside the bamboo hut that had become his palace.

'Soon after the death of the crown prince it seemed like the guards put more pressure on the king. They wanted him to die,' Khamphan would later conclude.

If so, they achieved their objective.

In March 1980, the last king of Luang Prabang died quietly in his sleep, aged seventy-two. The work team that had already buried a score of other prisoners was assigned to wrap his body in a sheet, bind it with bamboo twine and carry it to the improvised cemetery just north of the camp. Missing from the funeral party this time was Khamphan. Asked by his work mates to help them with the body, he had panicked.

'In my mind I thought that maybe it's a secret in history. Maybe I don't like to know where the king is buried. If I know, maybe the Pathet Lao will eliminate me. So I refused to participate.'

The four other work team members—Phoumi, Bao Thong, Phimpha and Amkhar—buried the last king of Laos. Queen Khamphoui attempted to accompany her husband's body to the grave, as she had tried to accompany her sons, but again was prevented by the guards from doing so. When they returned to camp, Khamphan's work mates told him they had buried the king about five metres from his heir, under the same spreading tree.

Soon after the king's death, Queen Khamphoui, then aged sixty-seven, was told to pack her personal belongings. She was to be relocated to another camp at Pafaek, just north of the road from Sop Hao to Xam Nua. After the queen's departure from Camp Number One, Phoumi and Bao Thong were ordered to clear the former quarters of the royal family of personal effects left behind. Among them, they found a hand-made smoker's pipe on which were carved in English the words 'LONG-WAY-FROM-HOME'.

Forty prisoners had entered the gates of Camp Number One in October–November 1977. Less than three years later, twenty-four were dead from disease and collapse of the will to live, but mainly from malnutrition. From the day the first prisoner died, the others had continued dying at the rate of one a month. The government of the Lao People's Democratic Republic chose not to intervene. It was knowingly and deliberately starving to death its own citizens.

18

Deliverance

It was our last afternoon in Viengxai, and a long and arduous drive back across the Annamite range awaited us.

With Sousath playing tour guide, we spent the remainder of the day poking around in various great leaders' caves. The elusive Pathet Lao leader Kaysone Phomvihan's subterranean villa was spacious and airy, and its vast family and meeting rooms with their sunny aspect would have provided quite comfortable living. On a tattered map still tacked to a wall, Hanoi was marked with a big red dot. Sop Hao was also marked, and there was the obligatory gas-attack room. The then President Nouhak Phoumsavanh and his Vietnamese wife were still regular visitors to their cave, although they stayed in a pretty, bougainvillea-covered bungalow near its entrance.

Back at the Number One Guesthouse, the staff were preparing a party, not for us, but in honour of a fraternal delegation from neighbouring So'n La province in Vietnam. The dried-mud top of a large earthenware *lau lao* jar had been lopped off, and long straws capable of drawing the more potent brew off the bottom protruded from the top. As the alcohol is drunk from the bottom, the jar is topped up with water, which turns to wine as the rice mash continues to brew. In the macho culture of *lau lao*, visitors are often challenged to prove themselves by consuming large quantities of the stuff. The hosts can tell how much they have drunk by how much water it takes to top up the jar.

'You must drink cleverly,' Sousath said, suggesting that I drink alongside a Lao and fake it.

The tables were laid with an impressive spread: chopped chicken, strips of marinated beef, and *laap*. As Richard fussed about the lack of food options for a vegetarian, a member of the kitchen staff sidled up to him, winked, and suggested there might be women on offer that night. Apparently the Number One Guesthouse had descended from palace to prison to whorehouse. I went upstairs to rest before dinner, and had fallen asleep when Richard came in and woke me.

'Your friend is here to see you,' he said.

'What friend?'

'The guy from Xam Nua. Lamphan, is it? He wants to see you.'

A shiver went through me.

'Richard.'

'Yes?'

'I'm not feeling too well,' I said, feigning a sudden illness. 'Do you think you could find me a couple of aspirin?'

'Sure. What have you got? A migraine?'

'Yes. Something like that.'

For the next several hours, I lay fully clothed and wrapped in a blanket under a mosquito net, listening intently as my mind raced with grim possibilities. I felt utterly alone, a misfit isolated by his unwelcome curiosity. I even began to doubt my own cause. Why should I carry a brief for a discredited feudal family, or any royal family for that matter? Why should I have become so fixated on finding their graves? Was I in too deep? They had given us the largest bedroom in the place, and it occurred to me that it was probably the royal suite. But now, plunged in darkness, it felt more like a chamber of horrors, windows rattling in a cruel breeze. Listening intently, I heard a few discordant voices wafting up through the stairwell, then a more general commotion echoing along the halls that led to the seminar room. Then, emerging from the background din, I heard footsteps coming up the staircase, and a knock on the door. It seemed my time in Laos was over. Lamphan had won.

'Are you okay?' asked a familiar voice. It was Richard.

'Not great,' I groaned, trying to mask the relief in my voice. 'My head's splitting.'

'You don't think it's malaria, do you?'

'Maybe. Might get a check-up at Xam Nua hospital in the morning.'

'Well, I'd stay put if I were you. They're making a real racket down there. You can hear that god awful music. It's the same tape going over and over. It's like some sort of Lao rave! And your friend Lamphan—he's a shifty-looking fellow isn't he—he's bitching about you. He reckons you lied to them when you came here last time.'

I bridled briefly at the insolence of a paid liar, but held my temper. If I could just keep my head down for a few more hours, I might escape this awful place. It was becoming a very long, very anxious night. Richard returned downstairs, leaving me alone in the darkness with my worst imaginings.

In the seminar room of the Re-education Guesthouse, the alcohol flowed freely as Lao and Vietnamese officials competed to consume the most. The men from Xieng Kho district were getting familiar with the waitresses, who smiled dutifully while picking up the empties. At one point, a particularly drunk Vietnamese accidentally head-butted one of the waitresses as he leaned across to tell her how gorgeous she was, knocking her out. Another poorly executed confidence sent a mugful of beer cascading over Richard. More chaos ensued in the rush to clean up the mess.

'There must have been fifteen people in my lap,' he told me the following morning.

Sousath had been 'drinking cleverly' with the others. Then a singing competition had ensued in which Richard was forced to take part. I could hear his reedy voice echoing up the stairwell, and despite everything, could not suppress a smile; he had chosen as his contribution William Blake's 'Jerusalem'.

> *And did those feet in ancient time*
> *Walk upon England's mountains green?*
> *And was the holy Lamb of God,*
> *On England's pleasant pastures seen?*
> *And did the Countenance Divine*
> *Shine forth upon our clouded hills?*
> *And was Jerusalem builded here*
> *Among these dark Satanic Mills?*

Towards dawn Richard returned, fumbling around the room. 'God! I'm shit-faced,' he said. 'Do you know, I've spent the past two bloody hours teaching the bloody district commissioner of bloody Xieng Kho how to speak bloody English. He now knows how to say, "I have got bad breath!" Sousath is blind.'

'What about Lamphan?' I asked

'Oh, God, he left hours ago. I saw his jeep heading back to Xam Nua. Jesus, I'm covered in beer! Never again, I tell you. Not with that local firewater.'

As he drifted off to sleep, his expostulations lost coherence and eventually subsided into snores.

The wind had dropped and it was a beautiful morning. The official delegation had slipped away, taking their hangovers back to Vietnam. Sousath steadfastly resisted all efforts to wake him, and would have slept until sunset unless something was done. So after packing up and paying the bill, Richard and I carried him to the jeep. Fishing the keys from his pocket, I took the wheel and we set off for Xam Nua, discovering at the first turn that the vehicle that had brought us across the Annamite mountains had no brakes.

*   *   *

In the summer of 1980, a caravan of the sick and crippled set out from a small, steep-walled valley north of village Nakaa Nua in Sop Hao district, Houaphan province, heading west towards the Ma River in north-eastern Laos. At the head of the procession, the immobilised were carried on stretchers while, behind, the emaciated supported the sick who needed help to walk. They looked like the casualties of a war or natural disaster. They were the fifteen survivors of the secret prison known as Camp Number One.

Shouldering one of the stretchers as the pathetic procession inched forward, Khamphan Thammakhanty pondered the latest twist in his fate. Three months had passed since the death of the king. That same month, the former army chief, General Bounpone also died, leaving only two prisoners out of the original seven living in the small barracks. For reasons that were never explained, the commandant decided to make the small barracks a separate quarters for the five-member work team. Brigadier General Chao Sinxay-Sana, who had been kept in stocks for more than two years, was freed from his shackles and hobbled over to the main dormitory. There the stocks were reassembled and he was shackled again. Liane Phavongviangkham, a former ambassador to China, accompanied him. The last prisoner to die in the camp was Khamchan Pradith, a former ambassador to Australia. An enthusiastic poet and patriot, Khamchan had been in Canberra when the Pathet Lao seized power in 1975. Australian diplomat and friend Barrie Dexter urged him to seek political asylum. But convinced his support for the neutralist cause would stand him in good stead, Khamchan returned to Laos, and was immediately arrested and sent to Viengxai. He spent his last days in Camp Number One, tormented by the thought of how naive he had been, and the Pathet Lao's inexplicable hostility towards him. Before returning to Laos, Khamchan had inscribed a copy of his self-published book of poetry to his friend Barrie Dexter. One of the poems, 'Memoirs of My Asian Tours', read, in part:

To visit all the continents and learn is not so much,
For me, friendship is the most priceless human touch,
As mankind must learn to live happy together,
So our world wisely can be peaceful forever.

That last morning in the camp, Khamphan had been surprised by a
personal visit from the well-disposed commandant, Bounyay. The
commandant told Khamphan that he wanted him to slaughter and
cook two chickens for himself and the other work-team members.
It was a rare treat, but as they sat down to eat in the small barracks,
the commandant reappeared with fresh orders. The prisoners were
to finish their meal quickly, and pack up their belongings. They
were leaving Camp Number One.

By noon, the inmates were assembled in the compound. Then,
leaving their bags to be sent on, they began their march to an
unknown destination. Four hours later, they had covered just two
kilometres, but their journey was almost over. They were entering a
large complex of barracks that dotted the eastern bank of the Ma
River and the hills beyond it. Struggling along the track as it
climbed higher into the hills, they eventually arrived at their new
home, a single barracks divided into two rooms with a view across
Camp Number Seven to village Sop Hao on the opposite side of
the river. Their new bunks were much higher off the ground than
before, but the walls were made from thin, irregular tree branches,
and the many wide gaps between them turned the barracks into a
wind tunnel. Half a dozen prisoners would die within six months
of arriving there from illnesses related to exposure.

From early on, the revolutionary government demonstrated a
degree of sensitivity to the way its prison camps were viewed by
the outside world. But rather than reform the camps to conform
with international humanitarian standards, it obfuscated and lied
about them. In 1977, all seminar camps run by the Ministry of

Interior were renamed 'production units' to avoid international condemnation, according to the CIA. Six years later, high-security facilities run by the Ministry of National Defence were handed over to civilian control. Officially, seminar camps and political prisons ceased to exist, but they continued to operate. Camp Number Seven at Sop Hao held murderers and opium traders, as well as political prisoners and disgraced Pathet Lao. It also held women. The political prisoners included dozens of Lao students called home in disgrace after questioning the hospitality of fraternal Vietnam. Having manipulated the student movement in order to secure power, the government now saw political activity among students as a threat, and dealt with it harshly.

Although Camp Number One had been only a few kilometres away, its existence was unknown to the inmates of Camp Seven, and because the new arrivals were kept in isolation from the rest of the camp, remained so. Apart from their location, little else changed for the country's highest security prisoners. Chao Sinxay-Sana was no longer kept in stocks, but all prisoners except the work team remained confined to barracks, and were still allowed outside to bathe only once a week. Even the guards at the now disused Camp Number One were transferred to keep watch over them. Above all, the slow advance of death continued, with Brigadier Bounchan—who had been one of those carried out of Camp Number One—dying within a week of arriving at the new location. Two prisoners—including the rebellious Nouphet Daoleuang—died on the one day. The feeble construction of their new barracks meant not only less protection from extremes of climate, but the intrusion of pests, including snakes and rats. Relishing his new freedom, Chao Sinxay-Sana caught one of the snakes and donated it to the barracks food pot. Inspired by his example, Khamphan tried to catch a rat, but was bitten by it instead. Life ground on.

In 1982, members of the former Camp Number One work team were ordered to participate in a curious expedition. Escorted by armed guards they were told to lead the way back to the site where they had buried the king and crown prince two years earlier. To reach the site, they had to pass through the valley where their darkest days were spent between 1977 and 1980. Entering the clearing where the now defunct Camp Number One had stood, they were amazed to find not a single structure standing. Everything—the barracks and watchtowers, the fences and food stores—had been dismantled. Once the highest security prison in Laos, it was now a lumber yard, and by order of their guards they paused to retrieve precious iron nails from the fallen timber planks and bamboo poles. The socialist experiment in Laos that had begun with the Pathet Lao seizing power seven years earlier had so impoverished the country that people were forced to scavenge for nails. Surveying the pitiless site, Khamphan noticed only one visible legacy of the prisoners' time there. Standing on the opposite side of the rivulet, in what had been the royal family's compound, were several papaya trees planted by the king. They were thriving.

From the deserted death camp, the prisoners and guards made their way due north towards the place where they had buried their dead on the western bank of the intermittent creek that occasionally ran south into the Ma River. There, the work-team members—Phoumi, Bao Thong, Phimpha, Amkhar and Khamphan—immediately recognised the spreading branches of the *kok caw* tree, beneath which they had buried the king and the crown prince. As they directed the guards to the unconsecrated graves, Khamphan lagged behind, saying nothing.

'I suspected it was a trick to see which of us remembered,' he would later recall, 'so I pretended to be unable to find the exact area. The guards didn't say why they wanted to visit that area. We thought maybe they wanted to come back later and loot the grave—take away teeth and other relics of the king that could be sold in Vientiane. But I didn't know why exactly.'

That same year, the separate compound housing survivors of Camp Number One at the new camp was disbanded. Mixing together for the first time, inmates of the two camps swapped stories. Prisoners of Camp Seven said they had recognised Queen Khamphoui who had been held there briefly in a separate compound in 1980. They had heard rumours carried by drivers that the last queen of Laos spent her declining years at Pafaek in a women's prison, among common criminals, prostitutes and murderers, and that she died in 1982 and was buried near the camp fence under a clump of bamboo.

After seven years in detention, Khamphan finally encountered the first inklings of a judicial process within the seminar system. At Sop Hao, magistrates would arrive regularly from Xam Nua, setting up in meeting halls and even on volleyball courts to stage mock trials. Even as they died of malnutrition, disease and starvation, inmates were being condemned to twenty-year prison terms which few would complete. However, even this pretence of justice was denied to the senior political prisoners from Camp Number One.

The impunity enjoyed by the Lao government in the treatment of its own citizens did not extend to the much more sensitive issue of downed American pilots captured by the Pathet Lao. The plight of America's former allies in Laos faded quickly from the political agenda in the United States, but the search for Americans missing in action in Indochina became a subject of enduring interest. The Lao government had always denied that it secretly held American pilots shot down over Laos, and live sightings of US POWs were often inspired by political or financial motives. Prisoners of the seminar camp system could not have been aware of such incentives, yet stories of detained Americans circulated in the camps. In Camp Seven, Khamphan met one prisoner who claimed to have encountered several Americans in detention in Houaphan province. Afraid of being entrapped by an agent provocateur, Khamphan expressed bemusement at the story, but asked no questions. He remembers only one detail: how excited the Americans had been when the Lao prisoners had shared some cooked sweet potatoes with them. Why a seminar camp prisoner would want to make up such a story, and include in it such detail, is difficult to imagine. Could he have been talking about the camp in the small valley of Thao La La hamlet where, as late as April 1982, six Americans were reportedly still being held?

Only seven of the original forty prisoners of Camp Number One remained alive, but the incorporation of the survivors into the main camp marked a turning point for Khamphan. Camp Seven prisoners were able to go out on work details, building small bridges and other structures, and carrying rice on their backs to a mill on the west bank of the Ma River south of Sop Hao. Although aged in his fifties, he relished the opportunity to play volleyball and the freedom to speak to other prisoners. Lao 'country' doctors, skilled in local herbal remedies, served the camp. One prisoner in particular—Khamphan's work buddy and fellow colonel, Amkhar Khantha-Mixay—thrived in the new atmosphere, applying his magic touch in animal husbandry to the camp's farm. Soon, the numbers of chickens, ducks, pigs and deer rapidly expanded. Amkhar even raised a tiger cub as the camp mascot. For the next three years, normal life seemed almost conceivable. Then the reality of revolutionary violence once again bared its teeth.

Of the original prisoners in Camp Number One, the two individuals who had probably suffered most were brigadier generals Ratana Banleung and Chao Sinxay-Sana. They had been confined to barracks for eight years—with Chao Sinxay-Sana in shackles for much of that time. They had survived starvation and disease and immobility, and had spent at most one day a year outdoors, if you added up the time spent undertaking their weekly bath. The only other prisoners to survive were those who had enjoyed the benefits of working in the fresh air and sunshine outside the barracks. One day in 1985, a group of military police from Xam Nua arrived at

Camp Seven and went to the barracks holding the two elderly generals. Calling them outside, they proceeded to beat them viciously before pushing them onto a *pirogue* and rowing them across the river. They were never seen again, and the rumour that they were executed on an isolated stretch of the river south of Sop Hao was widely touted in the village. The most plausible conclusion is that the authorities simply tired of waiting for the last two senior military officers of the old regime to die. They had survived too well, and paid the price.

Watching in horrified disbelief as the two elderly men were attacked was Khamphan's gentle assistant Amkhar. For eight years, he had fed them twice a day. Now he watched powerless as the life was beaten out of them.

'After that, Amkhar began thinking a lot,' Khamphan later recalled. 'He could not forget what he had seen, and became convinced that the guards were coming back to do the same to him.'

Suddenly, the animal nursery that Amkhar had husbanded no longer mattered to him. He ceased going to work, and stayed in his barracks. There he began to mull over the complete lack of contact from his wife during his decade in detention. He was also plagued by memories of an arrest he once participated in as an army colonel. Officers of the foreign intelligence directorate of the Vietnam People's Army had come to Vientiane to arrest one of their own diplomats. At their request, Amkhar had the man thrown into a prison run by the Royal Lao Army. It haunted him still. The spectre of Amkhar's rapid decline struck fear in Khamphan. It confirmed what he had always known: that survival depended mainly on the strength of the mind. For the first time in a decade, Khamphan cast aside his emotional armour, and went to the aid of a friend.

'He lived in an open barracks, so I was able to visit him every day for the next month or two,' Khamphan said. 'I would tell him how the camp needed him, how his work with the animals was excellent and that it was an inspiration to everybody in the camp. But always he would say, "No, no, no. I don't believe you. They are going to kill me too.'"

'The day he died, I went to see him in the morning. I told him, "Amkhar, you have to work. You work very well." But he just said, "No! I don't believe you. I have to die." And he did die later that day.'

The mental collapse of a respected and capable work mate shook Khamphan to the core. The traumatic decline of Amkhar brought into question the viability of his own survival strategy.

'If Amkhar can lose his mind,' Khamphan thought, 'maybe so can I.'

Elsewhere in Laos, a different kind of desperation was building. Beyond the camp, the folly of communist central planning adopted by the Pathet Lao leadership was becoming obvious all over the country by the mid 1980s. The economy was shot, and shortages of basic commodities had become endemic, while other South-East Asian countries boomed. At Camp Seven, prisoners began noticing increasingly predatory behaviour among the guards. Two brothers— the teacher, Chan Bounmee, and student, Wandi—had been confined to barracks for so long that their legs became completely paralysed. One night, a group of guards arrived at their hut and asked if the brothers would consider selling them their trousers. After all, they didn't go out much. What possible need could they have for them?

'They were nice trousers from Vientiane,' Khamphan recalled, 'much better than the rags the guards were wearing. So the guards offered the brothers a can of sweet condensed milk and some bananas, and took their trousers.'

In the mid 1980s, with the Soviet Union beginning to crumble and its global power in decline, the political elites in satellite regimes like Laos faced a stark choice: follow Moscow's lead, or remain loyal to their revolutionary principles. With a few exceptions like North Korea, they gambled on the twin reforms of *glasnost* (political openness) and *perestroika* (economic liberalisation). In Europe, *glasnost* would lead to the rapid erosion of the one-party state, but in Asia, especially China, Vietnam, Cambodia and Laos, the emphasis on reform was overwhelmingly economic, with the ruling party's monopoly on power stoutly defended. Easing restrictions on private trade offered the prospect of staving off both economic collapse and counter-revolution. Freed to pursue their own betterment, people would not blame others for their hardships, and the one-party state would retain the apparatus of repression just in case they did. In Laos they called the new policy *chintanakan mai*.

In the remote prison and labour camps of north-eastern Laos, the events far away slowly began to have an impact. One day in 1985, word spread around Camp Seven that a senior foreign dignitary was visiting the camp, accompanied by a daughter of the Justice Minister, Khammouane Boupha. The official, who appeared to represent the Soviet Union, toured the camp, asking questions in Russian, which were interpreted into Lao by the minister's daughter. Soon after the visit, discipline in the once rigorous prison began rapidly to slacken. Prisoners were told they must fend for themselves, and small-scale craft activities with commercial spin-offs were encouraged. At first, the wicker baskets, fishing nets and straw hats they made were sent off for sale, but the middlemen's take ate into revenues. Soon, internees were being allowed to travel into nearby villages themselves to hawk their wares, while camp authorities kept a close eye on their inventories. The Ma River, for so long an impregnable barrier between detainees and the outside world, became a thoroughfare of trade. As the guards became accustomed to a degree of laxity—and saw in it benefits for themselves—small freedoms began to grace the lives of their prisoners.

Ever cautious, Khamphan finally decided to take a risk. For almost ten years since leaving Vientiane, he had held onto his secret stash of foreign currency. Now, he decided to try changing a note into *kip*. His first attempt at changing five dollars through a fellow prisoner failed. The money, left with a Sop Hao resident, was never seen again. But when an ethnic Hmong inmate claimed to know a man in the village who was willing to change dollars, Khamphan tried again, this time with better results. With local currency in small denominations, Khamphan and the Hmong—who collected a 25 per cent commission for his efforts—could buy the medicines and small luxuries available in the village. Then, out of the blue a package arrived at the camp addressed to Khamphan. Sent by his younger sister Oudon, it contained a new jacket and pair of trousers. He was permitted to write his first letter in eight years, a note of thanks to his sister. She, too, had been banished to Houaphan province, to join her husband—a policeman under the old regime—who had been interned in a low-security re-education camp at Sop Pane, the central command headquarters for the entire camp system in Houaphan province. Having Oudon at Sop Pane would prove invaluable to Khamphan's other sisters who, unknown to him, had begun a vigorous campaign to locate and then secure the release of their brother.

Since he had last been seen by his wife at Vientiane airport, Khamphan's whereabouts had been a mystery to his family. His sister Khemphon and her daughter Rattana had travelled to Houaphan in a vain attempt to find him, while another sister, Bouakham, sought answers from the bureaucracy in Vientiane. In the early 1980s, a Lao exile newspaper had reported his death in detention. But snippets of information gleaned by relatives suggested he was still alive. Despite enormous obstacles, the sisters persisted. In 1983, Oudon obtained permission to visit Sop Hao, where she had heard her brother was being held.

'When she first arrived there, everybody freaked. Nobody wanted to get involved,' her son later told me.

It was the first of many visits, made under the cover of Oudon's trading business. Although she lived only a day's drive away, she had to go all the way to Vientiane to get permission to visit the off-limits village of Sop Hao. At every stage she was hit on for bribes by everyone from Interior Ministry bureaucrats to camp guards. They wanted a chain saw, or a thousand dollars, or a house in the village, or in Xam Nua, or even in Vientiane. There was no way of meeting such absurd demands. Satisfying one would not reduce the clamour of the others. Oudon and her family were themselves living in a camp, but what she lacked in resources she made up for with guts and commitment. Still, after two years of persistent attempts, sometimes camping in village Sop Hao for a month at a time, she had been unable to see her brother.

Luck is a valuable commodity, and at decisive moments in his life Khamphan appears to have been blessed with it. The last commandant at Camp Number One, the relatively enlightened Bounyay, had been transferred after the prison was emptied and dismantled. His new posting was Sop Pane, where he soon met Khamphan's sister Oudon, and confirmed for her that her brother was alive and living in Camp Seven. It was Bounyay who had arranged for his sister's parcel to reach Khamphan. Then, one morning in 1985, Khamphan was summoned to the office of the commandant of Camp Seven to be told that a visitor had come to see him. Oudon was waiting to meet him in Sop Hao.

Boarding a canoe, accompanied by Bounyay and an armed guard, Khamphan paddled across the Nam Ma, disembarked on the other side and was led to a guesthouse where his sister was waiting. It was a small bamboo hut, like so many in Laos, into which Khamphan walked, physically and emotionally a different man than the last time they had met. He was still handsome, with a full head of wavy, greying hair replacing his old military crop. His eyes were hooded, as they had always been, and Oudon recognised his funny, floppy ears. But there was something different in his face; the mischievous light in his eyes had gone out. Now, they stared blankly, giving nothing away. The ready smile no longer played on his lips, and the edges of his mouth fell down. Although rake-thin and walking with a stoop, he was otherwise physically unscarred. Yet his face—like that of a child who has been beaten—was both resentful and afraid, revealing the terrible scars within.

'I was so happy to see him, but also sad,' Oudon would later recall.

Her first duty was a sad one. She informed Khamphan that his father, the Mekong River salt trader, Manoi, had died. He had spent the last ten years of his life anxiously wondering what had happened to his eldest son. For the rest of the time, brother and sister made small talk, oppressed by the presence of the guard who sat with his gun in his lap chatting with Bounyay in a corner of the hut. Cautious as ever, Khamphan said little, and asked few questions. He did not even ask what had happened to his wife and children, and Oudon didn't tell him. The slightest personal detail overheard could potentially cause problems, more questioning or demands for bribes. Instead, Oudon acted solicitously, making him a bowl of chicken soup. After they had been chatting for two hours—mainly about Oudon's family—the guard called the meeting to an end, and Khamphan realised he had not touched his soup.

Walking back to the river, brother and sister managed to get sufficiently far ahead of the guards for Oudon to whisper to her brother. His wife and children had left Laos and emigrated to the West, she told him, after spending four years in a refugee camp in Thailand. They were waiting for him in the United States.

By 1986, the inmates of Camp Seven were enjoying more freedom of movement than they'd had in a decade. Once a month, Khamphan would join the work parties that collected rice from the mill near Sop Hao, stopping off in the village to buy items like bananas and meat on the way back. The commandant had launched a camp bank account into which friends and relatives could deposit funds for prisoners, and 20 000 *kip* had arrived for Khamphan by that route. With this money, his own dollars and other money Oudon had given him, he began to eat better. As people began to spend, strange new products— shampoo sachets and snack foods from Thailand—began appearing in the market. Finally, Khamphan was deputed by the commandant to set up and run a shop stall north of the village to sell prison wares and small items like cigarettes and sweets to travellers.

By 1989, the only survivors from Camp Number One were four members of the work team—Phoumi, Bao Thong, Phimpha and Khamphan. One day that year, three of the four were suddenly freed. Khamphan remained in custody with about eighty other low-security prisoners at Sop Hao. In May 1989, he was ordered to prepare an inventory of the items in stock at his roadside stall, as his presence was required in camp the following day. Another prisoner would look after the stall. The order struck a chord of fear in him. He remembered clearly how, twelve years earlier, a similar order to stay back from work at Xam T'ai had resulted in his arrest and imprisonment at Camp Number One. Fearful, as ever, he spent a sleepless night wondering if he had come so far only to fall, like Amkhar or the two brigadier generals who had been killed beside the river. Next day, he was summoned to the commandant's office.

'You are free,' the commandant told him. 'I am releasing you into the custody of a court official from Xam Nua. Collect your personal belongings and go.'

Khamphan could not believe his ordeal was over. Hurrying back to collect his things, he distributed them to guards, rather than to the other prisoners, and handed the commandant a hefty sum—all insurance against a bitter twist of fate. In the back of his mind, he was still worried about having taken part in burying the royal family. The others in the work team may have been released, but he had no idea what had happened to them, and the murder of the two brigadier generals haunted him. Anything could happen on the road to Xam Nua. So, fifteen years after first being detained at Chinaimo camp in Vientiane, Khamphan Thammakhanty walked free into the remote fastness of Houaphan province, his moment of liberation clouded by anxiety. He had been forty-six when first detained, an army intelligence officer in the prime of his life and career. Now he returned to the world as a 60-year-old man, with no job prospects, and no idea whether he would be able to leave the country to be reunited with his wife and family. All Laos seemed like a prison.

Accompanied by the court-official, Khamphan stepped onto a motorless *pirogue* and paddled across the Ma River for the last time. In village Sop Hao he waited while the official organised a jeep, then embarked with him and another freed prisoner on the sixty-kilometre drive to Xam Nua. As the jeep bounced along the rutted road, he waited in silent terror for something to go wrong, praying that it wouldn't. Every pause along the road intensified his paranoid imaginings, but eight hours later, in the early hours of the following morning, the jeep finally rolled into the deserted streets of Xam Nua. After dropping the court official at his home, the jeep driver offered Khamphan a room at a guesthouse he ran in the town. An ethnic Chinese, the driver also arranged to find him a seat on a flight to the capital, even though his would-be passenger had insufficient funds to cover the fare. In the coming days, Khamphan would wander around Xam Nua like a tourist in between visits to the local police station to obtain the required *laissez passer* to travel to Vientiane. Locals recognised men like him. They had seen so many of them pass through over the years, and left them alone. After a wait of several days, plagued by continuing fears of a last-minute glitch, the prisoner who dared not hope boarded a Russian helicopter not dissimilar to the one that had brought him to Houaphan province so many years before. He had never been charged with any crime, nor appeared before a judge. He had been cheated out of the best years of his life. But he had survived.

At Wattay airport in Vientiane, Khamphan walked out through the same terminal where, fourteen years earlier, he had farewelled his wife without so much as a kiss or caress. In the carpark he loaded his suitcase into a taxi and was driven home to suburban Dong Mieng. Flanked by palm trees, the family house looked rundown like the rest of the city. Alighting from the taxi, he carried his bags through the front gate and knocked on the door. From inside, the voice of a little girl greeted him, but not knowing the wiry, wizened old man with the dark complexion and worn denim clothing, she refused to let him in. No-one else was home, but the commotion attracted the attention of a neighbour who recognised the stranger immediately, and telephoned the girl's mother. When Khamphan's sister Bouakham arrived, all cultural taboos were cast aside as she rushed to embrace him. Before fleeing the country, Khamphan's wife, Singpheng, had insisted that his sister move into the house to look after the place. The little girl who had defended the home was informed that the intruder was her uncle, and was persuaded to allow him to come inside.

Within days, a procession of disbelieving relatives and friends were making their way to Dong Mieng to meet the miracle man. Some of those who came had attended the memorial service held after his death was reported in the early 1980s. Now, informed that her son was not only alive, but 'free, Khamphan's 90-year-old mother rushed to Vientiane from Australia, where she had been visiting another son. Hardly had they been reunited, than she ordered him to give thanks to Lord Buddha by becoming a monk.

At some time in their lives, it is traditional for all Lao Buddhist men to cleanse their spirits by having their heads shaved and entering a monastery for several months. It also brings great merit to their parents. From the austere isolation of the death camps, Khamphan Thammakhanty entered the tranquil isolation of the *wat*.

Many Happy Returns

My return to Vientiane from the wilds of Houaphan province coincided with the twentieth anniversary celebrations of the Lao People's Democratic Republic.

In the main hall of the National Assembly, a who's who of the party and army leaderships—those imbued with 'the spirit of Xam Nua'—along with the entire foreign diplomatic corps, assembled for' a performance of revolutionary ballet in which pirouetting soldiers in slippers danced with bayonets. The Politburo members— old men perched on overstuffed pink sofas—were offered cognac, but made a show of declining. On stage, the strident voice of a Defence Ministry diva commanded diminutive Lao soldiers to throw their grenade launchers in the air like Cossacks. Lao women in knee-length black boots goose-stepped across the stage, but as the guerilla ballerinas segued into the graceful *lamvong* the line between the official and the popular began to blur. The *khene* bamboo harmonicas buzzed, and the dancers' hands flowed rhythmically and hypnotically, as they have done in the villages for centuries. The government had decided against holding a military parade, and ordered that only the national flag, not the party's, be flown, leaving twin flagpoles all over the city strangely lopsided.

'At the Lan Xang Hotel, an island of good old-fashioned bad service, Foreign Minister Somsavat Lengsavad was deputed to play cat and mouse with foreign correspondents flown in for 'the occasion. Blinking furiously, the ethnic Chinese Somsavat said without a hint of irony that big houses and cars were among the achievements of the revolution. Clearly, the party's anger against privilege and inequality had been packed off to the museum with all the other hollow promises. Then came one of those unscripted moments that can make politicians of all colours, from Vientiane to Washington, squirm. Jonathan Miller, a BBC correspondent, stood up and asked what the government had done with the royal family. Had they been cremated in accordance with Buddhist rites?

The foreign minister baulked, no doubt pausing to check his recollection of Buddhist funeral rites, in which the body is bathed in warm water, then in cold water, before being embalmed, massaged with fragrant oils and dressed in two sets of the deceased's favourite clothes, one donned back to front. These rites represent the balance of life and death. The hair of the deceased is dressed with a broken comb that should not be used again, and the body is bound hand and foot with an unbroken length of white cotton, to ensure that the dead do not disturb the living. The body is then wrapped in a shroud, and laid in the family home. Money is placed in the mouth lest greedy spirits wander. Before cremation or burial, the face of the deceased is washed with coconut water and perfume. Mourners may throw handfuls of lemons, banana leaves, coins and roasted rice, and the body is carried three times around the pyre. The day after cremation, the bones are collected from the ashes for washing, then thrown into the nearest river, or buried in a *stupa*. Then begins the drinking 'and dancing, designed not to express joy, but to fool evil spirits.

Was that the kind of funeral that was held for the royal family, the correspondent wanted to know.

There was a stirring in the room. The four or five ministers at the head table looked at their hands, or at the ceiling. A few throats were cleared amid some whispering. The translators held their breath, and suddenly we were all in a courtroom, the court of international opinion. Somsavat, smiling and blinking, prepared to answer for his party's history.

'I'm not responsible for this affair,' he said. 'Birth and illness and death is the common lot of people…and Laos is composed of many ethnic minorities, who have different customs concerning the cremation or the burying of dead people.'

Then he did an extraordinary thing. He giggled. A constricted, terrible giggle that was soon covered by a chorus of similar giggles belonging to his fellow ministers.

My last few days in Laos were spent in the south, awash with tamarind and sunshine. The Mekong at Pakse is a carefree stream, broad and shallow. On the streets of the provincial capital, men with sandwich carts sold baguettes filled with bacon and hot sauce; women roasted chicken and sweet potatoes and told me not to stand in the sun lest my brains boil; and cafes served rich black coffee from the old French plantations on the Boloven Plateau. Gun emplacements built by the French to defend the town from the Thais could still be found, and the party's directive on removing its flags had yet to filter down, so the colonial streets were a riot of red and gold banners and green palm trees.

On my last day in Laos, I boarded a *pirogue* for the journey further south to Champassak and the old royal monuments at Wat Phu, 80 kilometres from the Cambodian border. Rounding the first bend in the river south of Pakse, there appeared a great mountain, rearing up from the plain, with a sharp peak on top. Phou Malong rose 1300 metres from the banks of the Mekong, its sheer cliffs resembling battlements. As we pulled into shore at Champassak town, women paddled out in canoes selling cooling turnips and barbecued chicken with sticky rice wrapped in palm leaves. Taking the only available *tuk-tuk*, I drove to the base of the tiered mountain slope of Wat Phu, then proceeded on foot to the site of a sixth-century temple, where black butterflies rode the warm air currents rising from the plain. Nagas and Shivas covered the walls of the ancient stone monuments, older than Angkor. It was a rain-watching pavilion overlooking the valley of the Mekong, with the Bolovens in the distance. In the cloying moss, the great stone blocks tumbled in disarray, little visited by tourists and unprotected by guards. A stone mahout rode high atop a triple elephant in embroidered *dupatta*; a stone rat sheltered between its curling trunks and tusks; oriental demons poked pointy tongues between their fangs. I found the sacred spring that had once been used to wash a phallic deity collecting in 44-gallon drums. After three months on the road my clothes felt like they owned me, so I took them off and plunged my head beneath the water, said by locals to give good luck, then walked to the edge of the escarpment and let the breeze dry me.

An old car ferry, made up of three aluminum dinghies lashed together with a timber deck nailed over them, took me back to the eastern bank of the river, making landfall 30 kilometres south of Pakse. Hitching a ride in a timber truck, I climbed into the back to find about twenty people, mainly children, perched on logs like large, rather exotic birds. The air rushed through the truck, carrying my lonely thoughts away. The end was near. I thought I might never again feel so free.

At the Chongmek border crossing into Thailand, blind singers busked and presenting your passport seemed entirely optional. The Lao immigration officer looked over his shoulder at a clock that had stopped hours, possibly years earlier, and a uniformed woman, seeing me watching him, giggled. Then everyone started laughing and wishing me *sogdee*—good luck—and I began, for the first time, to feel what so many Lao had felt through the turbulent years of recent history: the wrench of leaving.

Postscript

In March 2003, seven years after leaving Laos, I arrived in Portland, Oregon, and took a taxi across the Ross Island Bridge over the Willamette River to the middle-class suburb of Sellwood. Waiting to meet me at a typical bungalow in the heart of the American Dream was Khamphan Thammakhanty.

At seventy-three, he looked great, dressed smartly in a checked shirt and woollen jacket, and sporting spectacles and a shock of silver hair. The home was packed with the memorabilia of a Lao family, and in Portland's bleak weather had the cosy atmosphere of a beloved refuge. Having been put in touch by members of the Lao royal family living in exile in Paris, we had already become friends over many telephone conversations. Now it was time to piece together and examine his incredible life story face to face.

The indefatigable sisterhood that had found him, and then engineered his release from the death camps, had continued working on his case. Oudon, the sister who had met him at Sop Hao, had emigrated to the United States, where his wife and children were living. While Khamphan rested and meditated in the quiet stillness of a *wat*, another sister, Khemphon, was shuttling between the Foreign and Interior Ministries, and the American embassy in Vientiane, moving the paperwork forward towards obtaining for her brother a passport and visa. The process was not without anxiety, as Khamphan learned when his seclusion ended.

One day, as he waited at home for his travel papers to be approved, there was a knock on the door of the house at Dong Mieng. Opening the door, he was stunned to see, standing before him, Kong Tong, the harsh overlord of Camp Number One. It was Kong Tong who had been in charge at the time Touby Lyfoung was murdered. After the dissolution of the camp, and the transfer of its inmates to Camp Seven, he had gained a reputation for extorting money from prisoners with threats to block their release. He had been visiting Vientiane, Kong Tong said breezily, and thought he would just drop by to see his old prison friend. Appalled, Khamphan tried not to let his emotions show, pretending instead to be pleased to see his former jailer. At Khamphan's suggestion, they went off together to one of the hut restaurants that perch along the high levee banks of the Mekong. They drank beer and Khamphan bought dinner, laughing and joking about anything and everything except their time together in camp. When his guest had been well watered and fed, Khamphan insisted that he accept a gift, and stuffed 2500 Thai *baht* into his hands. Kong Tong accepted the pre-emptive bribe without demur, and was never seen again.

In January 1990, the salt trader's son, Khamphan Thammakhanty, flew out of Vientiane's Wattay airport for the last time. A few days later, he walked into the arrivals hall of the airport at Portland, Oregon in the north-western United States to be mobbed by his family and friends. Whatever shock there was at his physical transformation, it was overwhelmed by pure joy. Besides, everyone else had gotten older too. His wife Singpheng's hair was streaked with grey, and his son and daughter had both grown to adulthood as immigrants in a new country, without the advantages that might have been theirs in Laos had things been different. Everyone knew they were witnessing something miraculous—the triumph of the human spirit over adversity.

America was not without its challenges for a sixty-year-old unemployed Lao colonel. In order to qualify for social security, Khamphan needed to demonstrate ten years continuous employment in the United States. Without hesitating, he found a job as a welder and stuck at it until his seventieth birthday. The factory was a kind of United Nations, with employees from Laos, Vietnam and the Soviet Union, among others places, most of whom had little interest in the old national enmities. It was an ideal Khamphan embraced when he became an American citizen.

I had brought with me the maps I had purchased years before at the Service Géographique National in Vientiane. Seizing on the one of Houaphan province, Khamphan pored over it, peering through his spectacles as his right index finger traced a path to a small valley, squeezed between tight topographical lines indicating mountains.

'Right there!' he said, excited, as if he'd found an old acquaintance. 'Camp Number One was right there.'

It was only a kilometre or two east of the Ma River, so close to where my own journey had been scuttled by government minders when I'd visited Sop Hao village seven years earlier. Depicted in the cold formalism of a map, those places still retained their chill for me. Xam Nua, Viengxai, Sop Hao, Muang Et. How much more powerfully must those names speak to Khamphan, and tens of thousands of other Lao whose lives disappeared into the black hole of the camp system?

Over several days, Khamphan talked openly about the terrible time of seminar. Being questioned in minute detail, and having to relive the emotional trauma of those awful times, was exhausting work but he held up well. He had written his own 300-page manuscript in Lao, in which his experiences in Camp Number One play a supporting role to the broad sweep of Lao history. His openness and directness contrasted sharply with the opacity one so often encounters in Laos itself. Later, he introduced me to other Lao men who had spent time with him in other camps and who vouched for who he was. In between interview sessions, we would break for lunch, and Khamphan would drive me in his Lexus to Portland's Vietnamese *pho* restaurants. Chatting over bowls of noodle soup, we shared the jovial good company I'd enjoyed in so many soup kitchens and bamboo bars in Laos itself.

In time, I found other former camp inmates who confirmed key details such as Khamphan's arrest and removal from Xam Tai in 1977, along with the rest of the high-ranking former military officers. Perhaps it was his military training, or the legacy of his maltreatment over so many years, but Khamphan's catalogue of life in Camp Number One was devoid of one key element: emotions. The fortress he had built around his heart and mind in order to survive was still standing.

In subsequent conversations extending over several months, I struggled to imagine what he must have been through, if only to find the right questions that would unlock the door to his suffering. At times I felt like a detective cross-examining a suspect, at others, like a medium for a tortured soul, condemned to relive his torment for him in order to explain it. It was sad work. Too sad. I hope not to see its like again soon.

Khamphan Thammakhanty's story is the definitive account of the last days of one of South-East Asia's oldest dynasties. Not surprisingly after what he experienced, Colonel Khamphan is no admirer of the Lao PDR and its rulers. His principal goal now is to defend his nation's history from those who would whitewash it. The Lao government's efforts to cover up the crimes of the revolution are, by comparison, without honour. When they obfuscate and conceal, officials of the regime are not practising some quaint cultural predilection for subtlety, but a more universal instinct for political survival. Khamphan is the sole survivor of Camp Number One living in the West. Two others—Bao Thong and Phimpha, both members of the prisoner work team—may still be alive, but they are believed to have never left Laos, where freedom of speech no longer exists.

There will be those who believe Colonel Khamphan fought on the wrong side in the Indochina wars, and that therefore his suffering has no meaning. Such a view—which today has its echo in the detention of Islamic militants without trial at Guantanamo Bay and elsewhere—denies the basic human rights that protect the security of all of us. The Lao PDR had fourteen years to charge Khamphan with any crime they liked. They chose not to do so. Terror and deceit are their currency, but thanks to Khamphan's testimony, their crimes are no longer in the realm of speculation.

In January 2003, the Lao People's Democratic Republic declared a national holiday to honour the fourteenth-century Lao king Fa Ngum, who founded the Lan Xang line of royal rulers that ended in 1975. Fa Ngum's empire included much of present-day Thailand.

'This is the most amazing thing I've seen in my time in Laos,' the American ambassador, Douglas Hartwick, told the *New York Times*, noting the many ironies. 'They are making a direct linkage between the king and the current leadership, and these are the same people who deposed the last king of Laos,' he said. Commentators saw the move as signalling the government's concern about the rampant Thai influence that has invaded Laos since the early 1990s. Thailand has ten times as many people, and more people of Lao ethnicity than Laos itself. 'The Lao government is urgently in need of new symbols for its legitimacy after long years of authoritarianism,' commented Dr Pavin Chachavalpongpun, a lecturer in the Faculty of Arts at Chulalongkorn University in Bangkok. 'To Vientiane, the king's spirit is being resurrected just in time before Laos' identity further fades into the Thai orbit of cultural supremacy.' Laos seeks no such separation from neighbouring Vietnam. Its uncompromising stance towards the last king, Savang Vatthana, and his descendants remains unchanged. Noted the *South China Morning Post*, 'The Lao regime has never denied the royal past, but by choosing to honour a man who became king in 1353, it appears eager to avoid political controversy accompanying some of the more recent monarchs.'

In July 2000, the son of Crown Prince Vongsavang and Princess Mahneelai called for Washington's help to 'liberate' his homeland. The current heir to the Lao throne, Soulivong Savang remained in Laos for six years after the communist takeover, working in the rice fields to help feed the rest of his family. In 1981, he escaped Laos by rafting across the Mekong, aged eighteen, and now lives in France. After lobbying congressmen on Capitol Hill, prince Soulivong said American lawmakers had been 'receptive to our views, and their support is remarkable…We hope that with their effort, Laos will return to being ruled by the law…I want to get back to Laos, and, along with the people, work for the reconstruction of the country.'

Unbelievably, the unlawful system of detaining political prisoners in cruel camps in remote Houaphan province continues today. Camp Seven, where Khamphan Thammakhanty spent nine years without trial, remains a functioning gulag. In 1990, soon after Khamphan left Laos, a new generation of prisoners went into Sop Hao. Three pro-democracy activists—Thongsouk Saysangkhi, Latsami Khamphoui and Feng Sakchittaphong—were arrested. All one-time supporters of the Lao People's Revolutionary Party, their crime was to write letters to the government expressing their view that Laos needed more democracy, perhaps even a multi-party system. Brought to trial in November 1992 in Xam Nua, they were convicted of plotting a rebellion and sentenced to fourteen years' imprisonment. According to Amnesty International:

All three men are imprisoned in Prison Camp Number 07, Ban Sop Hao, Houaphan province. The other inmates of the prison are common criminals, apart from three prisoners who have been in detention as part of a "re-education program" since 1975, who were recently transferred to the camp. Latsami Khamphoui, Thongsouk Saysangkhi and Feng Sakchittaphong are being held together in one cell measuring six metres long by six metres wide. There are three beds in the cell with mattresses and blankets, but the floor is concrete and a gap between the bottom of the walls and the floor makes the cell very cold during several months of the year. Although they are held in the same room, the prisoners are not allowed to speak to each other, and a guard is always posted by their cell to ensure that silence is maintained. The men have reportedly been threatened with beatings or being shot if they speak. They are not allowed access to reading or writing materials. Once a fortnight the prisoners are permitted to leave the cell to bathe; the cell is often searched during this interlude and personal belongings have been confiscated. There are no medical facilities available in the prison, and all three men are suffering from medical conditions which require ongoing treatment. Latsami Khamphoui is known to have angina; the two other men are reported to be suffering from a variety of illnesses including kidney problems and diabetes. Family visits to the men have been severely restricted. Permission to visit must be obtained from both the Ministry of Interior and the Provincial Police Chief. Visitors are allowed to take small quantities of food and medicine to the prisoners. Until recently, Amnesty International believes that there had been no visits allowed for almost two years. Since then, family members of one prisoner were permitted one visit, but the contact was limited to one hour and took place under heavy surveillance. In September 1996 permission for family visits was again denied…The organization [Amnesty] calls upon the Lao authorities to ensure that the cruel, inhuman and degrading treatment of all three prisoners ceases immediately and that they are given immediate access to the medical treatment they urgently require, and visits from their family members.

This protest, which was ignored by the Lao PDR, came too late for Thongsouk, who died in February 1998. According to Amnesty, his death in detention for writing a letter to the government 'highlights not only the Lao government's complete lack of care of its political prisoners, but its contempt for the opinion of the international community'.

The US-led war on terror has given the Lao exile movement hope that small authoritarian regimes like the Lao PDR may face pressure to democratise. Yet America's use of detention without trial to hold suspected Islamic militants at Camp Delta at Guantanamo Bay, Cuba, can only undermine Western protests against regimes that use similar methods against their own people.

According to an old saying, Laos has three wives—Vietnam, Thailand and China. How to satisfy all of them? To put the question differently, how to keep all of them at bay? The past quarter-century of rule by a secretive party led by a ruthless gerontocracy hasn't provided the inclusive style of government that might have been an improvement on the *ancien régime*. The bulk of the country's educated, affluent diaspora remains reluctant to return to their homeland, even to visit. Those who do, go warily. Genuine national reconciliation remains difficult so long as a one-party Marxist–Leninist political system continues to control the courts, police and the media. Six of the nine members of the party Politburo are serving or former army generals. All citizens and outsiders are at the mercy of arbitrary, unaccountable power, and corrupt officialdom.

A quarter-century after the revolution, male citizens of the Lao PDR live for only 52 years on average, the lowest life expectancy in South-East Asia. Infant mortality is 90 per 1000 live births, the worst rate in the region. Laos remains the most illiterate country in East Asia. More than half the population depends on agriculture and per capita income is $350 a year. The majority of the people live in villages untouched by government services. A minority in the towns and cities have begun to prosper partly due to the liberalised economic policy, but also because of increased foreign aid, which in 1994 accounted for 45 per cent of the national budget. In the Asian economic crisis of 1997, Laos was hardest hit and is still to recover. The value of its currency, the *kip*, plummeted from 1000 to 10 000 to the dollar. Triple-digit inflation destroyed the value of whatever modest savings people had. Insulated by revenue from corrupt dealings, senior party leaders remained comfortable.

In October 1999, members of the Lao Students Movement for Democracy staged demonstrations in Vientiane, the first public anti-government protests since the fall of the monarchy in 1975. Thirty young people attempted on 26 October to raise banners calling for peaceful political change. Five students were arrested— Thongpaseuth Keuakoun, Khamphouvieng Sisaath, Seng-Aloun Phengphanh, Bouavanh Chanhmanivong and Keochay—and since their arrest the Lao government has refused to reveal their fate, or publicly acknowledge that they are being detained. They are believed to be held in Vientiane's Xam Khe prison, where inmates are routinely confined in rigid wooden leg stocks. Amnesty International has designated them as prisoners of conscience, detained solely because of the non-violent expression of their political beliefs. It fears for their safety and considers them at risk of torture and ill-treatment. Members of the public are welcome to join Amnesty's campaign for their immediate and unconditional release.

In the year 2000, a series of bomb blasts rocked Vientiane, although speculation linking the blasts to government servants and business people disenchanted with the economic turmoil could not be confirmed. Press reports spoke of a crisis summit called by party elder statesman Nouhak Phoumsavanh, at which the former president advocated a new policy of national unity including political and social reforms, possibly including a multi-party state, although no such moves were subsequently adopted. In September 2000, a son of the Red Prince, Khamsai Souphanouvong, left Laos dissatisfied with his declining role in the government, and defected to New Zealand. Rumours in 2003 suggested he had moved to Vietnam, his mother's country of origin where, exiles speculate, he may make himself useful in that country's ongoing policy of engagement with Laos. He is the party's highest-ranking defector since 1975.

In early 2003, a spate of armed attacks along Route 13 between Vientiane and Luang Prabang left at least 23 people dead, including two Swiss nationals. Again, rumours that Hmong anti-government rebels were involved could not be confirmed. But *Time* magazine quoted a military officer as saying that a calling card left at the scene of one of the attacks read, 'We have lost our nation and are fighting to get it back.' The magazine also quoted from the report of a US-based 'Fact Finding Commission' which claimed that two divisions of the Vietnamese People's Army had been deployed in northern Laos to combat rising Hmong resistance to the Vientiane regime. The report claimed 739 people had been killed in skirmishes in the first four months of 2003.

The forerunner to this book, *Stalking the Elephant Kings*, published in 1997, first revealed the damage inflicted upon the standing stones of Houaphan province by a road project funded with US government aid monies. That report attracted the attention of US officials.

'My predecessor went up there, and when he saw what had happened he said, "Oh my God, this is not good",' the American ambassador to Laos, Douglas Hartwick, told me later. In 1999, the US State Department established an ambassador's fund for the preservation of Lao arts and culture, and money was spent rerouting the road, making an inventory of the site and devising a plan for its preservation. Signs explaining the history and significance of the site were erected at Phonsavan and Xam Nua airports to attract tourists. In December 2002, Ambassador Hartwick and Houaphan provincial governor Cheu Ying Vang formally opened the Hintang Archaeological Park.

'We didn't build the road, we only funded it, but we wanted to see what we could do to make amends and help preserve the site and encourage tourism to Houaphan province. They are a national treasure. Any damage is horrific, but fortunately only a small part of the site was damaged,' said Hartwick.

However, two independent researchers who began working at the site after the initial damage was revealed claimed more destruction followed because of an ill-considered commercial logging operation that was directly facilitated by the American road.

'Numerous stone blades were snapped off by trees dropped directly onto menhir clusters. Nothing has been ameliorated,' researchers Catherine Raymond, Associate Professor of Art History at Northern Illinois University, and Dr Alan Potkin, team leader of the Digital Conservation Facility, Laos, told me.

According to these experts, the new archaeological park at the site has no official boundaries and appears to have no formal institutionalised basis.

'Nor are there any specific, legally binding management or conservation requirements for such a protected area category,' the researchers said. 'As for whether the site will be helped or harmed, the damage done in the last decade by the roadway and the subsequent logging was so extensive, it is hard to imagine that park status and tourism could make things worse.'

In 1988, Laos attracted only 600 tourists. By the start of the twenty-first century, a new open-door policy was attracting tens of thousands of tourists a year, although the government's target of one million in the year 2000 never looked like being achieved. The violence along Route Thirteen and the unexplained bomb blasts in the capital kept a lid on the expansion of tourist numbers.

The royal puppets no longer dance in Luang Prabang, their restless *phi* still imprisoned in a box. But in 1999, the Lao national puppet theatre troupe, the Bulgarian-trained hand puppeteers who studied briefly under the Luang Prabang masters, were awarded the UN Development Award in recognition of their work in promoting public awareness of such issues as immunisation, education for girls and the threats posed by malaria, AIDS and unexploded ordnance. Roberta Borg, who first drew my attention to the story of the *tookatahs*, has since passed away.

There are still 1891 Americans listed as missing or unaccounted for from the war in South-East Asia, including 1444 in Vietnam, 382 in Laos, 57 in Cambodia and eight in territorial waters of China, according to officials of the Joint Task Force Full Accounting.

In November 2002, the Thai crown princess, Sirindhorn, paid an official visit to Houaphan province. Lao exile reports claimed the princess had visited the graves of the Lao royal family. However, a spokesman for the Thai Foreign Ministry said the visit had been to 'caves, not graves', indicating the princess had taken in the Pathet Lao memorial caves in and around Viengxai.

In November 1998, the veteran revolutionary propagandist Sisana Sisane died aged 76. Sousath Phetrasy's tourism business has grown and prospered. His 24-room Maly Hotel in Phonsavan boasts hot showers, a restaurant, airport pick-ups and its own website, www.malyht.laotel.com. He accepts most major credit cards (except American Express).

Khamphan Thammakhanty continues to live a comfortable, healthy and happy retired life with his wife and two children in Portland, Oregon in the United States. His younger sister Oudon, the one who broke down the walls of secrecy to find him in Camp Seven, now lives in Connecticut with her family. Occasionally, Khamphan misses the sunshine and laughter of Laos, but knows it would be unwise for him to return at this point. His 300-page opus about his own experiences, and the history of Laos, awaits publication.

Glossary

baci Lao ceremony of welcome or thanksgiving

ban village (Lao)

baw no (Lao)

bonze Buddhist monk

chintanakan mai literally, 'new thinking' or economic liberalisation

felang originally, French man or woman, now foreigners in general

feu Lao name for Vietnamese rice noodle soup

khouan soul

kip Lao currency unit

kop chai thank you (Lao)

laissez passer Lao internal travel permit (abolished in 1990s)

lamvong dance (Lao)

Lao Loum mainly Buddhist people of the Mekong Valley

Lao Seung mainly animist cultivators of Lao highlands (aka Hmong)

Lao Theung people of the mountainsides, mainly animists (aka Kha)

lau lao rice wine

liusee wandering ascetic (Lao)

muang county (Lao)

nam river (Lao)

nop gesture of greeting and respect (hands raised in prayerful manner towards bowed forehead)

padaek fermented fish paste

Pathet Lao 'Lao Nation' leftist guerilla army

phi spirit

Pimai Lao New year

pirogue canoe

pra bang golden Buddha statue, palladium of Lao nationhood

pukhai Buddhist monk's robes

Ramayana Hindu battle epic

sabaidee good day/evening (Lao)

sampot traditional Lao baggy trousers

sangkha Lao Buddhist clergy

seminar Lao term for detention in re-education or prison camp

sim chapel of a Buddhist monastery

sin woman's skirt

sogdee good luck (Lao)

stupa Buddhist monument and shrine often containing relics and
votary objects

tookatah puppet

tuk tuk motorised three-wheel rickshaw

wat Buddhist monastery and temple complex

Timeline

1353 King Fa Ngum unites principalities that form modern Laos, recognises Buddhism as the state religion.

1707 Kingdom of Lan Xang breaks up. Royal line continues to rule in Luang Prabang.

1893 Beginning of French colonial administration in Laos.

1907 Last king of Laos, Savang Vatthana, born in Luang Prabang.

1945 Japanese Imperial Army briefly ousts the French administration in Laos, forces King Sisavangvong to declare independence from France.

Lao nationalists depose king and declare independence.

1946 French return to Laos, monarchy restored.

1949 Lao nationalists split along Cold War lines.

1950 United States signs agreement to provide economic and military aid to Laos.

1954 Laos gains full independence from France as a constitutional monarchy. Pathet Lao fight on with Soviet and Vietnamese aid.

1962 Geneva agreement guarantees neutrality of Laos, but is widely ignored.

1965 US begins secret bombing of Laos to disrupt communist military operations.

1973 Paris Accords end US support for anti-communist forces in Indochina.

Vientiane Accords agree ceasefire between Lao factions.

1975 US forces withdraw from Vietnam, Saigon falls to Vietcong and North Vietnamese Army.

Khmer Rouge occupy Cambodian capital, Phnom Penh.

Last king of Laos, Savang Vatthana, forced to abdicate and placed under house arrest.

Founding of Lao People's Democratic Republic.

Re-education and prison camps set up in Laos to detain members of the former regime.

1977 Lao royal family arrested and flown to north-eastern Houaphan province.

1980 Lao crown prince and king die in Prison Camp Number One, Sop Hao, Houaphan province.

1980s Lao government adopts economic reforms.

1982 (approx.) Queen Khamphoui of Laos dies in Prison Camp Pafaek, Houaphan province.

1995 United States lifts decades-old ban on US aid to Laos.

1997 South-East Asian economies collapse. Laos hardest hit. Laos joins Association of South-East Asian Nations.

1999 First anti-government demonstrations in Laos since the fall of the monarchy.

2003 Lao government honours fourteenth-century king, Fa Ngum.

Inmates of Prison Camp Number One

King Savang Vatthana, died March 1980

Queen Khamphoui, died 1982 (approximately) at Camp Pafaek

Crown Prince Vongsavang, died January 1980

Prince Sisavang, the king's second son, died September 1978

Prince Souphantharangsi, secretary-general of the royal palace,
    brother of the king, died February 1980

Prince Bovone Vatthana, former provincial governor,
    half-brother of the king, died August 1978

Prince Thongsouk, director of protocol, royal palace, half-brother of
    the king, died October 1978

Prince Manivong Khammao, the king's nephew,
    died July 1979

Prince Souk Bouavong, former provincial governor and minister,
    died December 1978

Phagna Bong Souvannavong, former government minister, died
    October 1978

Phagna Pheng Phongsavan, Minister of the Interior, signatory to
    Vientiane Accords, died March 1979

Phagna Soukan Vilaisarn, deputy Minister for Veterans' Affairs, died
    March 1979

Phagna Touby Lyfoung, deputy Minister of Telecommunications,
    died April 1979

Phagna Liane Phavongviangkham, Ambassador to China, died May
    1980

Phya Khamchan Pradith, Ambassador to Australia, died May 1980

Lieutenant General Ouane Rathikoun (Rtd), former chief of Royal
    Lao Armed Forces, died October 1978

Lieutenant General Bounpone Makthepharak, former Chief of
    Royal Lao Armed Forces, died March 1980

Lieutenant General Bounleuth Sanichan, died June–August 1980 (at
    Camp 7, Sop Hao)

Major General Phasouk Solatsaphak, died March 1979

Brigadier General Assaphangthong Pathammavong, died 1980 (at
    Camp 7, Sop Hao)

Brigadier General Thongphan Knocksi, died January 1980

Brigadier General Bounchan Savath Phayphan, died June 1980 (at
    Camp 7, Sop Hao)

Brigadier General Kaan Insixiangmay, died October 1978

Brigadier General Bountieng Venevongsoth, died 1981 (at Camp 7,
    Sop Hao)

Brigadier General Lee Lithi-Luxa, died October 1978

Brigadier General Ratana Banleung Chounlamany, executed 1985,
    (near Sop Hao)

Brigadier General Chao Sinxay-Sana, executed 1985, (near Sop Hao)

Brigadier General Nouphet Daoleuang, died 1980 (at Camp 7, Sop
    Hao)

Colonel Khamphan Thammakhanty, released 1989, living in United
    States (as at July 2003)

Colonel Amkhar Khantha-Mixay, died 1985 (at Camp 7, Sop Hao)

Major Sivilai (Pathet Lao defector), died October 1979

Captain Seri Xayakham, died July 1979

Police Lieutenant General Lith Lunammachak (Rtd), former
    director-general of police, died February 1979

Police Colonel Kavin Keonakorn, died June–August 1980 (at
    Camp 7, Sop Hao)

Police Colonel Khammouk Phengsri-Aroun, died 1981 (at
    Camp 7, Sop Hao)

Police Colonel Heng Saythavi, died June–August 1980 (at Camp 7,
    Sop Hao)

Police Sergeant Phoumi Phanvongsa, released 1989, died 2001 (in
    United States)

Police Sergeant Bao Thong, released 1989, remained in Laos (fate
    unknown)

Mr Issara Sasorith, died June 1979

Bao Phimpha, former driver for a Pathet Lao official, released 1989,
    remained in Laos (fate unknown)

Selected Reading

Nina Adams and Alfred McCoy (eds), *Laos: War and Revolution*,
    Harper & Row, New York 1970

Fred Branfman, *Voices from the Plain of Jars: Life Under an Air War*,
    Harper & Row, New York 1972

MacAlister Brown and Joseph J. Zasloff, *Apprentice Revolutionaries:
    The Communist Movement in Laos, 1930–1985*, Hoover
    Institution Press, Stanford 1986

Wilfred G. Burchett, *Mekong Upstream: A Visit to Laos and Cambodia*,
    Seven Seas, Berlin 1959

Timothy N. Castle, *At War in the Shadow of Vietnam: U.S. Military Aid
    to the Royal Lao Government, 1955–1975*, Columbia University
    Press, New York 1993

Sisouk Na Champassak, *Storm Over Laos*, Praeger,
    New York 1961

Kenneth Conboy, *Shadow War: The CIA's Secret War in Laos*, Paladin
    Press, Boulder 1995

Arthur J. Dommen, *Laos: Keystone of Indochina*, Westview
    Press/Praeger, Boulder 1962

——*Conflict in Laos: The Politics of Neutralization*, Praeger, New
    York, 1971

Grant Evans, *Lao Peasants Under Socialism*, Yale Uni Press, New
    Haven 1990

————The Politics of Ritual and Remembrance: Laos Since 1975,
University of Hawaii Press, Honolulu 1998

Bernard B. Fall, *Anatomy of a Crisis: The Laotian Crisis of 1960–61*,
Doubleday, Garden City, New York 1969

————*Hell in a Very Small Place: The Siege of Dien Bien Phu*, DeCapo
Press, New York 2002

Viktor E. Frankl, *Man's Search for Meaning*, Washington Square Press,
New York 1985

Edward A. Gargan, *The River's Tale: A year on the Mekong*, Knopf,
New York 2002

Francis Garnier, *Travels in Cambodia and Part of Laos* Vol. 1 and
*Further Travels in Laos and in Yunnan: Mekong Exploration
Commission Report (1866–1868)* Vol. 2, White Lotus Press,
Bangkok 1996

Jane Hamilton-Merritt, *Tragic Mountains: The Hmong, the Americans,
and the Secret Wars for Laos, 1942–1992*, Indiana University
Press, Bloomington 1993

William M. Leary, *Perilous Missions: Civil Air Transport and the CIA
Covert Operations in Asia*, Smithsonian Institution Press,
Washington 2002

Norman Lewis, *A Dragon Apparent: Travels in Cambodia, Laos and
Vietnam*, Jonathan Cape, London 1951

M.L. Manich, *History of Laos*, Chalermnit Books,
Bangkok 1967

John B. Murdoch (trans) & David K. Wyatt, *Iron Man of Laos: Prince
Phetsarath Ratanavongsa*, Cornell, New York 1978

Milton E. Osborne, *River Road to China: The Mekong River
Expedition, 1866–73*, Liveright, New York 1975

Kaysone Phomvihan, *Revolution in Laos: Practice and Prospects*,
Progress, Moscow 1981

C. Pym, *Henri Mouhot's Diary—Travels in the Central Parts of Siam,
Cambodia and Laos during the years 1858–1861* (abridged and
edited), Oxford University Press, Kuala Lumpur 1966

Judy Austin Rantala, *Laos: A Personal Portrait from the Mid-1970s*, McFarland, Jefferson NC 1994

Christopher Robbins, *Air America*, Putnam, New York 1979

———*The Ravens*, Crown, New York 1987

Maha Sila Viravong, *History of Laos*, Paragon Books, New York 1964

Perry Stieglitz, *In a Little Kingdom*, M.E. Sharpe, London 1990

Martin Stuart-Fox and Mary Kooyman, *Historical Dictionary of Laos*, The Scarecrow Press, New Jersey & London 1992

Martin Stuart-Fox (ed), *Contemporary Laos*, Uni of Queensland Press, St Lucia & London 1982

Martin Stuart-Fox, *A History of Laos*, Cambridge University Press, Cambridge 1997

Joseph Westermeyer, *Poppies, Pipes and People: Opium and its Use in Laos*, University of California Press, Berkeley 1983

Joseph Zasloff & Leonard Unger (eds), *Laos: Beyond the Revolution*, Macmillan, Basingstoke, London 1991

Index

About the Author

Born in Sydney, Christopher Kremmer is an author and journalist whose previous books include the award-winning *Stalking the Elephant Kings* and the international bestseller, *The Carpet Wars*. His print journalism has appeared in the *Sydney Morning Herald* and he has broadcast extensively for the Australian Broadcasting Corporation. He now lives in the Southern Highlands of New South Wales and is working on several book and film projects.